THE MEANING OF THE TIMES

THE
MEANING *of* THE TIMES

AND

OTHER SPEECHES

By

ALBERT J. BEVERIDGE

Jeremiah

Essay Index Reprint Series

Originally published by:
THE BOBBS-MERRILL COMPANY

 BOOKS FOR LIBRARIES PRESS
FREEPORT, NEW YORK

MANUFACTURED
BY
HALLMARK LITHOGRAPHERS, INC.
IN THE U.S.A.

CONTENTS

INTRODUCTION

The volume before us contains some of the public addresses made by Senator Beveridge during the past ten
years. They have a wide range of subject, yet from two
standpoints they will be found to possess coherence and
unity. The convictions and intellectual processes of a
man whose mind and character give him the right to
claim the attention of his fellow citizens, are never un-
related and detached. And the carefully prepared public
addresses of a sincere man who really expresses himself in his utterances will show how his mind works, what
he believes, and what tendencies he represents. This
collection of addresses, therefore, has unity in the sense
that it reveals the intellectual quality and the public personality of the speaker, and shows us what his attitude is
toward the political and social problems that have occupied our attention in the past decade.

On the other hand, this varied series of addresses has
unity in the great fact that every speech is an attempt
at the interpretation of some phase of the indivisible life
of our own times in the United States. For those who
are interested in the author, the volume interprets Senator
Beveridge. For those who are interested in our contemporary life and problems, the volume reminds us of
much that we have been doing as a nation, and presents
what is, in effect, a consistent analysis and theory of
contemporary American progress.

INTRODUCTION

Mr. Beveridge is an orator in a time when orators are very few. We have many cogent speakers, and many more who are cultivated, fluent, and agreeable. But oratory is an art of itself, often analyzed and described, and which I have no need to discourse about. Usually there must be strong conviction in the heart of the orator, there must be constructive imagination, and there must be the kind of faith that helps the speaker to inspire his hearers.

Mere rhetoric and the flowers of speech do not constitute oratory in a high sense — and the reader will find that Mr. Beveridge does not rely upon tricks or devices — although this entire volume is on the plane of the orator, and not upon that of the essayist, the debater, or the expositor. Mr. Beveridge has amply shown in other published writings a rare power to narrate and describe; and on countless occasions he has shown his force and talent as an expositor or a debater. But here we have the orator's interpretation of the men and the movements of his own time, and the setting forth of his own hopes and convictions in the realm of social and political life. He believes in the country, in the greatness of its destiny, in the fulfilment of its providential tasks, in the adequacy of its institutions, in the fitness of its constitutional system for the treatment of new problems as they arise. He believes in the plain people, and knows that the country's future lies in the broadening of opportunity for the children everywhere.

In his own experience and observation as a western boy, he finds it easy to understand the qualities of men

like Lincoln and Grant, and not less easy to understand
an Oliver P. Morton or a Marcus A. Hanna. His addresses on *School and Nation* and *Child Labor* show his
firm grasp of Jefferson's idea that the child is the most
precious asset of the State, and that his right training and
symmetrical development are to be placed above all other
social duties. His addresses on *Methodism, Frances E.
Willard,* and *James Whitcomb Riley* further reveal his
sympathetic appreciation of great movements and influences that affect the national life and character.

Mr. Beveridge was elected to the United States Senate
from the State of Indiana in January, 1899. He was
thirty-six years old, had practised law for about twelve
years, and had held no public offices. His election to the
Senate from a great state noted for its able public men
was a high tribute to his talent and to his personal force.
We had only then concluded our treaty of peace with
Spain and acquired the Philippines.

Our problems of colonial administration were bound to
give us much concern, and to occupy a leading place in
the discussions of Congress, as well as in the Presidential
campaign of the following year. It was characteristic of
Mr. Beveridge that he should have determined not to
take his seat in the Senate until he was as well qualified
to speak on those questions as any other man in the body.
Not only did he prepare himself by a study of the legal
and constitutional questions involved and by the reading
of the whole literature of colonial administration as practised by other countries, but he resolved to go to the
far East, see what we had taken upon ourselves in the

INTRODUCTION

Philippine archipelago, and also acquaint himself with the politics and conditions of Japan and China, and of the Russians in the far East.

This thorough-going, masterful method of approaching the thing in hand enabled Mr. Beveridge to take on the floor of the Senate a place which at once made him a marked man. However he may have violated the traditions of the Senate, which require a new member to be seen but not heard for a year or two, there could be no doubt of the hearty approval of the country at large. Mr. Beveridge's position with respect to our insular territories and their treatment is set forth in several of the addresses included in the present volume.

Upon the great domestic problems of the day, Senator Beveridge has always taken a stand that is clear, open, and strongly presented. He is a national man, who does not fear to think in terms of continents rather than of parishes. He sees no possible reason why the Government of the United States should not use its powers for the regulation of things national in their scope which in the nature of the case require uniformity of treatment. He is not afraid of the large modern organization of capital and industry, but he believes in the supremacy of law and in the appropriate regulation of great interstate agents of commerce by the hand of the only government which has coextensive jurisdiction. His views upon these subjects are well worth a careful reading.

A statesman must have large views and he must have a sense of the processes of history. He must distinguish the permanent from the transient; he must rely upon public opinion rather than upon manipulation in politics,

INTRODUCTION

and there must be no doubt about his sincerity. Those
who read these addresses will feel that they have before
them the utterances of a man entitled to be placed in the
statesman's class. If they have also followed his public career, they will not be in any doubt, but will include
him with a few others in a group of our public men not
so large as we could wish to have it. These are the
men whose public careers have turned upon the constructive tasks and the great opportunities afforded in the
period immediately following the war between the United
States and Spain.

ALBERT SHAW.

THE MEANING OF THE TIMES

VITALITY OF THE AMERICAN CONSTITUTION

Address delivered before the Allegheny County Bar Association at the Tenth Annual Dinner, Pittsburgh, Pennsylvania, January 4, 1898.

GOVERNMENT under a written constitution was a noble but daring experiment. Free institutions had survived in England because the British Constitution had "proceeded from progressive history "— because it had grown as the people had grown, developed as liberty had developed. If the barons had attempted to fix, with the precision of a pen-point, all the metes and bounds of governmental powers when they wrested Magna Charta from King John; had Sir Edward Coke and the lawyers of England before and after him been strict constructionists of such an instrument, English history would have been lurid with unending revolution — the revolt of Anglo-Saxons against artificial restraint upon their enlarging intelligence and increasing power.

The first question of the thoughtful student of American affairs is: Why did we adopt a written constitution? Why did not England adopt a written constitution also? We know that the English Government operates under a constitution which, though unwritten, is as definite and real as our own. We know, too, that the English people are among the most practical of nations. We know, further, that the English people are the most aggressive in the assertion of personal rights of any people in the world, not excepting Americans. We know that liberty has steadily grown, without a single reaction for hundreds of years, in the mother country, and that the rights of property, of labor and of life are secured by English law more firmly than elsewhere in the world; and we know, finally, that English statesmen have been fruitful of practical methods for the advancement of the English people. Why, then, have they not adopted a written constitution, and why did our fathers, who themselves were English, adopt a written constitution?

The English people did not ordain a written constitution because their customs, their steadily developing modes of procedure, constituted their constitution. These customs, methods, institutions had been growing for centuries. They changed only as the tree changes from sprig to sapling, from sapling to oak. The roots of their constitution were in remote history, and growth was the law of its being. The violation of established modes of procedure or of universal privileges was certain to cause impeachment or revolution if attempted by Parliament or Crown. Thus the British Constitution, springing from the memories of the past, is vitalized by the affections of the present. It has its security not in cold type but in the hearts of the people.

But when the hour came for the founding of our Government, we found no such established system of connected custom and methods of governmental procedure. Personal rights and privileges we had, of course, and modes of thought and living; but these had been transplanted from England and Holland and were unsystematized, ineffective, not unified, and they did not afford a working machine of government or give national cohesion to the people. So it became necessary that a constitution should be adopted which should give expression to our nationality, mark out the boundary lines of governmental procedure, and even enumerate certain fundamental powers and prohibitions.

The germ for such an instrument already existed in most of our state constitutions, which were themselves an outgrowth, in part, of the people's enlarging powers from the colonial charters granted one hundred and fifty years before. No one can read Mr. Fisher's essay without acknowledging that our state constitutions, from which our National Constitution was so largely taken, were the development, through many scores of years, of the original charters granted to the colonists. We all understand, of course, how largely the British Constitution influenced our own; and Mr. Douglas Campbell has demonstrated our constitutional indebtedness to Holland. And even these sources are not the most remote. But such parts of our written Constitution as are indigenous had been growing here on our own soil for a century and a half. The occasion and cause for our adoption of a written constitution, therefore, become clear, and the reason why an equally liberty-loving and practical people, such as the English, preferred an unwritten constitution is explained.

When you come to the interpretation of this most remarkable instrument of history, the American constitution, you will see through a glass darkly unless you consider its purpose and the cause and nature of its origin.

It was not, as that great phrase-maker, Gladstone, said, " struck off at a given time by the brain and purpose of man," and therefore limited in its usefulness to the wisdom and circumstances of that time. On the contrary, our Constitution proceeded from " progressive history," and therefore is capable of future growth, just as it is the result of past growth. The Constitution was not a contract between thirteen allies called states, and so to be construed as a contract is to be construed; it was and is an ordinance of nationality springing from the necessities of the people and established directly by the people themselves. And as the Constitution gradually grew out of the necessities of the people in the past and was formulated out of the necessities of the people at the time of its adoption, so it embraces the necessities of the people for all time. But as the necessities of the people for all time could not possibly have been foreseen by the men who wrote the Constitution, it follows that they could not have intended to confine the purposes of the Constitution and the powers it confers to the necessities of the people of 1789; that they so wrote it that it might meet the requirements of the people for all time.

If that is so, it follows that the Constitution must steadily grow, because the requirements of the people steadily grow. As Mr. Justice Story says of the Constitution: " It was not intended to provide merely for the emergencies of a few years, but was to endure through a long lapse of ages, the events of which were locked up in the inscrutable purposes of Providence." The safety and vigor of the British Constitution is not only in the inviolability of the customs which constitute it, but even more in its powers of change and growth. So the vitality of the American Constitution and all constitutions must reside in their power to grow as the people grow, and furnish scope for the people's power and the Nation's necessities in exact proportion as the people's power and the Nation's necessities enlarge.

The Golden Rule of constitutional interpretation is this: *The Constitution exists for the people, not the people for the Constitution.*

But how can a written Constitution grow? Its words are there not to be changed. But the people change; conditions change; new problems arise; the happiness and welfare of the Nation constantly demand new methods, enlarging powers, activities in directions hitherto unknown. And if the Constitution can not keep pace with the needs of the people, it ceases to be useful to the people and becomes oppressive to them. If the Constitution had locked up the people's energies and prevented the recognition of their ever-increasing necessities and paralyzed their ever-enlarging powers, the people would have made short work of the Constitution. They would have overthrown it by revolution, if necessary, just as the people will overthrow anything which stands in the way of the prosperity of their homes, the happiness of their firesides.

The march of nationality is not to be withstood; and so the salvation of the Constitution is in its capacity for growth; and he is the enemy, no matter how much he may think himself the friend, of our fundamental law, who does not recognize its capacity for self-enlargement, determined by the enlarging necessities of the people. He is the enemy of the American Constitution who binds the American people to the letter of that instrument; for if that were done, the people's expanding necessities

would overthrow a constitution which retarded and oppressed them. It is therefore important to discover in
the instrument itself the principle of self-expansion.
Where is that principle found?

This question demanded answer at the very beginning
of the Government's life. A simple circumstance determined the inquiry. The Constitution contained no
authority for chartering a national bank. But such a
bank was chartered by Congress, and this act was assailed
as unconstitutional by those who said that the Nation's
Government had no power except that expressed in
words. Vexed by the contentions of these literalists,
Washington required of his cabinet opinions upon that
subject. Alexander Hamilton, the greatest synthetic intellect in legal history, in his opinion answered the question. He announced the principle of implied powers.
He realized that the controlling words of the Constitution were, " We, the people," and that the Constitution
in its larger and profounder meaning is an ordinance of
nationality.

So it follows that whatever may be essential to the
development of the people's nationality lies latent in the
Constitution's general terms, awaiting the necessity of
events to call it into action. Hamilton said: " If the
power is necessary to the purposes of the Constitution
it may be implied from powers expressed." This vital
principle of implied powers which Hamilton discovered,
John Marshall, the greatest judicial mind of all time,
developed, in his historic opinion in McCullough vs.
Maryland. Marshall reasoned that to deduce from the
Constitution power in Congress to charter a bank, it was
first necessary to establish the proposition that this is

a Nation of the people, deriving its powers directly from them and not from the states. If that is so, if nationality is the great purpose of the Constitution, if the people directly are the source of its power and the object of its beneficence, then unexpressed powers and duties in the National Government were called into being, which upon any other theory could not possibly exist.

And so Marshall declared that "the Government proceeds directly from the people." He said: "Its powers are granted by them, and are to be exercised directly on them and for their benefit." And so the necessities — yes, even the convenience of the people ("the interest of the Nation," as Marshall expressed it) — is the light by which the assertion of national power must be examined; and therefore, while the power to charter a bank is not found in so many words in the Constitution, a bank is a convenient method of executing powers expressly granted. Said Marshall: "The emergencies of the Nation may require that the treasure raised in the north should be transported to the south, that raised in the east conveyed to the west." A national bank is a convenient means to meet these "exigencies of the Nation," and "the interest of the Nation" therefore requires that the power to charter a bank be deduced from general powers expressly granted.

This was the reasoning upon which the power to charter a bank was declared to be a constitutional power of Congress. "We, the people" was the major premise; "the Nation" was the minor premise; a vital Constitution, comprehensive enough to embrace all the future of the American people, was the conclusion. Marshall's immortal exposition of the Constitution was merely the national thought and aspiration of the people expressed in words.   John Marshall, in writing his constitutional opinions, was a prophet of national life.   He made it possible for the Constitution to keep pace with the people.   Vitalized by the doctrine of implied powers, it ceased to be the barrier in the way of progress, which a mighty people in their resistless march towards nationality might have trampled underfoot.   It became instead that people's protecting spirit, directing their development and proceeding with it.

This aspiration of the common people toward nationality has expressed itself through every branch of the Government, legislative as well as judicial, executive as well as legislative.   Indeed, the Constitution may be said to have been construed, as it was created, by the people's common instinct of nationality.   The doctrinaires declared that internal improvements by the National Government were unconstitutional.   Three of our Presidents were sure of it.   Jefferson so believed.   Madison vetoed the first internal-improvement bill on the ground of its unconstitutionality.   Monroe made it the subject of a message to Congress.

But the common people knew better than the theorists. No matter what refined logic, spun from mere words and names, might conclude, the farmer and the trader, the feller of forests, the tiller of fields, the builder of homes, the makers, one and all, of the Nation, knew that they were fellow-citizens of the American Republic, and not mere members of friendly localities, and so they said: " It is the business of our common Nation to build canals, construct the national highways, clear the rivers, dredge the harbors of our common country; it is absurd to leave to each neighborhood its portion of the work, which if undone impairs and possibly destroys the whole;" and so internal improvements have become an unquestioned practice of the National Government.

And yet internal improvements by the National Government are constitutional exclusively upon the theory that the American people are a unit, and that their nationality is the purpose of their fundamental law. Power to make them is absolutely unauthorized in the Constitution's words, as Madison pointed out in his veto message. Indeed Madison went further and said that not only is such a power not expressed but can not be *implied*. Yet to-day the most extreme of strict constructionists never question the river and harbor bill, although less than two generations ago its constitutionality was a burning question. So have time and events and the necessities of the people marched on, leaving behind the quibblers over words.

The legal-tender decision advanced the doctrine of implied powers to the extreme logical limit of Marshall's thought. If the Constitution is a contract — if you must find all powers expressed in its words — the legal-tender acts were so plainly unconstitutional that it needed not the remarkable argument of Mr. Potter to demonstrate it. The Constitution gives Congress the power to " coin money." Printing on pieces of paper promise to pay is no more the coining of money than the offer of a promissory note is a legal tender for the payment of a debt; but if the Constitution is what James Wilson, of Pennsylvania, called it, " the charter of the people's nationality," if the purposes of the Constitution are truthfully stated in its preamble, then considerations large as destiny an-

swered the mere word-logic of the lawyer.   Then woke
the powers implied, and Congress, like another Richelieu,
drew round the imperiled Nation the magic circle of
Marshall's constitutional principles.

In the legal-tender decision the Supreme Court went
back to Marshall's method of considering " the exigencies
of the Nation."   The thunder of artillery of rebellion,
the blue battalions marching into the flames of havoc,
the Republic's flag fading from sight in the smoke of
internal conflict, the Nation's very life itself — these were
circumstances calling forth all the might of the saving
doctrine of implied powers.   The time of the passage
of the legal-tender acts was a time to remember the
difference between constitutions and statutes.   The Constitution gave the Government power to live; that, indeed,
was its purpose.   Congress remembered it when it passed
the act.   The Supreme Court remembered it when, in
deciding the legal-tender cases, it said:

"If it be held by this court that Congress has no constitutional
power under any circumstances or in any emergency to make
Treasury notes legal tender for the payment of all debts, the Government is without those means of self-preservation which, all
must admit, may in certain contingencies become indispensable.   It
is not indispensable to the existence of any power claimed for the
Federal Government that it can be found specified in the words
of the Constitution, or clearly or directly traceable to some one
of the specified powers.   Its existence may be deduced fairly from
more than one of the substantive powers expressly defined, or *from
them all combined*.   It is allowable to group together *any number
of them* and infer *from them all* that the power claimed has been
conferred."

This assertion of nationality by the exercise of powers
not specified in the Constitution has not been confined
to the legislative or judicial department.   Steadily, in-

creasingly, and without reaction, the executive department has also asserted national power where no specific warrant in the Constitution could be found for doing so. While Washington was President national troops were sent to suppress lawlessness in Pittsburgh, although the Constitution gives no such authority, but, on the contrary, expressly says that the president shall send the national guardians of law and order to a state only when the legislature of the state asks for aid, or, when it is not in session, the governor of the state applies for help.

A more notable instance was the action of President Cleveland in sending the national soldiers to Chicago, not only without the request of the legislature or the governor, but over the violent protest of the latter. It is said to be true that a mail car was hitched to the train which bore the soldiers to the imperiled city, but protection of United States mails was not the substantial ground upon which President Cleveland acted. When the soldiers arrived in Chicago they did more than protect mails; they protected the city itself, suppressed mob violence, and overcame the popular frenzy which was fast approaching the magnitude of insurrection.

The action of President Washington and the later assertion of national power by President Cleveland can be justified on two grounds only — first, that the Constitution granted to every state a republican form of government, which was in danger and which it was the President's duty to maintain; and, second, that the Nation is so consolidated that the destruction of peace in one great central city, where lines of communication which reach throughout the country are focused, affects the entire Republic, and that therefore "the interests of the Nation," again to use Marshall's phrase, demanded the restoration of order at the disturbed point. On any other ground the Constitution was not only disregarded, but actually violated.

The exercise of the doctrine of implied powers has surrounded the written Constitution with a body of judicial decisions and legislative and excutive practices which have grown to be as firm a part of our fundamental law as the written word of the instrument itself; and so it is that the Constitution has grown steadily and will grow steadily just as long and just as fast as the people themselves make progress. If this had not been so, the Constitution would have been a curse instead of a blessing. It would have been an iron band pressed around a young and growing tree, checking its growth and finally strangling it to death, instead of the bark which surrounds the trunk and expands as the great and substantial body within makes progress toward maturity. For the people are the real tree; the Nation is the real trunk; the Constitution is the vital incasement which surrounds and protects it, but which keeps progress with the growth of the tree itself.

In interpreting the Constitution, then, we are not confined to its written words. Those written words are controlling, and where they expressly forbid or confer power they must be obeyed; but where they say nothing directly, Marshall has shown that they may be the key which unlocks the machinery of our reason and sets our thought in motion. When the people's government asserts a power we should not only scan the Constitution to discover if that power is defined in words; we should also look at any special provision, at any number of provisions, at the preamble, or even consider the broad general purposes of the Constitution; and from any one or all of these discover whether or not the power asserted by the people's government can be deduced.

Besides the powers expressed in the Constitution and the powers plainly to be deduced from it, there are other examples of every-day legislation which are on the border-land between powers implied and powers inherent. For example, we have national laws for preventing the use of the people's mails for sending obscene literature. Nowhere in the Constitution is such a power given to Congress. The Constitution confers nothing but the power to establish and maintain post-offices and post-roads. Moreover, the Constitution guarantees freedom of speech and of the press. Correspondence is, of course, speech as much as verbal communication is speech. So that we not only have no express powers given to Congress by the Constitution to exclude obscene literature in communications, but we have the prohibition against limiting freedom of speech.

Nevertheless, this law is approved as a valid exercise of the powers of Congress. The Supreme Court approved it, of course, upon the ground that it was a power implied from the power to establish post-offices and post-roads; but considered from the viewpoint of mere logic, this conclusion is violent. From the viewpoint of logic and the philosophy of government, its validity might have been rested as reasonably upon the ground that it was the exercise of a power inherent in sovereignty. We are a decent people. At all hazards our national morality must be maintained. And the validity law could have been rested upon the same ground upon which rests the validity of the act for the relief of Ireland.

Another example is our national statute excluding lottery literature from our mails. The extraordinary argument of Mr. James C. Carter, before the Supreme Court, that no such power was conferred by the Constitution, seems to me unanswerable if you consider only logic applied to the written words of the Constitution. Again, the Supreme Court upheld this enactment as a power implied from the power to establish post-offices and post-roads. But again it might as well have been rested upon the ground that it was a power inherent in nationality — an exercise of sovereignty necessary for the preservation of the morality and uprightness of our people on which our continuance as a nation depends. Many other illustrations might be given similar to these, concerning the constitutionality of which lawyers will say, if you ask them, " The Supreme Court probably did strain the Constitution; but the laws were necessary, and what is the use of arguing about it ? "

Such powers as these, upheld by decisions which are based not upon well-connected reasoning, deduced not from powers expressly granted in the Constitution, but upon the court's autocratic " We think that these powers may be implied," may almost be called floating powers — that is, powers not expressly granted by the Constitution, powers not plainly implied from its provisions, and yet powers which the Supreme Court has upheld. The doubtful nature of those powers leads us to the consideration of inherent powers.

Some years ago Congress sent a ship-load of provisions to the starving people of Ireland, an English possession. At another time, during a yellow-fever plague, the National Government sent tents to Memphis, Tennessee. For this exercise of power there is not the slightest warrant in the Constitution, either in powers expressly granted or in powers implied; yet there was practically no objection either in Congress or the country, but the existence of such a power in Congress was generally considered a matter of course.

These facts reveal practically unquestioned powers in Congress beyond the Constitution — powers not granted to Congress by the Constitution, nor yet reserved to the people or the states. They show that there are powers inherent in the Government itself as an incident to sovereignty. Indeed, a portion of our every-day legislation, as is pointed out by Mr. Justice Strong in the legal-tender decisions, is exercise of power necessary for national life, and into which the Constitution could not go without becoming a statute instead of a constitution.

These inherent powers exist in the nature of government. They are a part of the thing called sovereignty, without which government could not exist. The government is a real and not a fictitious thing. It lives. It is not an automaton operated through written instruments alone. Whatever is necessary to its continued life and to its beneficent operation exists by virtue of the existence of the government itself. If you name government, you imply powers needful for that government's operation; and therefore when government is established that very act creates those powers which sleep till necessity awakens them.

So that there appear to be four classes of powers which properly may be exercised by Congress: First, those that are expressly given by the written words of the Constitution; second (and by far the greater number), those not expressly given in the written words of the Constitution, but reasonably implied from them; third, powers neither expressly implied nor clearly deducible from them and yet upheld by the court as implied powers; and, fourth, powers beyond all of these, the necessity and wisdom of which are so evident that nobody objects. I have already given examples of this last class of powers.   There are many others.

Where, for example, is there power in the Constitution for the purchase of Alaska?   There was no constitutional power for the reconstruction of the seceding states.   An example of inherent *rights* is the right of the citizen to go wherever he likes throughout the Republic, which the Supreme Court in Crandall vs. Nevada declares to be an *inherent* right which the Constitution does not give and which it is not necessary for the Constitution to give.   A volume might be written consisting of nothing but statutes and instances of the exercise by the National Government of national powers which are inherent.

The recognition of these powers does not destroy or impair the Constitution.   Such recognition vitalizes it. When Marshall announced the doctrine of implied powers the literalists of that day declared that he had overthrown the Constitution.   It is a fact that Chief Justice Marshall was denounced as a " monarchist " because of his judicial opinions which all men now concede to be the foundation of sane constitutional inspiration.   But now, after a hundred years, we see that the Constitution could not possibly have lived except for this principle, which, when it was announced, was declared to be fatal to that instrument. Perhaps no constructive statesman was more malignantly abused than was John Marshall for announcing the very principles which have been the salvation of the Republic. The same has been true to a diminishing extent of every judge or statesman who has recognized the expanding powers of the people's government. All of them, at one time or another, have been called the " destroyers of the Constitution," when in fact events have demonstrated them to be its preservers.

Of course no one will be so unfair as to assert that this recognition of the plain facts of our legislation — recognition of powers implied as well as expressed and of powers that are extra-constitutional — is a recognition that Congress, under any circumstances, may violate any of the expressed provisions of the Constitution. The Constitution points out the general methods of governmental procedure; they must be followed to the letter. For example, the Constitution directs how laws shall be enacted, signed, vetoed and the like; laws can be enacted in no other manner than that. The Constitution enumerates fundamental prohibitions; they must be observed to the smallest punctuation point. The Constitution declares that no title of nobility shall be granted, no bill of attainder shall be passed, and all legislation of attaint or conferring titles of nobility which Congress could pass in a hundred years would be merely waste paper. But where an act of the legislative or executive department of the Government is not prohibited by the Constitution, it may be exercised if expressly granted by that instrument; or if deducible from its written words; or if it is the exercise of a power which is an essential part of the thing called government.

Whether you agree to this or not, all must concede that, *as a matter of fact,* both Congress and the Executive are almost daily exercising powers not mentioned in the Constitution. And it is certain that the only two theories upon which this exercise of power may be justified are either, first, that these powers are inherent in sovereignty, or else, second, that they are powers reserved to the people and exercised by the people through their agents.

Let no one be apprehensive that the recognition of these powers will endanger the liberties of the people. It was the people themselves who established the Government. It has been the people themselves who have preserved it. It is the people themselves who must and will make the Republic ever grander, nobler and more beneficent. No people on earth, no people of history so great, so powerful, so moral, so high-purposed as the American people! Their past has been glorious, their present is propitious, their future is almost sublime.

But the future of the American people is heavy with difficulties; so is all opportunity for great and splendid work. Increasing population; the knitting together by railway, telegraph and telephone of places most remote until the Republic is a single and consolidated community; the combination of capital and labor, which this development makes necessary; the shrinking of the very globe itself by these same agencies, until nations are neighbors and alien peoples are at elbow touch; the new problems and novel responsibilities which all this brings; the still undreamed-of emergencies of a yet undreamed-of future — all these will demand of the American people all their resourcefulness, purity and power.

And the American people will solve and overcome them all if their hands are not fettered. The hands of the American people were not fettered, but armed with strength, when the Constitution was adopted. That free hand was not paralyzed, but connected with the mind and heart of the Nation, when Marshall established the doctrine of implied powers. So is our Constitution a source of life and power — the spirit and soul of a mighty people's progress. And so God defend and God preserve the American Constitution — a living spirit and not a dead and fading parchment!

FOREFATHERS' DAY

Response to a toast on the occasion of the twelfth annual celebration of the New England Society at St. Louis, December 21, 1896.

Mr. Toastmaster, Ladies and Gentlemen:

"FOREFATHERS' DAY" is the birthday of modern citizenship. We observe it because we need reconsecration to its ideals. No event deserves celebration unless the world still needs the principles which gave that event its meaning. We have no "Columbus Day," because the Santa Maria carried no principle necessary to our national welfare now; no "Cavaliers' Day," because from Jamestown shines no light for our pathway as the century's evening darkens into night. But "Forefathers' Day" will dawn as long as the Republic lives, because the Puritan principle is to the Republic the very breath of life.

Puritanism is only another name for citizenship. The Puritan is the foremost citizen of history. He was inspired to build free institutions — to tear down rotten forms of civil abuses. He had the instinct of government; his revolutions were more orderly than the conditions he attacked. Men have believed that he set sail into the inky horizon because of the fanatical fierceness of his desire for freedom of faith. I choose to believe that our forefathers obeyed a divine impulse to found the everlasting commonwealth of liberty.

Freedom of faith they had in Holland; but they

dreamed of an ideal state — and the Mayflower bloomed on wintry seas. It requires more than religion to found civil institutions. It requires ideals of civil conduct — ideals of civil government. And these are the Puritan's legacy to the world. He forgot the divine right of kings; he never forgot the divine right of citizenship.

He ceased to assert the sovereignty of royalty; he never ceased to assert the sovereignty of public duty. The Puritan was Thought in action; he was Honesty with Sword in hand; he was Liberty on the charge, officered by Law; he was Citizenship personified and crowned.

Men have painted his picture as a disturber of existing order — as a perpetual protester. But he protested only against public wrong — he disturbed only evil conditions; and the sight of either was, to the Puritan, a command of God to denounce it and destroy it, even if he destroyed himself. It was a part of his religion that each of us is commissioned from on high to think on every public question until our thought crystallizes into conviction, our conviction into execution.

Silence in the face of public wrong was, to the Puritan, infamous; and folded hands, when abuses flourished, were, to him, a kind of blasphemy. Peace purchased by acquiescence in the wrongs of power; prosperity procured by making peace with public sin, was worse to him, in reality and repute, than poverty or prison cell or death.

He would not truckle, even to a king. He owned no earthly master but the commonweal. He was a superb politician, because his ideals of citizenship required it; but he used his power to place in office only ability, integrity and courage, because, to him, the conduct of the state is a divine trust.

Our forefathers *believed* in something. Their lives were not interrogation points. They had ideals — those landmarks of progress. They denied the adage that nothing succeeds like success, and announced, instead, the proverb that nothing is success which is not right.

They had unfaltering faith in the final triumph of the truth, and they knew enough to know that one man speaking truth to-day, with all the multitudes and all the powers of earth opposing him, will be, to-morrow, a majority. Without that belief, faith in free institutions is impossible and absurd.

And so the Puritan never asked, " Shall I be on the winning side? " He only asked, " What is my duty as a citizen and a man? " He loathed the vulgar power of wealth, and riches gave no advantage, purchased no immunity, in his scheme of citizenship. He could not be bought. He could not be intimidated. He could not be silenced. He was sufficiently inspired to know that if he spoke right on and acted right on, the sordid world at last would listen, and, listening, be reclaimed.

The defiance of Garrison, " I will be as harsh as truth, as uncompromising as justice. I am in earnest. I will not equivocate. I will not excuse. I will not retreat a single inch; and I will be heard," was the voice of our forefathers speaking again to the nineteenth century. Wealth, power, society, dragged Garrison through the streets; but he saved them from themselves at last, and to-day the children of his opponents have built Garrison a monument before their very doors, and future generations will linger lovingly around his tomb.

They tell us of the Puritan's faults. But what were

his defects, which were personal and passing, compared
to his strong performance of his high mission. We
say he founded free institutions; we are answered that
his singing was nasal. We say he established religious
liberty; we are told his manners were austere. We declare that he is the father of modern citizenship; the reply is that his hair was short and his aspect somber.

And yet even some of those very defects have themselves triumphed, like his principles, and, to-day, are the
fashion of the world. Men's manners are direct and
frank to-day — it is the Puritan in social contact. Short
hair, plain dress, sincere speech, practical mind — even
the defects you criticize you have yourselves adopted; the
Puritan is the originator of modern styles.

Think of gentlemen with curled hair and perfumed
length of locks, silken breeches to the knees, gartered
hose, scarlet coat, plumed hat and cumbrous courtesy,
walking down your streets to-day; think of that impossible spectacle and know how thoroughly even the
Puritan modes have conquered your world of fashion.
Every counting-room is a testimonial to Puritan methods; every tailor shop a tribute to Puritan taste.

But he burned the witches say you? I deny it. It
was the Englishman and the Age that lit those fires —
not the Puritan and his faith. The Puritans of the
Netherlands were clean of that crime; while in England
the wisest held that shameful belief — Shakespeare, Bacon, Addison, Hale, none of them Puritans. Perish the
old lie that throws upon Puritanism the shadow of fagot
and stake; shine on for ever the truth that reveals in
Puritanism the noblest civil principle of human history.

The Puritan was a constructive iconoclast, a practical

dreamer, a realist of idealism. Order was to him as
necessary as honesty; law as essential as liberty; government as important as resistance to wrong. His revolutions stopped with the destruction of their causes;
they never swept in passion past the point of justice.
Puritanism knows no St. Bartholomew, no Terror, no
Commune. Instead of a Robespierre it produced a
Cromwell; instead of a Rousseau, a Milton; instead of a
Danton and a Marat, a Hampden and a Pym.

It beheaded a king? Yes, but ere the ax fell it gave
England the greatest government she had ever known.
Puritanism was no madness of fanaticism; it was the
sternness of truth, the conservatism of common sense.
It loved the Wat Tylers and Jack Cades as little as it
loved royal vice and golden shame. Public infamy
could not breathe the atmosphere of Puritanism and
live; riot, even against wrong, dared not show its head
where ruled the Puritan's orderly hand. In short, Puritanism is the religion of citizenship.

And what the United States needs to-day is the renaissance of the Puritan principle. I say this gladly; I, a
son of Virginia, proud of that mother of our nationality,
proud of her Washington, proud of her Marshall. The
Cavaliers have their mission, but what we need to-day
is Puritan citizenship. There are wrongs to right, excesses to resist, frivolities to dispel. The intense ma-
terialism of the times is palsying manhood, poisoning justice, driving faith from its throne.

Our civilization suffers from the curse of Mammon,
and we witness epicureanism in private conduct, corruption in public morals, dissolving beliefs in religion. This
is the age of the reign and the worship of material suc-

cess. We measure careers by dollars. We measure political questions by our pocket-books. We are losing
sight of the eternal. We are nearing the time which
Phillips foresaw. And as the Puritan principle saved the
English people two centuries ago, the Puritan principle
must and the Puritan principle will save the American
people to-day.

Our forefathers hoped to plant a society whose purity
would make it immortal. They set their ideals among
the stars. They believed that citizenship is the highest
product of human life. Upon that exalted belief they
built their institutions and they wrought as well as human foresight allows.

But natural processes have worked counter to their
plans. The continent was new. Man's first business
was to build, to plant, to reap, to garner and to preserve.
The demand for material necessities was imperative;
after material necessities we demanded material comforts, then material luxuries, and finally we passed under
the dominion of material ideas. It is evolution; it is
natural; but it is fatal — fatal, unless the only spirit that
has the power changes all into a blessing — the spirit of
Puritanism inspiring the American heart to nobler ideals
and braver action.

I say our present condition is a natural evolution.
Our first task was the production of wealth; it has
developed into the sovereignty of wealth. There are
abuses of combined and consolidated capital which usurp
the functions of government, levy tribute on every citizen
in the land, reduce individual manhood to parts of a
machine — forms of financial confederation which pervert supply and demand and compel the natural laws

of trade to rob and pilfer for their benefit. There is a growing form of gilded ambition which seeks the supreme seats of statesmanship; and these influences are diseasing the very heart of citizenship.

These conditions have set in motion a reaction as dangerous as the original wrongs — a reaction which has behind it an unreasoning discontent, a vague feeling that the scepter has passed from the people to the lords of riches. This reaction has already placed revolutionary representatives, here and there, in places of power. Its apostles already propose experiments with destruction, already question the laws of Nature, already advocate the repeal of the commandments of Sinai.

The Republic stands in equal danger from the abuses themselves and from their reaction. Cause and effect alike threaten this last experiment of freedom. The success of either would be fatal; both must learn once again the lesson of "Forefathers' Day." The Puritan principle, with its courage, its honesty, its sanity and its sense, must revive American citizenship once more and make the double conquest over greed and discontent.

The only hope of the American Republic is that in the American heart still lives the forefathers' spirit, which, aroused, will, at any cost, correct the evils of capital, destroy the lottery of public office, overcome the habit of acquiescence in successful political villainy, and at the same time will fight the insanity of reactionary extremes, the doctrines of dissolution, the tenets of madness, the Camille Desmoulins of the American Republic, and that old sectionalism, which, revived, will be the death of the Nation.

We need a strengthening of national *character*. We need, in statesmanship, the high seriousness of a Sumner, the large ability of a Hamilton, the unbending uprightness of an Adams. We need public men who *believe* in something — men whom Burke described as " pillars in the temple of state, not weather-vanes upon its dome." We need a national habit of faith. We need even an exaltation of taste. We need a renewal of the Puritan ideals.

The Trivial did not lay the foundations of this Republic. The Accommodating and Complacent never smote from Humanity's wrists the shackles of old abuses. Satisfaction with the comfortable present does not hasten the coming of the ideal future; nor does distrust of that future speed the darkened world onward toward the dawn.

Only men invincible in their faith — men who believed that all must finally fail which is not right; men who believed themselves the agents of the eternal principles and powers; and therefore men who counted unpopularity, financial failure, even death itself, as nothing in the performance of their high agency — only these have sweetened the waters of human life. Only these have plucked thorned and poisoned wrongs from the pathway of mankind; only these have builded lasting governments on the foundations of permanent liberty — and only such as these can preserve what they achieved. Such were our forefathers. Come back to us, their children, O Puritan spirit of citizenship! Come back that we may keep what they bequeathed!

> "Oh, raise us up, return to us again,
> And give us manners, virtue, freedom, power!"

LINCOLN, THE CONSERVATIVE

Address before the New York City Republican Club, New York City, on the occasion of Lincoln's Birthday, February 12, 1898.

TO-DAY, when the honor of the American people is the issue; to-day, when free institutions are on trial; to-day, when questions that search out the very heart of organized society are involved, the spirit of Abraham Lincoln commands all who agree on the principles of conservatism to forget incidental differences and strike together until repudiation, sectionalism and the spirit of class are defeated. Any issue that beclouds the issue of all issues will weaken us. In Lincoln's time one issue was supreme — loyalty to the Republic. Had he not acted on that, and that alone, New York to-day would have been the port of a section instead of the metropolis of the mightiest Nation on the globe.

To-day disintegrating issues are advocated. Bizarre beliefs abound. The destroyers are abroad. And it is time the steady elements of the American people answered the command of common sense to " fall in." We hear of a new Declaration of Independence. I prefer the old Declaration of the fathers. We need no new philosophy of society or of politics to-day. We need only a renaissance of common sense. Let the political philosophy of Abraham Lincoln be our guide.

If you ask me to state that philosophy in a phrase I

should answer that his life spells out these two words, patriotic conservatism. He knew that the conservative elements of the American people are always in the majority. No matter what individual views on incidentals might be, he knew that the sight of the country's imperiled flag would marshal those elements into an irresistible host. He knew that the people need only to see the main issue and they respond.

And so out of the men of all parties who agreed on the issue of the integrity of the Nation Abraham Lincoln fashioned the party which met the emergency of war and won, met the emergency of reconstruction and won, met the emergency of resumption and won, met the problem of national prosperity for thirty years and solved it — the party that stands to-day strengthened, as it was created, by the conservative elements of all parties, ready to meet the emergency of repudiation and of industrial chaos and ready to triumph as of old.

Across the page of events the spirit of Lincoln has written the mission of the Republican party. The mission is the rejection of extremes — the conduct of Government by common honesty and common sense rather than by fanaticism and revenge. And this is merely progress by the processes of growth. It is government by experience instead of experiment. It is moderation instead of violence.

How does the present situation require Lincolnian methods?

On the one hand there is a tendency toward destruction. The Huns and Vandals of society are ·on the march. An implied promise of piracy lurks in every utterance of some of their leaders. They awaken ex-

pectations which nothing but the abolition of property
and the reversal of civilization can fulfil. Every sane
man knows that their measures, if adopted, would not
quench the flames which reckless extremists are fanning.
The readjustment of society is the ultimate answer to
the implied question which the new commune thoughtlessly puts to civilization. That is one extreme.

On the other hand, there are abuses of capital which
furnish the pillagers a war-cry — abuses of riches which
furnish the Catilines examples to the discredit of all
wealth; vulgar ostentations of money which unsheathe
envy and whet hatred; a meddling with the making and
the execution of the statutes; a controlling of the natural
laws of trade by unlawful devices. Free institutions are
not responsible for these abuses. They are merely a
natural tendency developed beyond their rightful sphere
and requiring rebuke, regulation and restraint. These
developments have no party. They use all parties for
their purpose.

What is the policy of Abraham Lincoln's party in this
situation? Go, as Abraham Lincoln always did, to the
plain people and learn from them. They will tell you
that our policy is Lincolnian common sense — Lincolnian
conservatism. Abraham Lincoln's plain people are weary
of both extremes.

The producing millions demand a truce to wicked
agitation. Righteous agitation is always good. They
demand an opportunity to create prosperity. They demand that the honor of the Nation be put beyond peril.
They repudiate revenge as a motive of political action.
They expect improper commercial developments to be
corrected without violating the principles upon which

civilization rests. They demand laws so just and so equally enforced that the lips of sedition will be padlocked by the peace they bring.

The plain people! There is the source of Abraham Lincoln's wisdom. Lincoln, the rail-splitter, and Emerson, the scholar, agreed. The final and unprejudiced instinct of the masses is unerring. The common sense of the plain people, who in peace create the wealth, and in war carry the muskets of the Republic, is ultimately an unfailing guide. Abraham Lincoln was one of these. Their conscience was his oracle. Their thought was his counsel. He preferred the matured judgment of the plowman, the blacksmith and the merchant to the opinion of any doctrinaire who ever lived. And the lesson of his life to the party he so loved is to take our orders from the plain people for whom, alone, this Republic is worth preserving.

Abraham Lincoln coined the phrase "the plain people." But demagogues have learned its power, and used it, too, until, like liberty, crimes are committed in its name and its Lincolnian meaning is obscured. The professionally miserable are not the plain people. The plain people are not those who preach the gospel of despair; not those whose trade is discontent and whose occupation is idleness. A man does not become one of the plain people merely by getting into debt — or cease to be one of them by getting out of debt. Rags are not a necessary badge of plain people, although a pauper may be one of them — nor is wealth, although a millionaire may be one of the plain people, too.

Abraham Lincoln's plain people are those who understand that labor is the law for all, be they railroad presi-

dents or section hands. They are those who believe
in that old phrase " the brotherhood of man." They are
those who acknowledge and accept the opportunities of
American institutions. The plain people of Lincoln's
love are they who understand that Liberty did not intend to abolish Labor, Thought and Thrift, that blessed
trinity that presides over all prosperity. They are those
who believe that the order of Nature should not be re-
pealed — those who do not expect law to do for them
what they should do for themselves. These are the plain
people who produced an Abraham Lincoln, and it is time
that those who misuse that term should be reminded of
what it means.

Abraham Lincoln was the spirit of the people incar-
nate, and therefore he was the spirit of nationality in-
carnate, for the plain people know no sections — they
know only American citizenship. Sections exist only in
the minds of politicians too small for the Nation. Abraham Lincoln knew that the Constitution of the people begins with " We, the people "; that the people's Nation
" guarantees to every state a Republican form of government "; and so he sent the plain people, wearing the
Nation's uniform and carrying the Nation's flag wherever
the Nation's Constitution required it, and asked no treasonable governor's permission.

He taught the American people that the golden rule
of patriotism is unity. This imperial city is not New
York's alone, she is the pride of the entire Nation.
Your prosperity depends upon the prosperity of the
American people. You dare not be selfish even if you
would. We hear men talking about New York and its
business men wanting to injure the American people.

How absurd — since injury to the American people is suicide to you, and since injury to you is misfortune to them! Your wisest selfishness is to help the general welfare. Whatever truly blesses Nebraska blesses New York as well. You are not " the enemy's country." New York is too great to be anybody's enemy. To be an enemy to any American citizen is to be an enemy to yourself.

We of the Central West would not let you be our enemy even if you wished. Why? Because you are too useful — and because you are an American port. No foreign ship can shell Indianapolis, no foreign force invade us. Yet, because we believe as Lincoln believed, because the Pacific coast is our coast and Sandy Hook American soil, Indiana and the Republic's heart is in favor of coast defenses and a navy that can render every port of the Republic as secure as Indianapolis itself. And I will say for the benefit of Mr. Roosevelt, our Assistant Secretary of the Navy, who sits beside me, that we are not only in favor of the ships, but we are in favor of dry-docks big enough to hold them.

If invasion should come to you the West would give her blood to help defend you,— we prefer to help protect you first. All this is true because at the firesides of the West the national spirit of Abraham Lincoln is dwelling still, and this latter-day sectionalism has not gangrened our hearts. All this is true because the virile, unspoiled and exhaustless West, that gave you Morton, Grant and Lincoln, is still true to their teachings.

Abraham Lincoln knew no class — he knew only the people. Attempts to divide the land into sections and the people into classes is a curse, whether the time be

1860 or 1896. The Constitution says " We, the people," therefore whoever says " We, the classes, " is a
traitor to American institutions.   Classes in a Republic
is a contradiction in terms.   What is the dividing line?
Wealth?   If so, how much?   If a man is poor, is he one
of the masses?   When Labor, Thought and Thrift have
filled his pockets, is he one of the classes?   If so, all
men may destroy the dividing line.   If not, there is no
line to destroy.

Yet Lincoln's name is used to incite labor against
capital.   Let Lincoln's word rebuke the maligners of his
thought and deeds.   This is what he said: " That men
who are industrious and sober and honest in the pursuit
of their own interests, should, after a while, accumulate
capital, and, after that, should be allowed to enjoy it, is
right."   " Labor is the superior of capital, and deserves
much higher consideration;" but " capital has its rights,
which are as worthy of protection as any other rights."
That was Lincoln's idea — those are his words.

Labor is as necessary as food; capital is as necessary as
civilization.   Nothing but malevolence would create
hatred between them or prejudice against either.   It is
as infamous to lay the practices of financial pirates at
the door of capital as it is to lay the deeds of anarch-
ists and outlaws at the door of labor.   Evils of wealth
there are, and the party of Abraham Lincoln proposes to
remedy them.   Evils of wealth there are, and the American Robespierres propose not to remedy, but to annihilate.
The whole issue is summed up in this: Evolution or
revolution.   And in a republic there can be no excuse for
revolution.

Abraham Lincoln was as sound on finance as he was

on liberty. He had indulged in thought on the subject
of money. He had read the history of his country.
Therefore Lincoln told Congress that redundant issues
of paper money had " increased prices beyond real values,
thereby augmenting the cost of living to the injury of
labor, and the cost of supplies to the injury of the whole
country." These are Lincoln's words and their keenness
cuts the heart out of inflation.

History and thought had taught Abraham Lincoln
that inflated prices mean immediate loss to labor and
ultimate loss to all. He had mastered first principles.
He knew that a government can not make money; that
the only way a government gets money is to take it by
taxation or to get it by borrowing; that if the government can make money all taxation is a crime; and that if
it can not make money its credit is its principal asset.

And, taking first principles for his premises, he stated,
the necessary conclusion — for Lincoln was a logician
and did not stop on the road of his reasoning to refresh
himself with rhetoric. He did not understand this latter-
day logic which eliminates the conclusion from a syllogism, substitutes a philippic for the syllogism itself, calls
the whole process oratory, and writes *quod erat demonstrandum* beneath a jeremiad. But he stated his conclusion with true simplicity and said: " A return to
specie payments at the earliest period should ever be kept
in view. Fluctuations in the value of currency are always injurious, and to reduce these fluctuations to the
lowest possible point will always be a leading purpose in
wise legislation."

That is not the language of Wall Street, gentlemen —
nor of Lombard Street; it is the solemn warning of the

savior of his country. And Abraham Lincoln said all this, too, when the angel of war sowed fire and death throughout the land and the Nation bound up its wounds with the money of emergency. Shall we depart from his principles now, after a generation of prosperity and in a time of profoundest peace? By our belief in his wisdom, no! We appeal from his misinterpreters to Lincoln's very words. We appeal from passion to reason. We appeal from sectionalism to nationality. In the name of Lincoln we appeal to that infallible judge — the conscience of the masses whom our hero loved to call the plain people of the Republic! To that ultimate tribunal, whose voice is indeed the voice of God, we fearlessly leave the rendering of this decree of destiny.

GRANT, THE PRACTICAL

Address delivered in Boston at the banquet of the Middlesex Club of Massachusetts, on the anniversary of Ulysses S. Grant, April 27, 1898, six days after the declaration of the war with Spain.

PARTIZANSHIP should only be a method of patriotism. He who is a partizan merely for the sake of spoils is a bucaneer. He who is a partizan merely for the sake of a party name, is a ghost of the past among living events. He who is merely the partizan of an organization is only a pebble in the sling of a boss. But he who is the partizan of principle is a prince of citizenship; and such a partizan was Grant the practical.

To-day the horizon's rim flames with war. It is no time for partizanship, say men. Aye! it is the hour for the supremest partizanship — it is the hour for the partizanship of patriotism. It is the hour when all who differ on methods for the Republic's ordinary welfare perceive, at last, an issue so immense that, disagreeing still, they still agree. It is an hour when men who thought that they hated one another at the ballot-box will find that they love one another on the battle-field.

It is an hour when a master event has found and struck the key-note of harmony between labor and capital. It is an hour when Democrats, Republicans and Populists learn that, after all, our parties are but different an-

swers to the same great question, and that question is,
" What of the Republic? "

In a Republic nothing is so necessary as to know that,
after all, the ultimate object of each citizen is the same
— the welfare of the Nation.   When we place a noble
motive in an adversary's breast we have prepared the
way for reason.   You can not argue with a prejudice.
Thought is ineffectual against the heart of hate.   Class
knows no influence but arrogance or revenge.   And,
sometimes, it is good that the lightnings of some vast
emergency should clear the heavy air and reveal us all as
brothers, reveal us all as the partizans of patriotism —
reveal the flag, still floating as the emblem of our common love, and not the ensign of our internecine hate.

It is good that an hour so dread shall strike that, in its
silence, Fate can hear in the heartbeats of a united people this sentiment of destiny —" Our country — may she
ever be right!   But, right or wrong, our country! "   In
such an hour it is well to speak of him who, out of his
affection even for those he fought, and not out of hate
for any one, uttered these words, " Unconditional surrender " and " Let us have peace;" but, " Let us have
peace " after " unconditional surrender."

War is only an auxiliary of peace.   War is a means
merely — not an end.   It has been said of old —" In time
of peace prepare for war."   But in time of war we also
should prepare for peace.   This is not done by hushing
reason's voice while the guns roar.   It is not done by
neglecting the great principles upon which abiding prosperity depends.   War-time should be the time for civil
vigilance as well as martial valor.   It is the season of
emergency methods in finance no more to be endured as

permanent policy than the medicines of fever are to be
continued as the regular food for health. It is the
period of intoxication in industry, when no thought is
taken of the morrow — how war activity and war wages
may be continued after the delirium has passed.

Lincoln knew all this when he warned Congress of
the evils of a diluted currency at the very hour when
thousands of the boys in blue were charging to their
death. Grant knew all this when, before the first furrow
had been turned in the blood-soaked soil, he burdened
his messages to Congress with argument and appeal for
a return to the methods of sanity and nature. And to-
day the thunder of our guns, in a conflict for civilization,
will be a blessing and a benediction to the Republic, if we
forget not those principles upon which the welfare, the
honor and the destiny of the Nation must depend in
years to come. For in the light of battle our political
enemies will behold us as their brothers, and, as brothers, we shall reason together.

Grant understood that the three elements of the Republic's prosperity are labor, currency and commerce.
He knew that labor is hunger personified if unemployed;
that currency is the script and chips of gamblers if un-
steady in value; that commerce begins to die the moment
it ceases to expand. And so, to the welfare of the Nation's toilers, to the honesty of the Nation's money, and
to the extension of the Nation's trade, his energies were
directed.

Grant came from the working-men, as every true
leader of the people must; he knew that we are a
nation of workers, and therefore that the civilization of
the Republic is measured by the condition of the produc-

ers of the land; and so he said: "The true greatness
of a nation is found in the elevation of its laborers."
*He was the first President to sanction the principle of
eight hours for a legal day of work; the first President
to approve the principle of the organization of labor.*

He knew that the safety, as well as the prosperity, of
the land rests on its working-men; that the victors of the
Republic in every battle for liberty from Concord to
Appomattox were its working-men, as it is their sons
who again to-morrow will be fighting the battles of the
Nation; and logic drew for him the conclusion that the
welfare of the working-man is the first measure of the
country's safety. He understood that the employment
of the Nation's working-men is the secret of prosperity.
He said: "If employment can be given to labor prosperity necessarily follows. How to induce capital to
employ labor is the question."

And he knew that constancy in currency is the best in-
ducement to capital to enter industry; that the first condition for a constant currency is to base it on the steadiest
standard of value; and so, with the haze of war still in
the air, this genius of the practical saw that the use of
the best money known to man is the first great truth in
the science of prosperity.

And he could not see why the dollar which is best for
the millionaire is not also best for the working-man.
He failed to see the advantage to the laborer of wages
which would buy a fraction only of what the best wages
would buy. He told Congress, a generation ago, that
"the greater part of the burden of prostration for want
of a sound financial system falls upon the working-man,
who must, after all, produce the wealth of the land."

He said that, because his convictions were the crystallization of experience and thought, and not the nightmares of a political delirium.

He was just to capital as well as to labor, and believed that even the Government should pay its debts in the same money in which he wished all wages paid. A certain political movement in America to-day is called by one of its priests " a church with a creed and not a party with a platform." Well, thirty years before its disciples went forth to preach, Grant rebuked the creed of this financial church in these words, which now seem prophecy: " To protect the national honor every dollar of Government indebtedness should be paid in gold unless otherwise expressly stipulated in the contract. Let it be understood that no repudiator of one farthing of our public debt will be trusted in public place and it will go far toward strengthening a credit which ought to be the best in the world."

You who have looked upon Grant merely as a man of the camp and the field, what think you of these words of this son of our western prairies? Boil down to the essence of its wisdom all the eloquence of your schooled and polished statesman, and I will match it with the clear and simple words of Grant, the Patriot and the Republican. Thank God, America has followed his advice; and to-day, when war consumes our ordinary revenue, the capital of the world is at our door and offered to us at a discount instead of a premium.

This statesman of the practical knew that even the best money can not induce capital and labor to produce unless there are markets for their products; and so he knew that, ultimately, the trade of the world must be ours.

He foresaw the day when our productive energies must have an outlet, and so he said: " Our commerce should be encouraged; American ship-building and carrying capacity increased and foreign markets sought. When a new market can be created for the sale of our products a new means is discovered for utilizing our idle capital and labor to the advantage of the whole people." And he followed them by this necessary conclusion: " A Nation situated like ours should maintain a navy adequate to its responsibilities."

He never forgot that we are a conquering race and that we must obey our blood and occupy new markets, and, if necessary, new lands. He had the prophet's seer-like sight which beheld, as a part of the Almighty's infinite plan, the disappearance of debased civilizations and decaying races before the higher civilization of the nobler and more virile types of man. He understood that the axioms applicable to thirteen impoverished colonies have been rendered obsolete by history. An echo of the past is not to stay the progress of a mighty people and their free institutions. He declared that " the theory of government changes with general progress."

He had the instinct of empire. He dreamed the same dreams that God put in the brain of Jefferson and of Hamilton, of John Bright and of Emerson, and of all the imperial intellects of his race — the dream of American extension till all the seas shall bloom with that flower of liberty, the flag of the Great Republic. Let me quote you, in this historic time, these words of Grant: " I do not share in the apprehension held by many as to the danger of governments being weakened and destroyed by their extension of territory. Commerce, education and rapid transit of thought and matter have changed all this. Rather do I believe that our Great Maker is preparing the world in His own good time to become one nation, speaking one language, and when armies and navies shall no longer be required."

The dawning of the day of that dream's fulfilment is at hand. American factories are making more than the American people can use; American soil is producing more than they can consume. Fate has written our policy for us; we must get an ever increasing portion of foreign trade. We shall establish trading-posts throughout the world as distributing points for American products. We shall cover the oceans with our merchant marine. We shall build a navy to the measure of our greatness. Great colonies, flying our flag and trading with us will grow about our posts of trade. Our institutions will follow our flag on the wings of our commerce. And American law, American order, American civilization and the American flag will plant themselves on shores, hitherto bloody and benighted, but, by those agencies of God, henceforth to be made beautiful and bright.

If this means the Stars and Stripes over an Isthmian canal, over Hawaii, Cuba and the southern seas, if it means American empire in the name of the Great Republic and its free institutions, then let us meet that meaning with a mighty joy and make that meaning good, no matter what barbarism and all our foes may say or do.

If it means Anglo-Saxon solidarity; if it means an English-American understanding upon the basis of a division of the world's markets so that the results may be just; upon the basis of justice to Ireland so that the un-

derstanding may be enduring; if it means such an English-speaking people's league of God for the permanent
peace of this war-worn world, the stars in their courses
will fight for us and countless centuries will applaud.

All this is not the work of a day nor yet of a year.
It is the work of a period — the period of the commercial expansion of the Republic, and therefore of the expansion of the institutions of the Republic. For liberty
and order and civilization are not planted by speeches,
nor essays, nor editorials; their seed are borne in the
talons of Trade and planted by the fingers of Might.
The beginning of that period is upon us and its rounding
out is as sure as the processes of time. Fate puts the
American people upon their decision between a Chinese
policy of isolation, poverty and decay, or an American
policy of progress, prosperity and power. The young
men of America will decide that question as Grant wished
to decide it, and as the God of civilization has willed it
shall be decided. And let those beware who prove
apostate to our destiny.

What should be the policy of this war? What will
be its result? The geography of the globe answers the
first question; the vigor of the American people answers
the second. We are at war with Spain. Therefore our
field of operations is not confined to Cuba. We are at
war with *Spain*. It is our military duty to strike her
at her weakest point before we strike her at her stronger
points. Cuba must fall into our hands, but that will
be only when Spain is conquered. Our warships to-day
surround Cuba; our armies are massing for Cuba. And
yet Cuba will be the last to fall. In the Pacific is the
true field of our earliest operations. There Spain has

an island empire, the Philippine archipelago. It is poorly
defended. Spain's best ships are on the Atlantic side.
In the Pacific the United States has a powerful squad-
ron. *The Philippines are logically our first target.*

And when the Pacific fleet of Spain is destroyed, not
only is Spain beaten to her knees by the loss of the
Philippines, which would necessarily follow, but San
Francisco and Portland are at the same time rendered
safe.

It is not Cuba we must conquer — it is *Spain.* We
must never lose sight of the main objective — to bring an
early peace by conquering the enemy. We must strike
the most vulnerable points of that enemy. We must sail
to meet the enemy — not wait for her to come. These
were the methods and maxims of Grant. And, although not a gun has yet been fired, I predict that these
will be the American methods in the war we have just
declared.

The ultimate result we can leave to the wisdom of
events. Victory will be ours — that we know this moment, though no shot has yet been fired. And in that
victory I see a blessing, not only for the people of Cuba,
but for the oppressed of the Philippines. And in free-
ing peoples, perishing and oppressed, our country's blessing will also come; for profit follows righteousness.

The first gun of our war for civilization will be also
the morning gun of the new day in the Republic's imperial career. We wage no war of conquest; but

> "The hand that rounded Peter's dome
> And groined the aisles of Christian Rome
> Wrought in a sad sincerity —
> He builded better than he knew."

We go forth to fight for humanity; but where American blood establishes liberty and law in any land, the American people will see that that blood is not shed in vain. Events, which are the arguments of God, are stronger than words, which are the arguments of man. We are the allies of Events and the comrades of Tendency in the great day of which the dawn is breaking.

In the name of labor to be employed in clothing and feeding new peoples and new lands, we welcome it. In the name of capital, to be quickened into developing our commerce, we welcome it. In the name of a congested industrial situation to be relieved by our commercial expansion, we welcome it. In the name of the far-seeing minds of every party and of every English-speaking land whose dream we now go forth to realize, we welcome the dawn of the Republic's full-grown manhood. And finally we welcome it in the name of him whose natal day we celebrate. We shall not live to see its close; but it is enough to behold its daybreak, for in that

> "Our eyes have seen the glory
> Of the coming of the Lord."

THE MARCH OF THE FLAG

Speech opening the Indiana Republican Campaign at Tomlinson Hall, Indianapolis, September 16, 1898. This speech was made the Republican campaign document for Indiana, Iowa and other states.

IT is a noble land that God has given us; a land that can feed and clothe the world; a land whose coastlines would inclose half the countries of Europe; a land set like a sentinel between the two imperial oceans of the globe, a greater England with a nobler destiny.

It is a mighty people that He has planted on this soil; a people sprung from the most masterful blood of history; a people perpetually revitalized by the virile, man-producing working-folk of all the earth; a people imperial by virtue of their power, by right of their institutions, by authority of their Heaven-directed purposes — the propagandists and not the misers of liberty.

It is a glorious history our God has bestowed upon His chosen people; a history heroic with faith in our mission and our future; a history of statesmen who flung the boundaries of the Republic out into unexplored lands and savage wilderness; a history of soldiers who carried the flag across blazing deserts and through the ranks of hostile mountains, even to the gates of sunset; a history of a multiplying people who overran a continent in half a century; a history of prophets who saw the consequences of evils inherited from the past and of martyrs who died

47

to save us from them; a history divinely logical, in the process of whose tremendous reasoning we find ourselves to-day.

Therefore, in this campaign, the question is larger than a party question. It is an American question. It is a world question. Shall the American people continue their march toward the commercial supremacy of the world? Shall free institutions broaden their blessed reign as the children of liberty wax in strength, until the empire of our principles is established over the hearts of all mankind?

Have we no mission to perform, no duty to discharge to our fellow-man? Has God endowed us with gifts beyond our deserts and marked us as the people of His peculiar favor, merely to rot in our own selfishness, as men and nations must, who take cowardice for their companion and self for their deity — as China has, as India has, as Egypt has?

Shall we be as the man who had one talent and hid it, or as he who had ten talents and used them until they grew to riches? And shall we reap the reward that waits on our discharge of our high duty; shall we occupy new markets for what our farmers raise, our factories make, our merchants sell — aye, and, please God, new markets for what our ships shall carry?

Hawaii is ours; Porto Rico is to be ours; at the prayer of her people Cuba finally will be ours; in the islands of the East, even to the gates of Asia, coaling stations are to be ours at the very least; the flag of a liberal government is to float over the Philippines, and may it be the banner that Taylor unfurled in Texas and Fremont carried to the coast.

The Opposition tells us that we ought not to govern a people without their consent. I answer, The rule of liberty that all just government derives its authority from the consent of the governed, applies only to those who are capable of self-government. We govern the Indians without their consent, we govern our territories without their consent, we govern our children without their consent. How do they know that our government would be without their consent? Would not the people of the Philippines prefer the just, humane, civilizing government of this Republic to the savage, bloody rule of pillage and extortion from which we have rescued them?

And, regardless of this formula of words made only for enlightened, self-governing people, do we owe no duty to the world? Shall we turn these peoples back to the reeking hands from which we have taken them? Shall we abandon them, with Germany, England, Japan, hungering for them? Shall we save them from those nations, to give them a self-rule of tragedy?

They ask us how we shall govern these new possessions. I answer: Out of local conditions and the necessities of the case methods of government will grow. If England can govern foreign lands, so can America. If Germany can govern foreign lands, so can America. If they can supervise protectorates, so can America. Why is it more difficult to administer Hawaii than New Mexico or California? Both had a savage and an alien population; both were more remote from the seat of government when they came under our dominion than the Philippines are to-day.

Will you say by your vote that American ability to

govern has decayed; that a century's experience in self-rule has failed of a result? Will you affirm by your vote that you are an infidel to American power and practical sense? Or will you say that ours is the blood of government; ours the heart of dominion; ours the brain and genius of administration? Will you remember that we do but what our fathers did — we but pitch the tents of liberty farther westward, farther southward — we only continue the march of the flag?

The march of the flag! In 1789 the flag of the Republic waved over 4,000,000 souls in thirteen states, and their savage territory which stretched to the Mississippi, to Canada, to the Floridas. The timid minds of that day said that no new territory was needed, and, for the hour, they were right. But Jefferson, through whose intellect the centuries marched; Jefferson, who dreamed of Cuba as an American state; Jefferson, the first Imperialist of the Republic — Jefferson acquired that imperial territory which swept from the Mississippi to the mountains, from Texas to the British possessions, and the march of the flag began!

The infidels to the gospel of liberty raved, but the flag swept on! The title to that noble land out of which Oregon, Washington, Idaho and Montana have been carved was uncertain; Jefferson, strict constructionist of constitutional power though he was, obeyed the Anglo-Saxon impulse within him, whose watchword then and whose watchword throughout the world to-day is, " Forward! ": another empire was added to the Republic, and the march of the flag went on!

Those who deny the power of free institutions to expand urged every argument, and more, that we hear, to-day; but the people's judgment approved the command of their blood, and the march of the flag went on!

A screen of land from New Orleans to Florida shut us from the Gulf, and over this and the Everglade Peninsula waved the saffron flag of Spain; Andrew Jackson seized both, the American people stood at his back, and, under Monroe, the Floridas came under the dominion of the Republic, and the march of the flag went on! The Cassandras prophesied every prophecy of despair we hear, to-day, but the march of the flag went on!

Then Texas responded to the bugle calls of liberty, and the march of the flag went on! And, at last, we waged war with Mexico, and the flag swept over the southwest, over peerless California, past the Gate of Gold to Oregon on the north, and from ocean to ocean its folds of glory blazed.

And, now, obeying the same voice that Jefferson heard and obeyed, that Jackson heard and obeyed, that Monroe heard and obeyed, that Seward heard and obeyed, that Grant heard and obeyed, that Harrison heard and obeyed, our President to-day plants the flag over the islands of the seas, outposts of commerce, citadels of national security, and the march of the flag goes on!

Distance and oceans are no arguments. The fact that all the territory our fathers bought and seized is contiguous, is no argument. In 1819 Florida was farther from New York than Porto Rico is from Chicago to-day; Texas, farther from Washington in 1845 than Hawaii is from Boston in 1898; California, more inaccessible in 1847 than the Philippines are now. Gibraltar is farther from London than Havana is from

Washington; Melbourne is farther from Liverpool than Manila is from San Francisco.

The ocean does not separate us from lands of our duty and desire — the oceans join us, rivers never to be dredged, canals never to be repaired. Steam joins us; electricity joins us — the very elements are in league with our destiny. Cuba not contiguous! Porto Rico not contiguous! Hawaii and the Philippines not contiguous! The oceans make them contiguous. And our navy will make them contiguous.

But the Opposition is right — there is a difference. We did not need the western Mississippi Valley when we acquired it, nor Florida, nor Texas, nor California, nor the royal provinces of the far northwest. We had no emigrants to people this imperial wilderness, no money to develop it, even no highways to cover it. No trade awaited us in its savage fastnesses. Our productions were not greater than our trade. There was not one reason for the land-lust of our statesmen from Jefferson to Grant, other than the prophet and the Saxon within them. But, to-day, we are raising more than we can consume, making more than we can use. Therefore we must find new markets for our produce.

And so, while we did not need the territory taken during the past century at the time it was acquired, we do need what we have taken in 1898, and we need it now. The resources and the commerce of these immensely rich dominions will be increased as much as American energy is greater than Spanish sloth. In Cuba, alone, there are 15,000,000 acres of forest unacquainted with the ax, exhaustless mines of iron, priceless deposits of manganese, millions of dollars' worth of which we must buy, to-day, from the Black Sea districts. There are millions of acres yet unexplored.

The resources of Porto Rico have only been trifled with. The riches of the Philippines have hardly been touched by the finger-tips of modern methods. And they produce what we consume, and consume what we produce — the very predestination of reciprocity — a reciprocity " not made with hands, eternal in the heavens." They sell hemp, sugar, cocoanuts, fruits of the tropics, timber of price like mahogany; they buy flour, clothing, tools, implements, machinery and all that we can raise and make. Their trade will be ours in time. Do you indorse that policy with your vote?

Cuba is as large as Pennsylvania, and is the richest spot on the globe. Hawaii is as large as New Jersey; Porto Rico half as large as Hawaii; the Philippines larger than all New England, New York, New Jersey and Delaware combined. Together they are larger than the British Isles, larger than France, larger than Germany, larger than Japan.

If any man tells you that trade depends on cheapness and not on government influence, ask him why England does not abandon South Africa, Egypt, India. Why does France seize South China, Germany the vast region whose port is Kaouchou?

Our trade with Porto Rico, Hawaii and the Philippines must be as free as between the states of the Union, because they are American territory, while every other nation on earth must pay our tariff before they can compete with us. Until Cuba shall ask for annexation, our trade with her will, at the very least, be like the preferential trade of Canada with England. That, and the ex-

cellence of our goods and products; that, and the convenience of traffic; that, and the kinship of interests and
destiny, will give the monopoly of these markets to the
American people.

The commercial supremacy of the Republic means that
this Nation is to be the sovereign factor in the peace
of the world. For the conflicts of the future are to
be conflicts of trade — struggles for markets — commercial wars for existence. And the golden rule of peace
is impregnability of position and invincibility of preparedness. So, we see England, the greatest strategist
of history, plant her flag and her cannon on Gibraltar, at
Quebec, in the Bermudas, at Vancouver, everywhere.

So Hawaii furnishes us a naval base in the heart of
the Pacific; the Ladrones another, a voyage further on;
Manila another, at the gates of Asia — Asia, to the trade
of whose hundreds of millions American merchants,
manufacturers, farmers, have as good right as those of
Germany or France or Russia or England; Asia, whose
commerce with the United Kingdom alone amounts to
hundreds of millions of dollars every year; Asia, to whom
Germany looks to take her surplus products; Asia, whose
doors must not be shut against American trade. Within
five decades the bulk of Oriental commerce will be ours.

No wonder that, in the shadows of coming events so
great, free-silver is already a memory. The current of
history has swept past that episode. Men understand,
to-day, that the greatest commerce of the world must be
conducted with the steadiest standard of value and most
convenient medium of exchange human ingenuity can
devise. Time, that unerring reasoner, has settled the
silver question. The American people are tired of talk-

ing about money — they want to make it. Why should the farmer get a half-measure dollar of money any more that he should give a half-measure bushel of grain?

Why should not the proposition for the free coinage of silver be as dead as the proposition of irredeemable paper money? It is the same proposition in a different form. If the Government stamp can make a piece of silver, which you can buy for 45 cents, pass for 100 cents, the Government stamp can make a piece of pewter, worth one cent, pass for 100 cents, and a piece of paper, worth a fraction of a cent, pass for 100 cents. Free-silver is the principle of fiat money applied to metal. If you favor fiat silver, you necessarily favor fiat paper.

If the Government can make money with a stamp, why does the Government borrow money? If the Government can create value out of nothing, why not abolish all taxation?

And if it is not the stamp of the Government that raises the value, but the demand which free coinage creates, why has the value of silver gone down at a time when more silver was bought and coined by the Government than ever before? Again, if the people want more silver, why do they refuse what we already have? And if free silver makes money more plentiful, how will *you* get any of it? Will the silver-mine owner give it to you? Will he loan it to you? Will the Government give or loan it to you? Where do you or I come in on this free-silver proposition?

The American people want this money question settled for ever. They want a uniform currency, a convenient currency, a currency that grows as business grows, a currency based on science and not on chance.

And now, on the threshold of our new and great career, is the time permanently to adjust our system of finance. The American people have the mightiest commerce of the world to conduct. They can not halt to unsettle their money system every time some ardent imagination sees a vision and dreams a dream. Think of Great Britain becoming the commercial monarch of the world with her financial system periodically assailed! Think of Holland or Germany or France bearing their burdens, and, yet, sending their flag to every sea, with their money at the mercy of politicians-out-of-an-issue. Let us settle the whole financial system on principles so sound that no agitation can shake it. And then, like men and not like children, let us on to our tasks, our mission and our destiny.

There are so many real things to be done — canals to be dug, railways to be laid, forests to be felled, cities to be builded, fields to be tilled, markets to be won, ships to be launched, peoples to be saved, civilization to be proclaimed and the flag of liberty flung to the eager air of every sea. Is this an hour to waste upon triflers with nature's laws? Is this a season to give our destiny over to word-mongers and prosperity-wreckers? No! It is an hour to remember our duty to our homes. It is a moment to realize the opportunities fate has opened to us. And so it is an hour for us to stand by the Government.

Wonderfully has God guided us. Yonder at Bunker Hill and Yorktown His providence was above us. At New Orleans and on ensanguined seas His hand sustained us. Abraham Lincoln was His minister and His was the altar of freedom the Nation's soldiers set up on a hundred battle-fields. His power directed Dewey in the East and delivered the Spanish fleet into our hands, as He delivered the elder Armada into the hands of our English sires two centuries ago. The American people can not use a dishonest medium of exchange; it is ours to set the world its example of right and honor. We can not fly from our world duties; it is ours to execute the purpose of a fate that has driven us to be greater than our small intentions. We can not retreat from any soil where Providence has unfurled our banner; it is ours to save that soil for liberty and civilization.

OUR PHILIPPINE POLICY

Senator Beveridge's first public utterance on the Philippine situation after his return from a visit to the islands. Delivered in the Senate of the United States, January 9, 1900.

Mr. Beveridge. I ask for the reading of the joint resolution introduced by me on Thursday last.

The President pro tempore. The Chair lays before the Senate the joint resolution introduced by the Senator from Indiana, which was laid on the table subject to his call. The joint resolution will be read.

The Secretary read the joint resolution (S. R. 53) defining the policy of the United States relative to the Philippine Islands, as follows:

> *Be it resolved by the Senate and House of Representatives of the United States of America in Congress assembled,* That the Philippine Islands are territory belonging to the United States; that it is the intention of the United States to retain them as such and to establish and maintain such governmental control throughout the archipelago as the situation may demand.

Mr. Beveridge. Mr. President, I address the Senate at this time because Senators and Members of the House on both sides have asked that I give to Congress and the country my observations in the Philippines and the far East, and the conclusions which those observations compel; and because of hurtful resolutions introduced and

58

utterances made in the Senate, every word of which will
cost and is costing the lives of American soldiers.

Mr. President, the times call for candor. The Philippines are ours, "territory belonging to the United
States," as the Constitution calls them. And just beyond
the Philippines are China's illimitable markets. We
will not retreat from either. We will not repudiate our
duty in the archipelago. We will not abandon our opportunity in the Orient. We will not renounce our part
in the mission of our race. And we will move forward
to our work, not howling out regrets, like slaves whipped
to their burdens, but with gratitude for a task worthy of
our strength, and thanksgiving to Almighty God that He
has deemed us worthy of His work.

This island empire is the last land left in all the oceans.
If it should prove a mistake to abandon it, the blunder,
once made, would be irretrievable. If it proves a mistake
to hold it, the error can be corrected when we will.
Every other progressive nation stands ready to relieve us.

But to hold it will be no mistake. Our increasing
trade henceforth must be with Asia. More and more
Europe will manufacture what it needs, secure from its
colonies what it consumes. Where shall we turn for consumers of our surplus? Geography answers the question. China is our natural customer. She is nearer to
us than to England, Germany or Russia, the commercial
powers of the present and the future. They have moved
nearer to China by securing permanent bases on her borders. The Philippines give us a base at the door of all
the East.

Lines of navigation from our ports to the Orient and
Australia; from the Isthmian Canal to Asia; from all Ori-

ental ports to Australia, converge at and separate from the Philippines. These islands are a self-supporting, dividend-paying fleet, permanently anchored at a spot selected by the strategy of Providence, commanding the Pacific. And the Pacific is the ocean of the commerce of the future. Most future wars will be conflicts for commerce. The power that rules the Pacific, therefore, is the power that rules the world. And, with the Philippines, that power will be the American Republic.

China's trade is the important commercial fact of our future. Her foreign commerce was $285,738,300 in 1897, of which we, her neighbor, had less than 9 per cent., of which only a little more than half was merchandise sold to China by us. We ought to have 50 per cent., and we shall. And China's foreign commerce is only beginning. Her resources, her possibilities, her wants, all are undeveloped. She has only 340 miles of railway. I have seen trains loaded with natives and all the activities of modern life already appearing along the line. But she needs, and in fifty years will have 200,000 miles of railway.

Who can estimate her commerce then? That statesman commits a crime against American trade who fails to put America where she may command that trade. Germany's Chinese trade is increasing like magic. She has established ship lines and secured a tangible foothold on China's soil. Russia's Chinese trade is growing rapidly. She is spending the revenues of the Empire to finish her railroad into Pekin itself, and she is in physical possession of Manchuria. Japan's Chinese trade is multiplying in volume and value. She is bending her energy to her merchant marine, and is located along China's very coast.

But the Philippines command the commercial situation of the entire East. Can America best trade with China from San Francisco or New York? From San Francisco, of course. But if San Francisco were closer to China than New York is to Pittsburgh, what then? And Manila is nearer to Hong-Kong than Havana is to Washington. Yet American statesmen plan to surrender this commercial advantage in the Orient which Providence and our soldiers' lives have won for us. When History comes to write the story of that suggested treason to American supremacy and therefore to the spread of American civilization, let her in mercy write that those who so proposed were blind and nothing more.

But if they did not command China, India, the Orient, the whole Pacific for purposes of offense, defense, and trade, the Philippines are so valuable in themselves that we should hold them. I have cruised more than 2,000 miles through the archipelago, every moment a surprise at its loveliness and wealth. I have ridden hundreds of miles over the islands, every foot of the way a revelation of vegetable and mineral riches.

No land in America surpasses in fertility the plains and valleys of Luzon. Rice and coffee, sugar and cocoa-nuts, hemp and tobacco, and many products of the temperate as well as the tropic zone grow in various sections of the archipelago. The forests of Negros, Mindanao, Mindora, Paluan, and parts of Luzon are invaluable and intact. The wood of the Philippines can supply the furniture of the world for a century to come. At Cebu the best informed man in the island told me that 40 miles of Cebu's mountain chain are practically mountains of coal. Pablo Majia, one of the most reliable men on the islands,

confirmed the statement. Some declare that the coal is
only lignite; but ship captains who have used it told me
that it is better steamer fuel than the best coal of Japan.

In one of the islands valuable deposits of copper exist
untouched. In many places there are indications of gold.
The mineral wealth of the Philippines will one day surprise the world. I base this statement partly on personal
observation, but chiefly on the testimony of foreign merchants in the Philippines, who have practically investigated the subject, and upon the unanimous opinion of
natives and priests. And the mineral wealth is but a
small fraction of the agricultural wealth of these islands.

And the wood, hemp, copra, and other products of the
Philippines supply what we need and can not ourselves
produce. Spain's export trade, with the islands undeveloped, was $11,534,731 annually. Ultimately our
trade, when the islands shall be developed, will be $125,-
000,000 annually; for who believes that we can not do
ten times as well as Spain?

Behold the markets they command. It is as if a half-
dozen of our states were set down between Oceana and
the Orient, and those states themselves undeveloped and
unspoiled of their primitive wealth and resources.

Nothing is so natural as trade with one's neighbors.
The Philippines make us the nearest occidental neighbor
of all the East. Nothing is more natural than to trade
with those you know — this is the philosophy of all ad-
vertising. The Philippines bring us permanently face
to face with the eagerly sought-for customers. National
prestige, national propinquity, these and commercial activity are the elements of commercial success. The Philippines give the first.

The character of the American people supplies the last. It is a providential conjunction of all the elements of trade, of duty, and of power. If we are willing to go to war rather than let England have a few feet of frozen Alaska, which affords small market and commands none, what should we not do rather than let England, Germany or Japan have all the Philippines? And no man on the spot can fail to see that this would be their fate if we retired.

The climate is the best tropic climate in the world. This is the belief of those who have lived in many tropic countries, with scores of whom I talked on this point. My own experience with tropical conditions has not been extensive; yet, speaking from that experience, I testify that the climate of Iloilo, Jolo, Cebu, and even of Manila, greatly surpasses that of Hong-Kong. And yet on the bare and burning rock of Hong-Kong our constructing race has builded one of the noblest cities of all the world, and made the harbor it commands the focus of the commerce of the East. And the glory of that achievement illumines with a rarer splendor than that of Waterloo the flag that floats above the harbor; for from Hong-Kong's heights civilization is irradiating all the Orient. If this be imperialism, its final end will be the empire of the Son of Man.

And yet, only fifty years ago this English outpost of empire was a smooth and treeless mountain, blazing like a ball of fire beneath the tropic suns. The Philippines are beautiful and rich, with the healing seas pouring round and through them and fanned by a thousand winds. Even in the hottest season, under severest conditions, I found the weather tolerable and often delightful; and in

Luzon, Panay, Cebu, Negros and Sulu I have been in the sun and rain without protection from either for hours at a time, traveling from place to place on horseback, on foot, or in a boat, rising at dawn, retiring at midnight, week after week, without injury to health.

General MacArthur, commanding a force which had been fighting continuously for three months, and which was under fire practically every hour, was in excellent health the time I saw him at San Fernando, our extreme front. General Lawton, that perfect soldier, whom I have seen ride, order, plan and execute all day, and then ride, order, plan and execute all night, until the Tagals named him " the soldier of the night," told me that his health was perfect. General Otis, that devoted servant of the Republic, who toils ceaselessly, does not fall ill, nor grow weary, nor complain. I could give the names of scores of our officers and describe feats of their endurance witnessed by me that would have taxed their strength even in America. Yet they do not succumb.

I have seen newspaper correspondents exert themselves in all kinds of weather, without food or sleep, in a way that would prostrate them in the hottest days of our summer in Chicago or New York. Major Hoyt, chief medical officer with MacArthur, told me that San Fernando is as healthy as the average American town. The European business men of Cebu, Iloilo and Manila work as hard and as many hours a day as those of New York, and a finer body of physical manhood can not be gathered at random in America. This proves that this garden of the seas is not the sweltering, steaming, miasmatic swamp it has been described.

It will be hard for Americans who have not studied

them to understand the people. They are a barbarous race, modified by three centuries of contact with a decadent race. The Filipino is the South Sea Malay, put through a process of three hundred years of dishonesty in dealing, disorder in habits of industry, and cruelty, caprice, and corruption in government. It is barely possible that 1,000 men in all the archipelago are now capable of self-government in the Anglo-Saxon sense. I know many clever and highly-educated men among them, but there are only three commanding intellects and characters — Arellano, Mabini, and Aguinaldo. Arellano, the chief justice of their supreme court, is a profound lawyer and a brave and incorruptible man. Mabini, who, before his capture, was the literary and diplomatic associate of Aguinaldo, is the highest type of subtlety and the most constructive mind that race has yet produced.

Aguinaldo is a clever, popular leader, able, brave, resourceful, cunning, ambitious, unscrupulous, and masterful. He is full of decision, initiative and authority, and has the confidence of the masses. He is a natural dictator. His ideas of government are absolute orders, implicit obedience, or immediate death. He understands the character of his countrymen. He is a Malay Sulla; not a Filipino Washington.

Conclusions as to the character of the natives were forced upon me by observing people in all walks of life in the different islands, and by conversations with foreign merchants, priests, mestizos, pure Filipinos, and by contact with every variety of mind, character and opinion, from San Fernando, in Luzon, on down through the entire archipelago to the interior of Sulu. These conversations were had informally at dinner-tables, on journeys, and the like, and always under conditions favorable to entire frankness and unreserve.   Their chief value is that they are the real opinions of their authors and not prepared and guarded statements.

I shall read to the Senate salient points from a few of my notes of these conversations, reserving the names of the persons interviewed, except that of Pablo Majia, of Cebu, who was assassinated a week after I met him, and whose fate I shall not risk bringing down on others. Their names and residences are here in this book, and will be gladly given to any Senator or to the Senate in executive session.   The conversations themselves, of course, are many of them quite extended.   I give here only the brief extracts, which may be helpful to a correct understanding of the subject immediately in hand.

One of the principal merchants of the Philippines and the far East, said, among many other things:

> The whole country is incalculably rich. With only ordinary good government commerce would be immense. Spanish rule was corrupt, but commerce accustomed itself to the conditions and flourished in spite of them. So rich is the country that commerce will survive any situation, however bad, if it is only fixed and certain. The people are incapable of self-government. The few exceptions are no examples of the masses. For years to come a very strong government will be necessary. The climate is very good.   I have lived here eighteen years, and my health was never better.

[Senator Beveridge then went on to read interviews to similar effect that he had had with a large number of other prominent citizens of the Philippines, merchants, physicians, scientists, planters, native Filipinos, etc.]

I shall close these few extracts, which are a fair sample of a great number of others, all of which I am willing to submit to the Senate at any time, by reading a few suggestions made to me by the first statesman of the far East, who has had practical experience with similar problems. In the course of a long interview, he said:

> You must establish government over the islands, because it is incalculably to your interest in the future, and because, if you do not, another power will undoubtedly take them, involving the world in a war for which you will be responsible.
>
> As to the form of government, you should have a governor-general of great ability, firmness, and purity; under him sub-officers of districts, and under them still lower officials for the municipalities, all appointed by their superiors and not chosen by the people. You should employ the ablest natives in the government service in some way so as to enlist them on your side. The courts are the most important consideration of all. Don't put the natives in charge of them, whatever else you do. In the armed forces, don't give any natives superior positions for a long time. Don't do too much for them in the beginning. Do it gradually, as the years go by. I think your course is clear. Don't treat with them until you defeat them. You must do that. You can not treat and fight.
>
> Make English the language of the courts, schools and everywhere possible. Let me impress on you the necessity of conferring your benefits on these people quite gradually. If you give them too much they can not appreciate nor understand nor rightly use it, and it will thus be thrown away; but if you give them the blessing of free institutions gradually, you furnish a source of constant gratitude. In the other way you exhaust yourself at the beginning, and besides, fail in your good intentions.

Here, then, Senators, is the situation. Two years ago there was no land in all the world which we could occupy for any purpose. Our commerce was daily turning toward the Orient, and geography and trade developments made necessary our commercial empire over the Pacific. And in that ocean we had no commercial, naval, or military base. To-day, we have one of the three great

ocean possessions of the globe, located at the most commanding commercial, naval, and military points in the
eastern seas, within hail of India, shoulder to shoulder
with China, richer in its own resources than any equal
body of land on the entire globe, and peopled by a race
which civilization demands shall be improved.

Shall we abandon it? That man little knows the common people of the Republic, little understands the instincts of our race, who thinks we shall not hold fast and
hold it for ever, administering just government by simplest methods. We may trick up devices to shift our
burden and lessen our opportunity; they will avail us
nothing but delay. We may tangle conditions by applying academic arrangements of self-government to a crude
situation; their failure will drive us to our duty in the
end.

The military situation, past, present, and prospective,
is no reason for abandonment. Our campaign has been
as perfect as possible with the force at hand. We have
been delayed, first, by a failure to comprehend the im-
mensity of our acquisition; second, by insufficient force;
third, by our efforts for peace. In February, after the
treaty of peace, General Otis had only 3,722 officers and
men whom he had a legal right to order into battle.
The terms of enlistment of the rest of his troops had
expired, and they fought voluntarily and not on legal
military compulsion. It was one of the noblest examples of patriotic devotion to duty in the history of
the world.

Those who complain, do so in ignorance of the real
situation. We attempted a great task with insufficient means; we became impatient that it was not

finished before it could fairly be commenced; and I pray we may not add that other element of disaster, pausing in the work before it is thoroughly and for ever done. That is the gravest mistake we could possibly make, and that is the only danger before us. Our Indian wars would have been shortened, the lives of soldiers and settlers saved, and the Indians themselves benefited, had we made continuous and decisive war; and any other kind of war is criminal, because ineffective. We acted toward the Indians as though we feared them, loved them, hated them — all at the same time — with a mingling of foolish sentiment, inaccurate thought, and paralytic purpose. Let us now be instructed by our own experience.

This war is like all other wars. It needs to be finished before it is stopped. I am prepared to vote either to make our work thorough or even now to abandon it. A lasting peace can be secured only by overwhelming forces in ceaseless action until universal and absolutely final defeat is inflicted on the enemy. To halt before every armed force, every guerrilla band opposing us is dispersed or exterminated, will prolong hostilities and leave alive the seeds of perpetual insurrection.

The news that 60,000 American soldiers have crossed the Pacific; that, if necessary, the American Congress will make it 100,000 or 200,000 men; that, at any cost, we will establish peace and govern the islands, will do more to end the war than the soldiers themselves. But the report that we even discuss the withdrawal of a single soldier at the present time, and that we even debate the possibility of not administering government throughout the archipelago ourselves, will be misunderstood and misrepresented and will blow into a flame once more the fires our soldiers' blood has almost quenched.

Mr. President, reluctantly and only from a sense of duty, I am forced to say that American opposition to the war has been the chief factor in prolonging it. Had Aguinaldo not understood that in America, even in the American Congress, even here in the Senate, he and his cause were supported; had he not known that it was proclaimed on the stump and in the press by a faction in the United States, that every shot his misguided followers fired into the breasts of American soldiers was like the volleys fired by Washington's men against the soldiers of King George, his insurrection would have dissolved before it entirely crystallized.

The utterances of American opponents of the war are read to the ignorant soldiers of Aguinaldo and repeated in exaggerated form among the common people. Attempts have been made by wretches claiming American citizenship to ship arms and ammunition from Asiatic ports to the Filipinos, and these acts of infamy were coupled by the Malays with American assaults on our Government at home.

The Filipinos do not understand free speech, and therefore our tolerance of American assaults on the American Government means to them that the Government is in the minority or it would not permit what appears to them such treasonable criticism. It is believed and stated in Luzon, Panay, and Cebu that the Filipinos have only to fight, harass, retreat, break up into small parties, if necessary, as they are doing now, but by any means hold out until the next Presidential election, and our forces will be withdrawn.

All this has aided the enemy more than climate, arms, and battle. I have heard these reports myself; I have talked with the people; I have seen our mangled boys in the hospital and field; I have stood on the firing line and beheld our dead soldiers, their faces turned to the pitiless southern sky, and in sorrow, rather than anger, I say to those whose voices in America have cheered those misguided natives on to shoot our soldiers down, that the blood of those dead and wounded boys of ours is on their hands. In sorrow, rather than anger, I say these words, for I earnestly believe that our brothers knew not what they did.

But, Senators, it would be better to abandon the Philippines, and count our blood and treasure already spent a profitable loss, than to apply any academic arrangement of self-government to these children. They are not yet capable of self-government. How could they be? They are not a self-governing race; they are Orientals, Malays, instructed by Spaniards in the latter's worst estate.

They know nothing of practical government, except as they have witnessed the weak, corrupt, cruel, and capricious rule of Spain. What magic will any one employ to dissolve in their minds and characters those impressions of governors and governed which three centuries of misrule has created? What alchemy will change the oriental quality of their blood, in a year, and set the self-governing currents of the American pouring through their Malay veins? How shall they, in a decade, be exalted to the heights of self-governing peoples which required a thousand years for *us* to reach?

Let men beware how they employ the term " self-government." It is a sacred term. It is the watchword at the door of the inner temple of liberty, for liberty does not always mean self-government. Self-government is a method of liberty — the highest, simplest, best — and it is acquired only after centuries of study and struggle and experiment and instruction in all the elements of the progress of man. Self-government is no cheap boon, to be bestowed on the merely audacious. It is the degree which crowns the graduate of liberty, not the reward of liberty's infant class, which has not yet mastered the alphabet of freedom. Savage blood, oriental blood, Malay blood, Spanish example — in these do we find the elements of self-government?

We must act on the situation as it exists, not as we would wish it. I have talked with hundreds of these people, getting their views as to the practical workings of self-government. The great majority do not understand participation in any government whatever. The most enlightened among them declare that self-government will succeed because the employers of labor will control the vote of their employees, and that this will insure intelligent voting. I was assured that we could depend upon good men always being in office, because the officials who constitute the government will nominate their successors, choose those among the people who will do the voting, and determine how and where elections will be held.

The most ardent advocate of self-government that I met was anxious that I should know that such a government would be tranquil, because as he said, " if any one criticized it, the government would shoot the offender." A few of them have a sort of verbal understanding of the democratic theory, but the above are examples of the notions concerning the practical workings of self-government entertained by the aristocracy, the rich planters and traders, and heavy employers of labor,— the men who would run the government.

Example for decades will be necessary to instruct them in American ideas and methods of administration. Example, example; always example — this alone will teach them.

Our government must be simple and strong. It must be a uniform government. Different forms for different islands will produce perpetual disturbance, because the people of each island will think that the people of the other islands are more favored than they. In Panay I heard murmurings that we were giving Negros an American constitution. Such jealousy is a human quality, found even in America, and we must never forget that in dealing with the Filipinos we deal with children. And so our government must be simple and strong. Simple and strong! The meaning of those two words must be written in every line of Philippine legislation, realized in every act of Philippine administration.

A Philippine office in our Department of State; an American governor-general in Manila, with power to meet daily emergencies; possibly an advisory council with no power except that of discussing measures with the governor-general, which council would be the germ for future legislatures, a school in practical government; an American lieutenant-governor in each province, with a like council about him; if possible, an American resident in each district and a like council grouped about him; frequent and unannounced visits of provincial governors to the districts of their province; periodical reports to the governor-general; an American board of visitation to make semi-annual trips to the archipelago without power of suggestion or of interference with officials or people, but only to report and recommend to the Philippine office of our State Department; a Philippine civil service, with promotion for efficiency; a reform of local taxation on a just and scientific basis; the minting of abundant money for Philippine and Oriental use; the granting of franchises and concessions upon the theory of developing the resources of the archipelago, and therefore not by sale, but upon participation in the profits of the enterprise; a system of public schools with compulsory attendance rigidly enforced; the establishment of the English language throughout the islands, teaching it exclusively in the schools and using it, through interpreters, exclusively in the courts; a simple civil code and a still simpler criminal code, and both common to all the islands except Sulu, Mindanao, and Paluan; American judges for all but smallest offenses; gradual, slow, and careful introduction of the best Filipinos into the working machinery of the government; no promise whatever of the franchise until the people have been prepared for it; all the legislation backed by the necessary force to execute it; this outline of government the situation demands as soon as tranquillity is established. Until then military government is advisable.

We can not adopt the Dutch method in Java, nor the English method in the Malay states, because both of these systems rest on and operate through the existing governments of hereditary princes, with Dutch or English residents as advisers. But in the Philippines there are no such hereditary rulers, no such established governments.

There is no native machinery of administration except that of the villages. The people have been deprived of the advantages of hereditary native princes, and yet not instructed in any form of regular, just, and orderly government.

Neither is a protectorate practicable. If a protectorate leaves the natives to their own methods more than would our direct administration of their government, it would permit the very evils which it is our duty to prevent. If, on the other hand, under a protectorate, we interfere to prevent those evils, we govern as much as if we directly administer the government, but without system or constructive purpose. In either alternative we incur all the responsibility of directly governing them ourselves, without any of the benefits to us, to them, or to the archipelago, which our direct administration of government throughout the Islands would secure.

Even the elemental plan I have outlined will fail in the hands of any but admirable administrators. Spain did not fail in devising. Many of her plans were excellent. She failed in administering. Her officials as a class were corrupt, indolent, cruel, immoral. They were selected to please a faction in Spain, to placate members of the Cortes, to bribe those whom the Government feared. They were seldom selected for their fitness. They were the spawn of Government favor and Government fear, and therefore of Government iniquity.

The men we send to administer civilized government in the Philippines must be themselves the highest examples of our civilization. I use the word examples, for examples they must be in that word's most absolute sense. They must be men of the world and of affairs, students of their fellow-men, not theorists nor dreamers. They must be brave men, physically as well as morally. They must be men whom no force can frighten, no influence coerce, no money buy. Such men come high, even here in America. But they must be had.

Better pure military occupation for years than government by any other quality of administration. Better abandon this priceless possession, admit ourselves incompetent to do our part in the world-redeeming work of our imperial race; *better now haul down the flag than to apply academic notions of self-government to these children or attempt their government by any but the most perfect administrators our country can produce.* I assert that such administrators can be found.

There is one in Cuba now who, with the words "Money is not everything," refused $30,000 a year as president of a corporation that he might continue the work of our race in the regeneration of Santiago, and thus announced and typified the new ideal of the Republic, which pessimists declared had become sordid and base. And among our 80,000,000 we shall find others like him. Necessity will produce them.

I repeat that our Government and our administrators must be examples. You can not teach the Filipino by precept. An object-lesson is the only lesson he comprehends. He has no conception of pure, orderly, equal, impartial government, under equal laws justly administered, because he has never seen such a government. He must be shown the simplest results of good government by actual example, in order that he may begin to understand its most elementary principles.

Such a government will have its effect upon us here in

America, too. Model administration there will be an example created by ourselves for model administration here. It is not true that " charity begins at home." Selfishness begins there; but charity begins abroad and ends in its full glory in the home. It is not true that perfect government must be achieved at home before administering it abroad; its exercise abroad is a suggestion, an example and a stimulus for the best government at home. It is as if we projected ourselves upon a living screen and beheld ourselves at work.

England to-day is the home of ideal municipal governments. England's administration of Bombay did not divert attention from Glasgow, and Glasgow is to-day the model for all students of municipal problems. England's sanitary regeneration of filthy Calcutta made it clearer that Birmingham must be regenerated, too, and to-day Birmingham is the municipal admiration of all instructed men.

England's miracle in Egypt, surpassing the ancient one of turning rods into serpents because the modern miracle turns serpents into men, deserts into gardens, famine into plenty — England's work in the land of the Sphinx has solved its profound riddle, exalted not England only, but all the world, by its noble example, and thrilled to the soul every citizen of Great Britain with civic pride in the achievement of the greatest civilizing empire of the world. " Cast thy bread upon the waters and after many days it shall return unto you. With what measure ye mete, it shall be meted to you again."

Mr. President, self-government and internal development have been the dominant notes of our first century; administration and the development of other lands will be the dominant notes of our second century. And administration is as high and holy a function as self-government, just as the care of a trust estate is as sacred an obligation as the management of our own concerns.

Administration of good government is not denial of liberty. For what is liberty? The liberty of a people means law. First of all, it is a common rule of action, applying equally to all within its limits. Liberty means protection of property and life without price, free speech without intimidation, justice without purchase or delay, government without favor or favorites. What will best give all this to the people of the Philippines — American administration, developing them gradually toward self-government, or self-government by a people before they know what self-government means?

The Declaration of Independence does not forbid us to do our part in the regeneration of the world. If it did, the Declaration would be wrong, just as the Articles of Confederation, drafted by the very same men who signed the Declaration, were found to be wrong.

The Declaration does not contemplate that all government must have the consent of the governed. It announces that man's " inalienable rights are life, liberty and the pursuit of happiness; that to secure these rights governments are established among men deriving their just powers from the consent of the governed; that when any form of government becomes destructive of those rights, it is the right of the people to alter or abolish it." " Life, liberty and the pursuit of happiness " are the important things; " consent of the governed " is one of the means to those ends.

If " any form of government becomes destructive of

those ends, it is the right of the people to alter or abolish it," says the Declaration. "Any form" includes all forms. Thus the Declaration itself recognizes other forms of government than those resting on the consent of the governed. The word "consent" itself recognizes other forms, for "consent" means the understanding of the thing to which the "consent" is given; and there are people in the world who do not understand any form of government. And the sense in which "consent" is used in the Declaration is broader than mere understanding, for "consent" in the Declaration means participation in the government "consented" to. And yet these people who are not capable of "consenting" to any form of government must be governed.

And so the Declaration contemplates all forms of government which secure the fundamental rights of life, liberty and the pursuit of happiness — self-government, when that will best secure these ends, as in the case of people capable of self-government; other appropriate forms, when people are not capable of self-government. And so the authors of the Declaration themselves governed the Indian without his consent; the inhabitants of Louisiana without their consent; and, ever since, the sons of the makers of the Declaration have been governing not by theory, but by practice, after the fashion of our governing race, now by one form, now by another, but always for the purpose of securing the great eternal ends of life, liberty and the pursuit of happiness, not in the savage, but in the civilized meaning of those terms — life according to orderly methods of civilized society; liberty regulated by law; pursuit of happiness limited by the pursuit of happiness by every other man.

If this is not the meaning of the Declaration, our Government itself denies the Declaration every time it receives the representative of any but a republican form of government, such as that of the Sultan, the Czar, or other absolute autocrats, whose governments, according to the Opposition's interpretation of the Declaration, are spurious governments, because the people governed have not " consented " to them.

The Opposition is estopped from denying our constitutional power to govern the Philippines as circumstances may demand, for such power is admitted in the case of Florida, Louisiana, Alaska. How, then, is it denied in the Philippines? Is there a geographical interpretation to the Constitution? Do degrees of longitude fix constitutional limitations? Does a thousand miles of ocean diminish constitutional power more than a thousand miles of land?

The ocean does not separate us from the field of our duty and endeavor — it joins us, an established highway needing no repair, and landing us at any point desired. The seas do not separate the Philippine Islands from us or from each other. The seas are highways through the archipelago, which would cost hundreds of millions of dollars to construct if they were land instead of water. Land may separate men from their desire, the ocean never. Russia has been centuries crossing Siberian wastes; the Puritans crossed the Atlantic in brief and flying weeks.

If the Boers must have traveled by land, they would never have reached the Transvaal; but they sailed on liberty's ocean; they walked on civilization's untaxed highway, the welcoming sea. Our ships habitually sailed round the Cape and anchored in California's harbors before a single trail had lined the desert with the whitening bones of those who made it. No! No! The ocean unites us; steam unites us; electricity unites us; all the elements of nature unite us to the region where duty and interest call us.

No; the oceans are not limitations of the power which the Constitution expressly gives Congress to govern all territory the Nation may acquire. The Constitution declares that:

> "Congress shall have power to dispose of and make all needful rules and regulations respecting the territory belonging to the United States."

Not the Northwest territory only; not Louisiana or Florida only; not territory on this continent only; but *any* territory anywhere belonging to the Nation. The founders of the Nation were not provincial. Theirs was the geography of the world. They were sailors as well as landsmen, and they knew that where our ships should go our flag might follow.

They had the logic of progress, and they knew that the Republic they were planting must, in obedience to the laws of our expanding race, necessarily develop into the greater Republic which the world beholds to-day, and into the still mightier Republic which the world will finally acknowledge as the arbiter, under God, of the destinies of mankind.

And so our fathers wrote into the Constitution these words which I have quoted,— words of growth and expansion, of empire, if you will, unlimited by geography or climate or by anything but the vitality and possibilities of the American people.

The power to govern all territory the Nation may acquire would have been in Congress if the language affirming that power had not been written in the Constitution. For not all powers of the National Government are expressed. Its principal powers are implied. Had this not been true, the Constitution would have failed, for the people in any event would have developed and progressed. And if the Constitution had not had the capacity for growth corresponding with the growth of the Nation, the Constitution would and should have been abandoned as the Articles of Confederation were abandoned.

For the Constitution is not immortal in itself, not useful, even, in itself. The Constitution is immortal and even useful, only as it serves the orderly development of the Nation. The Nation alone is immortal. The Nation alone is sacred. The army is its servant. The navy is its servant. The President is its servant. This Senate is its servant. Our laws are its methods. Our Constitution is its instrument.

This is the golden rule of constitutional interpretation: *The Constitution was made for the people, not the people for the Constitution.*

Hamilton recognized this golden rule when he formulated the doctrine of implied powers. Marshall recognized it when he applied that doctrine to constitutional interpretation in McCullough vs. Maryland. Congress recognized it when it provided for internal improvements. The Supreme Court recognized it when it confirmed the act of Congress in making the promissory notes of the Republic legal tender for debts. Washington recognized it when he sent the Nation's soldiers to supress local riot in 1794; and Lincoln, the soul and symbol of the common people, recognized the doctrine of implied powers in every effort he made to save the Nation.

"The letter killeth; but the spirit giveth life."

By the same reasoning that Hamilton, Marshall, Washington and Lincoln employed we could infer our power to do the work of administering government in the Philippines as the situation may demand, even if that power had not been affirmed in express words. We could infer it from the purpose of the Constitution to "provide for the common defense and promote the general welfare" of the Nation and the power given Congress to make laws to secure these ends.

For the archipelago is a base for the commerce of the East. It is a base for military and naval operations against the only powers with whom conflict is possible; a fortress thrown up in the Pacific, defending our western coast, commanding the waters of the Orient, and giving us a point from which we can instantly strike and seize the possessions of any possible foe.

The Nation's power to make rules and regulations for the government of its possessions is not confined to any particular formula of laws or kind of government or type of administration. Where do Senators find constitutional warrant for any special kind of government in "territory belonging to the United States"? The language affirming our power to govern such territory is as broad as the requirements of all possible situations. And there is nothing in the Constitution to limit that comprehensive language. The very reverse is true.

Power to administer government anywhere and in any manner the situation demands would have been in Congress if the Constitution had been silent; not merely because it is a power not reserved to the states or people; not merely because it is a power inherent in and an attribute of nationality; not even because it might be inferred from other specific provisions of the Constitution; but because it is the power most necessary for the ruling tendency of our race — the tendency to explore, expand and grow, to sail new seas and seek new lands, subdue the wilderness, revitalize decaying peoples, and plant civilized and civilizing governments over all the globe.

You can not interpret a constitution without understanding the race that wrote it. If our fathers had intended a reversal of the very nature and being of their race, they would have so declared in the most emphatic words our language holds. But they did not, and in the absence of such words the power remains which is essential to the strongest tendency of our practical race — the power to govern wherever we are, and to govern by the methods best adapted to the situation. But our fathers were not content with silence, and they wrote in the Constitution the words which affirm this essential power.

Mr. President, this question is deeper than any question of party politics; deeper than any question of the isolated policy of our country; deeper than any question of constitutional power. It is elemental. It is racial. God has not been preparing the English-speaking and Teutonic peoples for a thousand years for nothing but vain and idle self-contemplation and self-admiration. No! He has made us the master organizers of the world to establish system where chaos reigns. He has given us the spirit of progress to overwhelm the forces of reaction throughout the earth. He has made us adepts in govern-

ment that we may administer government among savage
and senile peoples.

Were it not for such a force as this the world would
relapse into barbarism and night. And of all our race
He has marked the American people as His chosen Nation finally to lead in the regeneration of the world. This
is the divine mission of America, and it holds for us all
profit, glory, happiness possible to man. We are trustees of the world's progress, guardians of its righteous
peace. The judgment of the Master is upon us: "Ye
have been faithful over a few things; I will make you
ruler over many things."

What shall history say of us? Shall it say that we
renounced that holy trust, left the savage to his base
condition, the wilderness to the reign of waste, deserted
duty, abandoned glory, forgot our sordid profit even, because we feared our strength and read the charter of
our powers with the doubter's eye and the quibbler's
mind? Shall it say that, called by events to captain
and command the ablest, noblest race of history in one
of history's largest works, we declined that great commission? Our fathers would not have had it so. No!
They founded no paralytic government, incapable of the
simplest acts of administration. They planted no slug-
gard people, passive while the world's work calls. They
established no reactionary Nation. They unfurled no
retreating flag.

That flag has never paused in its onward march. Who
dares halt it now — now, when historic events again
are carrying it forward; now, when we are at last one
people, strong enough for any task, great enough for
any glory destiny can bestow? How comes it that our

first century closes with the process accomplished of consolidating the American people into a unit, and quick upon the stroke of that great hour presses upon us our world opportunity, world duty, and world glory, which none but a people welded into an indivisible Nation can achieve or perform?

Blind indeed is he who sees not the hand of God in events so vast, so harmonious, so benign. Dull indeed is the mind that perceives not that this vital people is the strongest of the saving forces of the world; that our place, therefore, is at the head of the constructing and redeeming nations of the earth; and that to stand aside while events march on is a surrender of our interests, a betrayal of our duty as blind as it is base. Craven indeed is the heart that fears to perform a work so golden and so noble; that dares not win a glory so immortal.

Do you tell me that it will cost us money? When did America ever measure duty by financial standards? Do you tell me of the tremendous toil required to overcome the vast difficulties of our task? What mighty work for the world, for humanity, even for ourselves, has ever been done with ease? Even our bread must we earn by the sweat of our faces. Why are we charged with power such as no people ever knew, if we are not to use it in a work such as no people ever wrought? We shall not dispute the divine meaning of the fable of the talents.

Do you remind me of the precious blood that must be shed, the lives that must be given, the broken hearts of loved ones for their slain? And this is indeed a heavier price than all combined. And yet, as a Nation, every historic duty we have done, every achievement we have accomplished, has been by the sacrifice of our noblest sons. Every holy memory that glorifies the flag is of those heroes who died that its onward march might not be stayed. It is the Nation's dearest lives yielded for the flag that makes it dear to us; it is the Nation's most precious blood poured out for it that makes it precious to us. That flag is woven of heroism and grief, of the bravery of men, and women's tears, of righteousness and battle, of sacrifice and anguish, of triumph and glory. It is these which make our flag a holy thing. Who would tear from that sacred banner the glorious legends of a single battle where it has waved on land or sea? What son of a soldier dead in its defense would surrender that proud record for the heraldry of a king? In the cause of civilization, in the service of the Republic anywhere on earth, Americans consider wounds the noblest decorations man can win, and count the giving of their lives a glad and precious duty.

Pray God that spirit never fails. Pray God the time may never come when Mammon and the love of ease shall so debase our blood that we shall fear to shed it for the flag and its imperial destiny. Pray God the time may never come when American heroism is but a legend like the story of the Cid, American faith in our mission and our might a dream dissolved, and the glory of our mighty race departed.

That time will never come. We shall renew our youth at the fountain of new and glorious deeds. We shall exalt our reverence for the flag by carrying it to a noble future as well as by remembering its ineffable past. Its immortality will not pass, because everywhere and always we shall acknowledge and discharge the solemn responsibilities our sacred flag, in its deepest meaning, puts upon us.   And so, Senators, with reverent hearts, where dwells the fear of God, the American people move forward to the future of their hope and the doing of His work.

MORTON, THE NATIONALIST

Remarks in the Senate of the United States, March 24, 1900.

The Senate having under consideration the following resolution:
"*Resolved by the Senate (the House of Representatives concurring*) That the statue of Oliver P. Morton, presented by the State of Indiana, to be placed in Statuary Hall, is accepted in the name of the United States, and that the thanks of Congress be tendered the State for the contribution of the Statue of one of the most eminent citizens and illustrious statesmen of the Republic.
"Second. That a copy of these resolutions, suitably engrossed and duly authenticated, be transmitted to the governor of the State of Indiana—"

Mr. Beveridge said:

MR. President: Great men are instruments of God. They are His voice to the suffering, His shield to the oppressed, His hand for the building of the nations. The Almighty needed His Maccabee, His Joshua, and His David as much as His John the beloved. Richelieu and Washington and Bismarck were His ministers as much as Luther or Wesley or Brooks. And just as truly was Oliver P. Morton one of the small group of mighty men who bore Heaven's commission to establish the imperishable nationality of the American people; and fidelity to that trust is the key to all he ever said or did or was.

I do not believe that inspiration is confined to the dreamer of dreams or the singer of songs. Inspiration

89

may glorify the doer of deeds as well.   In a sense Oliver
P. Morton was inspired when, in the midst of doubt,
hesitation and beaconless purpose, he said: "I would
rather come out of a seven years' struggle defeated in
arms and conceding independence to successful revolution,
than to purchase present peace by the concession of a
principle that must inevitably explode this Nation into
small and dishonorable fragments;" and, speaking thus,
voiced the loyalty of the land to the flag of the Nation.
He was inspired when, on the very day and hour that
Lincoln called for troops, he flashed back this message
in response:

EXECUTIVE DEPARTMENT OF INDIANA, *April 15, 1861.*
To ABRAHAM LINCOLN, *President of the United States:*
On behalf of the State of Indiana I tender to you for the defense
of the Nation and to uphold the authority of the Government 10,000
men.   OLIVER P. MORTON, *Governor of Indiana.*

And, speaking thus, he made disgraceful all delay and
left only action glorious.   He was inspired when he
hurled regiment after regiment into battle with all of
duty's heroic sternness, and inspired when he cared for
and comforted soldier boys with all a mother's tenderness
for her suffering child.   His sanitary commission was
as holy as religion; his military agency was as sacred
as the church; his bureau of finance an institution divinely
blessed as an instrument of the great purposes of God.
All this was done in a holy cause.   A single passionate
belief inspired his life — a single irresistible resolution.
A Nation in reality the American people ought to be,
and a Nation in reality he would give his powers to
make us.   To the current of this great purpose every
act and word and thought of Oliver P. Morton was

tributary. His statesmanship was Nationality. His loves and hates, his hopes and fears, were incidents to the mighty thought that glorified his life and made him mighty as itself.

He was himself an argument for his cause. All great men are God's incarnations of national life. A man like Morton makes sectional lines absurd. Washington was too great for Virginia alone; Hamilton too great for New York alone. Bismarck was too great for Prussia only — he was, by divine right, the statesman of all the German people. And so we see that all great men belong to the nation they serve — not to a local subdivision of it. As civilization broadens, governments widen, men are great only as their powers and sympathies are large enough for all the people of their race. At the beginning the greatest man was great in his family alone. From families sprang communities. From communities grew petty states, and from these great nations with all their possibilities of commerce and art, of interchangeable industry and mutual helpfulness, of united power, collective achievement, the civilization of coöperation, the royalty of labor and the sovereignty of citizenship.

And so in the hearts of the common people the inspiration toward nationality ever dwells. It is their instinct of power. That is why the common people of every land respond to their Alfreds, their Lincolns, their Cavours, and their Mortons. These seers of statesmanship behold in a consolidated nationality the sovereignty of the people, the prosperity of the people, the happiness and safety of the people; and so the people hear them gladly. No man is great except he serves the people and becomes the visible expression of the people's better thought and higher purpose.   He who thinks to be great by serving self alone is ambition's fool.

It was to the establishment of the people's nationality that Morton consecrated his giant powers.   He was the Gibraltar of the Government in the West.   Stanton and Morton were the imperial wills that held aloft the hands of Lincoln until victory came.   So far as deeds and facts could make it so, Morton was Deputy President of the United States in active charge of the Ohio Valley.   No man can tell what the result would have been had not some man like Morton been what and where our Morton was.   Consider our position.   Indiana was the keystone of the North.   Indiana invaded, Chicago and Detroit taken, and the Confederate flag would have prevailed from lake to gulf.

So this territory was a necessary factor in any grand strategy the Confederacy might attempt.   Portions of the State were tainted with sympathy for the rebellion.   The Knights of the Golden Circle, numbering 50,000 in Indiana, with $200,000 for the purchase of arms, actually planned a military uprising.   Powerful men hoped to see Indiana the open gateway by which the hosts of the stars and bars might split the North in twain.   Suppose a commonplace man had been in Morton's place!   Think of the certain consequences had a Confederate sympathizer been the executive of this strategic State!

But Oliver P. Morton was Governor of Indiana, and, instead of an inward swinging gate to the enemies of the Union, Indiana was made by Morton an entering wedge for the rending of the Confederacy.   He did more.   He made Indiana an example for every loyal state.   He obliterated state lines for the purpose of patriotism.   Be-

fore Ohio had equipped a single man, Morton had sent
four regiments flying across her territory *en route* to
Washington. The Confederates threatened Cincinnati.
The proper authorities were laggard in responding; the
frightened city turned to Morton. In fifteen hours 3,000
stand of arms, 24 pieces of artillery, with ammunition
for both, two regiments of Indiana soldiers in Cincinnati's
streets, proved that Morton's patriotism knew not the
boundaries of states.

Morgan crossed the Cumberland; the news was wired
to Morton, and back the answer flew: " One regiment
leaves to-night, another to-morrow, two more next day."
He knew neither night nor day in his terrific activity.
The Sixty-eighth and Sixty-ninth regiments were mus-
tered in by candle-light and started to the front before
the break of dawn. The Government needed ammunition. Morton, on his own responsibility, established a
great manufactory of the materials of war. Admiral
Foote needed power to bombard Fort Henry; Morton
furnished it, and that stronghold fell.

Most of the ammunition with which the battle of Shiloh
was fought and won was supplied by Morton. Indiana's
soldiers needed overcoats; the supply of the Government
was short; Morton did not wait, but himself bought
nearly 30,000 overcoats, paid for them, and Indiana's
soldiers were kept warm. Indiana's treasury was empty
from the very start; Morton raised on private paper more
than $4,000,000. Such were the deeds of Morton. He
was the Nation's flaming sword all along the border. He
was faith to the faltering, certainty to the doubtful,
courage to the weak of heart, and an inspiration to every
man throughout the entire Nation.

And all this time traitors planned his death. More than once they sought his life; one time their bullet barely missed its mark. These were the only men that Morton ever hated. He respected the enemy in the field — they were brave men fighting in a mistaken cause. But for the cowards who sought by stealth to kill the cause for which he had sent more than 200,000 Indiana boys to battle, Oliver P. Morton had a brave man's righteous hatred. Yet when their leaders, condemned to death, stood in the shadow of the gallows, Morton interceded with the President and saved their lives — so close to the fountains of righteous wrath in the breast of this tender and heroic man the springs of mercy welled.

Morton's whole career was based upon profound belief in the common people — not the theoretical belief of the doctrinaire, not the simulated belief of the demagogue; but the living, vital, human faith of one who in himself is of the people. That is why he was a Nationalist. That is why he sent that telegram to Lincoln the very hour the President called for troops — he believed the 10,000 men he tendered would respond. Faith is the heart of deeds.

That was why he built arsenals, bought provisions, equipped a quarter of a million of men for war — he believed the people would sustain him. That was why he pressed the ratification of the fourteenth amendment, and, as a Senator, the adoption and ratification of the fifteenth amendment to the Constitution of the United States. That was why he championed reconstruction, based, as he declared, "upon the everlasting principles of equal and exact justice to all men."

Nearly a quarter of a century ago Morton proposed

an amendment to the Constitution providing for the
election of senators by the people. All his measures,
all his deeds were based upon his faith in the people.
He did not doubt, he did not underestimate the intelligence, the purity, and the patriotism of the masses.
He did not believe in Matthew Arnold's doctrine of the
" saving remnant." He knew that if this Republic is
to be saved the plain people must do the saving; that
when men get too far away from the soil they cease to
love it enough to die for it. He knew that nearly all
the heroes of Lexington and Concord, of Vicksburg and
the Wilderness, were toilers before they were soldiers.

And so Morton looked at every problem from the viewpoint of the common people. He sprang from them —
was one of them himself. His father was a shoemaker.
He was himself a hatter. His association, till full manhood, was exclusively with the working classes. Let
me again and again repeat that no one can understand
Oliver P. Morton who forgets that, first of all, he believed profoundly in the plain people, whom Abraham
Lincoln loved; and, second, that the passion of his life
was to see this matchless people welded into an indivisible
and immortal nation. Characters like his attract the
people by a sort of moral gravitation. The people trust
them by an instinct that passes the wisdom of formal
thought. The people know that these great ones, perhaps unconsciously to themselves, are the agents of the
eternal verities.

Inspired by such a faith and such a purpose, he put
his will into his thought, and instantly they were facts.
And his was the kingliest will of that heroic period.
After all, courage is the royal element of human character.

Stricken with paralysis, this Indiana shoemaker's son, this child and lover of the common people, went from the governor's chair to the Senate, and there, without experience or wide learning, he instantly became leader. And what a Senate it was! — a Senate to be a mediocre member of which was to be a distinguished man! Sumner was there, Conkling was there, Thurman was there, Edmunds and Carpenter and Logan were there. Distinguished men of the Nation who still are Senators of the Republic began their services with Morton — warriors and scholars and lawyers and orators, some of them statesmen equal to the greatest the world has seen. It was a time when America pointed proudly to her Senate and said, "These are representative of American courage and character of mind." And among them sat the Senator from Indiana, stricken unto death, yet the strongest among the strong.

Morton was a partizan — a partizan of an idea. A partizan like Morton is one who would have theories reduced to practice. A partizan like Morton is one whose faith in essential things dissolves his discontent with incidentals — whose loyalty to an eternal belief is greater than any temporary representative of that belief. All the world's achievers have been such partizans.

From Savonarola to Luther, from Cromwell to Gladstone, from Washington to Lincoln, the lords of human conviction and achievement have been partizans of the cause they championed. Between a partizan of a cause and his opposite is all the difference between beliefs and interests, between convictions and investments, between a principle and an expedient.

In this sense Morton was a king of partizans. He was

a partizan of principle; but *he was not the puppet of a machine* — a distinction frequently forgotten. No man honored a conviction that differed from his own more than did Morton, the incarnation of conviction; no man more swift and terrible in wrath at wrong in his own party than he, its strong leader.

America needs to-day more partizanship like that.

Courage and honesty, the gift of seeing things, and an appalling energy — these were the reinforcements that Morton brought to the Union. He saw things with that clear vision which, in another age, would have made men call him a seer. Morton understood the conclusion of the syllogism of events, and so beheld the flag of the American people — man's last experiment in liberty — saw that dear banner, carrying with it the destinies of his country and the hope of all mankind, sinking from sight in the smoke of rebellion.

And so, with a passion we can not understand in these cold days, he spoke and wrought. But Indiana's soldiers understood him when he handed them their colors and spoke to them words of fire at parting. They understood him when, suffering in hospitals on beds of pain, comforts and cheer and nursing came from the old Indiana home, sent by the hand of their great war governor. They understood him when the soldiers of other states told them how they looked on Morton as their governor, too. I knew a family of soldiers, Ohio volunteers, in whose household to this very day the name of Morton is second only to Lincoln as the best beloved of all our country's civil names since Washington. This prince of patriotism was national in his activity.

I have it at first-hand from authority absolutely re-

liable that he made many secret trips to Washington to
strengthen the decision of the President, perplexed with
conflicting considerations and distraught with the double
necessity of acting, and at the same time of holding together discordant elements essential to success, which
elements decided action in any direction threatened to
explode. I am told that Lincoln declared that Morton
had more influence with that iron man, Stanton, than
the President himself.

If Lincoln was the great conservative, the genius of
statecraft, the scientist of popular feeling, whose skill in
the management of men made ultimate victory possible,
Morton was the spirit of decision, moving the President
to act when the hour had struck. Without fear Morton
spoke his mind to the greatest, as, without favor, he lis-
tened to suggestion and advice from the humblest.

Frankly he spoke his mind to all. That was the secret
of his power in public speech. Every thought was to
Morton a conviction. That is the characteristic of all
great speakers. The only perfect argument is a truthful
statement of your case. That is the method of all immortal words. Jesus spoke " as one having authority."
The Declaration of Independence is not weakened by the
expression of a doubt. John the Baptist never said, " I
may be wrong." The man who influences men to die
for a principle must be an intellectual absolutist. This
was the method of Morton. He was not an orator as
the term is used to-day, no round-voiced, graceful-ges-
tured carpet-knight of words.

Had he been he never could have touched the people's
hearts as so masterfully he did. But he was an orator
in the sense that the Great Apostle was. Oratory is the

telling of a needful truth at an appropriate time by an honest man, who believes what he says so fervently that to his hearers he becomes a magnet of conviction; all else is merely entertainment by a skilled performer upon that wonderful instrument called human speech. The three model speeches of the world are the Sermon on the Mount, the appeal of Paul on Mars Hill, and the words of Abraham Lincoln at Gettysburg. These have no tricks, no tinsel; they are immortal in the simple majesty of the truths they so perfectly reveal. Morton's speech had this direct and simple quality.

Mr. President, Oliver P. Morton was an elemental man. He had the sincerity and simplicity of nature. He was the personification of the people who are always natural, always elemental, and in the end always — necessarily always — right. All great men are this. They have in them something of the oceans, the mountains, and the stars. In their presence the schemes of schemers seem illogical and absurd — seem like houses of cards that children build. The road is always plain before such men because they perceive, with large vision of the seer, whither that road inevitably leads.

Such men have that courage which lesser men call folly, but which history always estimates aright, and to which the people in the end unfailingly respond. They do not hesitate to make their stand. Indeed, their destiny, their personal fortunes, are the last items they consider. Their cause or their country alone is a thing of consequence to them.

Such are the inspired and inspiring characters in history. Such was Alexander, Cæsar, Cromwell, Bismarck, Washington. Men like these found States or save them.

Men like these clear the rugged, and, to weaker men, the impossible way up the mountain; and, taking humanity by the hand, lead it upward to purer atmosphere and broader vision.   And such was Morton.

INSTITUTIONAL LAW

Speech delivered in the Senate of the United States, March 29, 1900.

The Senate having under consideration the bill (H. R. 8245) temporarily to provide revenues for the relief of the island of Porto Rico, and for other purposes —

Mr. Beveridge said:

TO treat Porto Rico as we treat Hawaii; to deal with the latter as we deal with the Philippines; to apply to all without delay the same fixed formula of laws which custom and the intention of statehood has prescribed for our territories from which our states are formed, is a proposition the unwisdom of which appears in its very statement.

Our Constitution does not so manacle our hands and narrow our vision. It is no such charter of death. Our fathers did not so anchor us within a narrow harbor when the high seas call us. No! Our Constitution is a chart by which we sail all seas and make all ports. We must provide for our possessions according to the wisdom of events — according to the common sense of situations. The people of each are unlike the people of any other; none of them is like the American pioneers who settled our continental wilderness. We must adopt measures fitting the condition and the necessities of each and change those measures as conditions and necessities change.

According to the Opposition, the Constitution ties our hands and nullifies our understanding; according to the Government, the Constitution places in our hands the commission of all needful powers.

The Government says that *we reserve the future for the future,* but that for the present we hold these islands as a trust, dealing with them as wisdom and righteousness from day to day shall dictate, developing them into gardens, their inhabitants into happy and prosperous peoples; and when the time shall come, if ever, that American ideas, American methods, and the American spirit change the habit of their minds, and their conception of government, then our successors in the American Congress may admit them into or reject them from the blood of our national life, as the wisdom and justice of posterity may determine.

In a word, the question is whether the Constitution gives Congress a free hand over our possessions, or whether, if we retain them, the Constitution gives them a free hand over us.

We are like a farmer with a farm, part adapted to corn, part to fruit, part to woodland pasture, part a swamp which draining will render fertile, part a highland which irrigation will make productive. We say that the farmer must have a free hand to deal with each portion of that farm as its situation and quality requires. The Opposition says that, over all, uniform methods must be employed, the same treatment given. The parable of the sower who sowed alike by the wayside, among thorns, in stony places as well as in prepared ground is repeated here in the attitude of those who seek to scatter self-government and the Constitution on the people of the Philippines, Hawaii, and Porto Rico, in equal measure, no matter whether they are prepared for it or not, with the bestowal upon the brothers of our blood in our American territories.

We are like a modern business man with many and dissimilar enterprises. The Opposition says he must deal with all alike, must devise and apply a common system to different situations; we declare that he should have a free will and a constructive mind, to meet each situation with appropriate and therefore different action.

The exact situation is, for us, unprecedented. Our action must be without example in our own history. The decisions of our Supreme Court are not to the precise point, and where analogy applies those decisions to the present situation they are conflicting and confused. This is rather fortunate than the reverse. New situations should be met with new methods. Search for precedents where none can exist, effort to apply opinions of judges to a condition not of their time nor dreamed of when they wrote those opinions, is not helpful. There are some cases containing expressions which appear to be on one side of the present controversy and others containing passages apparently on the other side; but none of them completely illumines the new fields of effort and of duty into which we have entered.

I admit and assert the authority of precedent. I understand that the philosophy upon which the authority of precedent rests is as deep as civilization itself. But that very philosophy demands that precedents shall apply only to like situations and that the solutions of new problems shall not be hampered by fitting them into inapplicable precedents. The very reason of precedent demands the creation of new precedents out of new occasions. Surely we can see more clearly the situation before us with our eyes than with the eyes of the fathers, those eyes looking not at our problems, but at theirs.

Precedent has its rightful authority, but it has its danger, too. It sanctifies the past, but, used beyond its rightful sphere, it forbids the future. China, we say, is living in the past. She is living in her precedents. She inquires not the best way; she asks only the way of the fathers. She is reminiscent; not inventive. Her memory is abnormal; her initiative is atrophied. Drugged with the opium of precedent, she sits and dreams of ancient glories and the ancient gods. The science of the modern world is a lie to her, because the fathers knew it not. Our medicines are poison, because they are not inherited from the distant past; and enchantment is efficacious still, because her ancestry dealt with the magic of the night. Spirits of evil fly upon the air, and workmen fix charms upon buildings where they labor, to frighten the fell influences of the nether world, because their fathers did the like for a thousand years.

Precedent has shod with lead the feet of this puissant people and put upon her eyelids the somnolent spell of dreams. Happy for China when she shall shake that slumber from her blood, and her people, refreshed and inspired by the energy of progress, shall meet each new emergency, opportunity, and duty by the wisdom of a living mind, and not by the wisdom of a brain which, for a thousand years, has been thoughtless dust, and, even when quick and vivid, was solving, not the problems of to-day, but those of the entombed and storied centuries.

Can we, therefore, unaided by judicial decisions, find in the Constitution the free hand needful for our new task?

Is this great movement to halt because a partizan faction so construes our Constitution as to forbid it? And halt it must, if we find not the amplest power, expressed or implied, in our Constitution; for we, above all the peoples of the world, are a people of law, and our Constitution is the supreme ordinance of national life.

But the Constitution does give us power as ample as our present opportunities; power so express and emphatic that the Opposition dare not quote it, lest it confound them, but fly to subtleties and refinements of other sections not bearing on the matter in dispute; power so clear that it carries almost the authority of command; power written through the instinctive anticipation of our development; power penned through the racial impulse in the blood of the fathers; power so complete, emphatic, and unusual that there is in it the suggestion of duty.

"The Congress shall have power to dispose of and make all needful rules and regulations respecting the territory or other property belonging to the United States."— *Constitution of the United States, Article 4, section 3.*

Of course Congress, in exercising this power, must pass laws in the manner prescribed in the Constitution. The Constitution determines the method of Congressional action in exercising all Congressional powers. And the Constitution fixes certain fundamental general limitations to and absolute general prohibitions on the power of Congress; and when Congress makes " needful rules and regulations respecting territory or other property belonging to the United States," it can not transgress these general limitations or prohibitions any more than it can pass laws in any different manner than the one marked out in the Constitution. This is, of course, self-evident, but I state it that even partizanship shall not say that we put Congress above the Constitution.

Does the Opposition say that, under power so broad, we could, in providing a new government for Porto Rico, set up a king there, and that therefore we must so construe the Constitution as to forbid such a power? I answer that we could not set up a king in Porto Rico even if another section of the Constitution did not, in terms, forbid it. Why not? Because our Constitution in terms forbids? Yes. But also because our institutions forbid.

Institutional law is older, deeper, and as vital as constitutional law. Our Constitution is one of the concrete manifestations of our institutions; our statutes are another; decisions of our courts are another; our habits, methods and customs as a people and a race are still another.

Our institutional law is like the atmosphere — impalpable, imperceptible, but all-pervading and the source of life itself. There is scarcely a decision of our courts of last resort, involving great constitutional questions, which does not refer to the spirit of our institutions as interpreting our Constitution. It is our institutional law which, flowing like our blood through the written Constitution, gives that instrument vitality and power of development.

Our institutions were not established by the Constitution. Institutional law existed before the Constitution.

Our institutions had their beginnings well-nigh with the beginning of time. They have developed through the ages. Magna Charta only marked a period in their growth; the assertion of the rights of the Commons marked another; our Revolution marked another; the adoption of our Constitution marked another still.

Our institutional law, therefore, the spirit of our written Constitution, as well as that instrument itself, forbids the establishment of monarchy by American authority in devising new governments for our possessions. Partizanship shrieks " imperialism," and asks where we find words to prevent the development of a czar, beginning with absolute power in our possessions and ending with absolute power in the Republic, if such power as the Constitution confers be exercised.

I answer: I find the impossibility of such a development in our Constitution itself; but also, and as fully, in our institutions. I find it in the speech of the people; in the maxims of liberty; in our blood; in our history; in the tendencies of our race. Words would not prevent autocracy if the desire for a king were in the hearts of the people. Words can not bestow republican institutions, if the idea of and preference for an absolute ruler is in the minds, traditions, and practices of a people, as they are in Asia.

And words can not impose a czar upon a people whose very speech is the speech of self-government, whose ideals of self-rule for centuries have grown clearer, brighter, dearer. And those who fear imperialism, meaning by that term the overthrow of our republican institutions, are either insincere, or else unbelievers in the soundness of American institutions, the purity of the

American heart, and the noble intention of the American mind.

I have no respect for constitutional " learning " which deals alone with the written words of the Constitution, or even with the intention of its framers, and ignores the sources and spirit of that great instrument. The Constitution did not give us free institutions; free institutions gave us our Constitution. All our progress toward liberty and popular government, made since the adoption of the Constitution, has been the spirit of our institutions working out its sure results, through the Constitution when possible, and over it when necessary.

Jefferson wrote, in the Declaration of Independence, a denunciation of slavery and called it an " execrable commerce; " it was stricken out at the request of Georgia and South Carolina, and years afterward slavery was recognized in our Constitution. But slavery was opposed to the spirit of our institutions, and while legalized by our Constitution and defended by armies as brave as ever marched to battle, constitutional slavery went down before institutional liberty; and Appomattox was the capitulation of the word of death in our Constitution to the spirit of life in our institutions. Every amendment of our Constitution marks the progress of our institutions.

The Constitution contemplated and provided for the election of Presidents by electors, who should select the best man to preside over the Republic, irrespective of the people's choice. That was the intention of the fathers. But in that they did not correctly interpret the spirit and tendency of our institutions, which is toward getting the Government as close to the people as possible; and so, in spite of the Constitution, in spite of the intention of the fathers, in spite of the fact that this plan was pursued for several elections, the spirit of our institutions prevailed over our Constitution, and no Presidential elector now dare cast his ballot against the candidate for whom the people instruct him to vote.

Wherever the Constitution has correctly interpreted our institutions, it has lived; wherever it has not correctly interpreted our institutions, the defective part has died. Wherever our Constitution has been weak and insufficient in its apparent expressed powers, the spirit of our institutions has given it life. Read Marshall's opinions; read most of our great constitutional decisions; read the whole history of American constitutional progress, if you would know the beneficent influence of our institutions on our Constitution. Our institutions are not the destroyers of our Constitution, as partizanship would have men believe. No; our institutions are the saviors of our Constitution. The doctrine of implied powers, which has saved the country and the Constitution too, has been made possible only by reading our Constitution by the light of our institutions, as Hamilton and Marshall did.

And so our security, the security of our island wards, the security of liberty, is not in the written word of the Constitution alone; it is there, of course, but it is in our institutions also, which are the spirit of the Constitution, which illuminate and emphasize the meaning of that noble instrument. England has no written constitution. And yet England has steady and continuous liberty and law, while other countries provided with written constitutions of an ideal character sometimes have suffered from bureaucracy and military absolutism. These other nations had the forms of liberty and popular government in written constitutions, but they did not have free institutions which alone make formal constitutions living and vital things. England, without a written constitution, is almost as free a government as ours. Law reigns supreme. The poorest gatherer of rags has equal rights before the bar of justice with belted earl or millionaire, and those equal rights are impartially enforced. Neither wealth nor title is favored more than poverty or humble rank in the courts of England; and royalty itself, like the meanest subject, must appear as witness when occasion demands.

The Government itself is subject to the will of the people; and no ministry remains in power in face of an adverse majority, or forces into law an act of which the people disapprove. The English Parliament goes to the people as often as the government, in any of its proposed measures, fails of a majority. The suffrage is constantly enlarged, and the rights of labor are more carefully guarded by the laws of England than by ours. England's treatment of Ireland has been harsh, severe, unjust; and yet even there the spirit of a larger liberty is growing, and in the interest of the Irish tenant Parliament has put through a measure approaching state socialism, compelling the landlord to sell his land whether he wants to or not, at a price fixed by others than himself, and enabling the tenant to buy the land by the payment of his rent. Tolerance, justice, and individual liberty are daily developing throughout the British Empire, instead of diminishing.

To-morrow's record could be filled with examples of

the exercise of free government throughout England's dominions and of laws in the interest of labor, of poverty, of life's unfortunates. And yet England has no written constitution. But she has institutions, free institutions, institutions similar to those we have here in America. We surpass England in having developed free institutions until our Constitution, which is the highest expression of free institutions, has been produced. And the most inspiring thing in all the history of human hope is the development of free institutions on either side of the ocean, by two great peoples, one in blood, speech, religion, law, and in their world-wide mission, but two peoples in nationhood, in interests, and in individual destiny.

It is the free institutions of England that preserve and increase the liberty of Englishmen, and diminish and destroy the authority of the monarch, who is now only, the symbol of the Nation — the emblem of the Empire. It is England's free institutions that, in Egypt, Hong-Kong, Ceylon, the Malay States, India, have given the people of those dark places to eat of the *fruits* of liberty for the first time in all the strange history of the oppressed and wasted Orient. And it is our free institutions, as well as our Constitution, that in America make kings impossible, and which have, for a hundred years, wrought for a larger liberty and a more popular government.

And it is the spirit of our institutions, as well as our Constitution, that will prevent the abuse of power by American authority in Porto Rico, Hawaii, the Philippines, or any other spot blessed by the protection of our flag. It is our free institutions, working now by one method and now by another, after the fashion of our practical race, that will establish order, equal laws, free speech, unpurchasable justice, and " life, liberty, and the pursuit of happiness " throughout our ocean possessions and that will prepare the way for the Constitution itself.

For, Mr. President, our institutions can go to these people before our Constitution goes to them. Our institutions can precede our Constitution, as they did here in America itself. Did not Washington and his countrymen have free institutions for years before the Constitution was adopted? Did not the signers of the Declaration of Independence have the spirit of free institutions, although the Constitution was not thought of at that time?

It is our institutional law, therefore, of which men should inquire who would know the meaning and the life of our constitutional law.

I respect not the expounders of constitutional law, who have not studied the history of our institutions, of which the Constitution is the richest fruit, until that history is a part of their being.

I respect not that constitutional charlatanism that fastens its eye on the printed page alone, disdains our institutions as interpreting it, and refuses to consider the sources of that Constitution — the development of our present form of government for a century and a half from the old crown charters; the English struggle for the rights of man, regulated by equal laws which preceded that; the spirit of Dutch independence, Dutch federation, and Dutch institutions, working upon that; and still back the councils of our Teuton fathers in the German forests in the dim light of a far distant time.

If a people adopt a written instrument, you must understand that people and their institutions before you understand the writing. You can not separate a people and their history from a written constitution which is only a part of that history. The same words used by one people may have a different meaning used by another people. Any writing can be an *index* only to the institutions of a people. A people's institutions are the soul of the written and unwritten law. You must understand the French people, their history, and their unwritten institutions, before you can understand their written constitution. You must understand the American people, our history, and our institutions before you can understand our Constitution.

Our institutions embrace individual liberty and self-government, but they also embrace organization and administration.

They are the expression of the characteristics and tendencies of our race, as the institutions of other peoples are of theirs. Our race is the most self-governing but also the most administrative of any race of history. Our race is, distinctly, the exploring, the colonizing, the administrating force of the world. We are this, not from necessity, but from irresistible impulse, from instinct, from racial and unwritten laws inherited from our forefathers. Our pioneers reclaimed Kentucky and the Mississippi wilderness; they crossed the Rockies and seized Oregon; even when their homes behind them were still surrounded by virgin forest and untouched plain, they explored new regions and claimed new empires, and left behind them the crimson trail of their own blood, shed that the march of our race might not be stayed.

They did this because they could not help it. And wherever our race has gone it has governed; and where-ever it has governed law, order, justice and the rights of man have been established and defended. All this has been in obedience to our *institutions,* which, in turn, are expressive merely of racial character. Our institutions are carried in the breasts of American citizens and soldiers wherever they go.

So we have in our Constitution not only express words of power to acquire and to govern new lands, as our race had always done; but words that must be read as the large expression of our institutions as a race. If our institutions are not adapted to administration as well as to self-government; if they are fixed and unyielding; if our racial instincts are against expansion, organization and administration of governments over non-self-governing peoples; if our history and traditions are reactionary, then these words of power in our Constitution must be read as power merely to dispose of and regulate territory possessed at the time the Constitution was written and in the way then established.

Whatever our history, our race tendencies, our institutions, these large and vital meanings must pour through the Constitution, which is their medium. Without them the Constitution is only an assemblage of lifeless words. We can not read our Constitution by a word-dictionary only; we must read it by the unabridged lexicon of our institutions and their history. We can not read it by the temporary intentions of the fathers only; we must read it by all the experience of all our past as a race, and our future as a people.

The wisest minds of the fathers comprehended our future but poorly; their instinct embraced and hastened that future. Jefferson said we had territory enough for our descendants to the thousandth and thousandth generation — and there spoke his academic thought; but he secured Louisiana, even when he was declaring that he had no constitutional power to do so — and there spoke his racial instincts. In a century the Republic will number more than 200,000,000 souls; problems undreamed of by the fathers will arise; they will be unsolvable if the Constitution is an instrument of words; they will be solved if the Constitution is the expression of our institutions.

When, therefore, we read those institutional words —

"The Congress shall have power to dispose of and make all needful rules and regulations respecting the territory or other property belonging to the United States"—

we must read them as the utterance of the most vigorous branch of the world's greatest expanding and administering people. Coiled up in those words of racial purposes and power is all the energy of Raleigh and of Drake, of Clive and Cook, of Winthrop, Smith, and Penn, of that whole resistless people that has poured around the world its healing tide of civilization and of order, always and everywhere giving equal rights under equal laws, protecting commerce, planting social method, and establishing the statutes of the Almighty Father to whom our race has ever looked, upon whose Name we have ever called, and of whose Divine Will we are the agents in our day.

And so, even if those words of power and discretion which I have quoted were not in the Constitution, still we should have the power those words affirm; we should have that power as an attribute of nationality and by virtue of our institutions and race tendencies, which nothing but express denial in our Constitution could check, reverse, or destroy.

If then, the Constitution gives Congress a free hand over our possessions, how shall that power be exercised over each? How shall we deal with Porto Rico whose care is immediately before us?

I favor immediate free trade with Porto Rico, and I shall go on record as voting for amendments giving immediate and unrestricted freedom of trade to our island of Porto Rico. But if we in the Senate who believe that Porto Rico should have reciprocity at once are not able so to amend the bill here, I shall, after voting for free trade amendments, vote for the civil-government bill as finally modified by the committee, because we must not deny civil government to the people of Porto Rico a moment longer, and because the bill, as now modified, insures free trade with Porto Rico as soon as the civil government of that island provides a system of taxation of its own, and because it gives free food, clothing and implements to the islanders at once. I am proud that our fight against the House bill has caused this modification.

Mr. President, the great movement on which the American people have embarked is a movement of conscience as well as of power; of civilization as well as of commerce. It touches the shores of every sea. Directly or indirectly it affects all humanity. We go forth on a world career; we must conduct it with a world statesmanship — a statesmanship that considers the effect of every law we pass upon the peoples over whom our influence is extending and upon the world at large, as well as upon ourselves.

Administration of government means more than balance sheets; more than weights or measures. It means this, but it also means the weighing of the hearts of men and the balance sheets of the affections of the governed people. Why to-day do England's colonists voluntarily tax themselves by preferential tariffs in order to give England the advantage of their trade? Why to-day do Canadians, Australians, and sons of the Empire everywhere voluntarily enlist to fight and die in far and savage lands that the dominion of England's flag may be extended? Why to-day are England's governed people themselves among the bravest of those who charge to their deaths in her defense? What, within a single half century, has thus reversed English colonial history and experience? Simply a statesmanship practical enough to consider sentiment as a real factor in the government of peoples.

The American masses, in whose breasts dwell the purity, power and hope of the Republic and of the world, understand this well. They mean to profit by the world's large lesson. They mean that our dominion shall be exercised in righteousness. They doubt not that human progress is one vast and swelling harmony which not even all the discords of history can destroy; and they mean that in that divine composition the noblest, highest, purest, tenderest note shall be that struck by the American people as the sovereign power of earth.

THE STAR OF EMPIRE

Speech opening the Republican Campaign for the West in the Auditorium, at Chicago, September 25, 1900, in reply to Mr. Bryan's Indianapolis speech accepting his second Democratic nomination for President. This speech was used by the Republicans as a National Campaign document.

"WESTWARD the Star of Empire takes its Way." Not the star of kingly power, for kingdoms are everywhere dissolving in the increasing rights of men; not the star of autocratic oppression, for civilization is brightening and the liberties of the people are broadening under every flag. But the star of empire, as Washington used the word, when he called this Republic an "empire"; as Jefferson understood it, when he declared our form of government ideal for extending "our empire"; as Marshall understood it, when he closed a noble period of an immortal constitutional opinion by naming the domain of the American people "our empire."

This is the "empire" of which the prophetic voice declared "Westward the Star of Empire takes its Way" — the star of the empire of liberty and law, of commerce and communication, of social order and the Gospel of our Lord — the star of the empire of the civilization of the world. Westward *that* star of empire takes its course. And to-day it illumines our path of duty across the Pacific into the islands and lands where Providence has called us.

In that path the American government is marching forward, opposed at every step by those who deny the right of the Republic to plant the institutions of the Flag where Events have planted that Flag itself. For this is our purpose, to perform which the Opposition declares that the Republic has no warrant in the Constitution, in morals or in the rights of man. And I mean to examine to-night every argument they advance for their policy of reaction and retreat.

It is not true, as the Opposition asserts, that every race without instruction and guidance is naturally self-governing. If so, the Indians were capable of self-government. America belonged to them whether they were or were not capable of self-government. If they were capable of self-government it was not only wrong, but it was a crime to set up our independent government on their land without their consent. If this is true, the Puritans, instead of being noble, are despicable characters; and the patriots of 1776, to whom the Opposition compares the Filipinos, were only a swarm of land pirates. If the Opposition is right, the Zulus who owned the Transvaal were capable of self-government; and the Boers who expelled them, according to the Opposition, deserve the abhorrence of righteous men.

But while the Boers took the lands they occupy from the natives who peopled them; while we peopled this country in spite of the Indian who owned it; and while this may be justified by the welfare of the world which those events advanced, that is not what is to be done in the Philippines. The American government, as a government, will not appropriate the Filipinos' land or permit Americans as individuals to seize it. It will protect the Filipinos in their possessions. If any American secures real estate in the Philippines, it will be because he buys it from the owner. Under American administration the Filipino who owns his little plot of ground will experience a security in the possession of his property that he has never known before.

The English in Egypt and India have not taken the land from its owners; they have confirmed the occupants in their ownership. In Hawaii we have not taken the land from its owners; we have secured its owners in their peaceable possession. And our administration in the Philippines will also establish there that same security of property and life which is the very beginning of civilization itself.

If it be said that tropical countries can not be peopled by the Caucasian race, I answer that, even if true, it is no reason why they should not be governed by the Caucasian race. India is a tropical country. India is ruled by England to the advantage of India and England alike. Who denies that India's 300,000,000 are better off under English administration than under the bestial tyranny of native rulers, to whom the agony of their subjects was the highest form of amusement?

Dare Mr. Bryan say that he would have India back to its condition before England took it? If he dare not, he is answered. Dare he say that he would withdraw English rule now? If he dare not, he is answered. Dare he say that he would take the English " residents " from the Malay States and turn them back again to the rule of their brutal lords? If he dare not, he is answered.

Dare he say that the Boers should restore the Transvaal to its original owners? If he dare not, he is answered. Dare he deny that the greatest progress shown upon the map of earth to-day is the progress of Egypt during the last twenty years under English rule? If he dare not, he is answered. And he dare not. If he proclaims his faith in the Filipino people, who know not the meaning of self-government, I declare my faith in the American people, who have developed the realities of liberty.

Grant, for the purposes of argument, the Opposition's premise that the white man can not people the Philippines. Grant, also, that the Malays of those islands can not, unaided, establish civilization there; build roads, open mines, erect schools, maintain social order, repress piracy and administer safe government throughout the archipelago. And this must be granted; for they are the same race which inhabits the Malay Peninsula. What, then, is the conclusion demanded by the general welfare of the world?

Surely not that this land, rich in all that civilized man requires, and these people needing the very blessings they ignorantly repel, should be remanded to savagery and the wilderness! If you say this, you say that barbarism and undeveloped resources are better than civilization and the earth's resources developed. What is the conclusion, then, which the logic of civilization compels from these admitted premises? It is that the reign of law must be established throughout these islands, their resources developed and their people civilized by those in whose blood resides the genius of administration.

Such are all Teutonic and Celtic peoples. Such are the Dutch; behold their work in Java. Such are the

English; behold their work all around the world. Such the German; behold his advance into the fields of world-regeneration and administration. Such were the French before Napoleon diverted their energies; behold their work in Canada, Louisiana and our great Northwest. And such, more than any people who ever lived, are the Americans, into whose hands God has given the antipodes to develop their resources, to regenerate their people and to establish there the civilization of law-born liberty and liberty-born law.

If the Opposition declares that we ought to set up a separate government over the Philippines because we are setting up a separate government over Cuba, I answer that such an error in Cuba does not justify the same error in the Philippines. I am speaking for myself alone, but speaking thus, I say, that for the good of Cuba more even than for the good of the United States, a separate government over Cuba, uncontrolled by the American Republic, *never should have been promised.*

Cuba is a mere extension of our Atlantic coast-line. It commands the ocean entrances to the Mississippi and the Isthmian Canal. Jefferson's dearest dream was that Cuba should belong to the United States. To possess this extension of American soil has been the wish of every far-seeing statesman from Jefferson to Blaine. Annexation to the greatest nation the world has ever seen is a prouder Cuban destiny than separate nationality. As an American possession, Cuba might possibly have been fitted for statehood in a period not much longer than that in which Louisiana was prepared for statehood.

Even now the work of regeneration — of cleansing cities, building roads, establishing posts, erecting a system of universal education and the action of all the forces that make up our civilization — is speeding forward faster than at any time or place in human history — American administration! But yesterday there were less than ten thousand Cuban children in school; to-day there are nearly one hundred and fifty thousand Cuban children in school — American administration! But yesterday Havana was the source of our yellow-fever plagues; to-day it is nearly as healthy as New Orleans — American administration!

When we stop this work and withdraw our restraint, revolution will succeed revolution in Cuba, as in the Central and South American countries; Havana again fester with the yellow death; systematic education again degenerate into sporadic instances; and Cuba, which under our control should be a source of profit, power and glory to the Republic and herself, will be a source of irritation and of loss, of danger and disease to both. The United States needs Cuba for our protection; *but Cuba needs the United States for Cuba's salvation.*

The resolution for Cuban independence, hastily passed by all parties in Congress, at an excited hour, was an error which years of time, propinquity of location, common commerce, mutual interests and similar dangers surely will correct. The President, jealous of American honor, considers that resolution a promise. And American promise means performance. And so the unnatural experiment is to be tried. What war and nature — aye, what God hath joined together — is to be put asunder.

I speak for myself alone, but speaking thus, I say that it will be an evil day for Cuba when the Stars and Stripes come down from Morro Castle. I speak for myself alone, but I believe that in this my voice is the voice of the American millions, as it is the voice of the ultimate future, when I say that Porto Rico is ours and ours for ever; the Philippines are ours and ours for ever; and Cuba ought to have been ours, and by the free choice of her people some day will be ours, and ours for ever.

We have a foreign nation on our north; another on our southwest; and now to permit another foreign nation within cannon shot of our southeast coast, will indeed create conditions which will require that militarism which the Opposition to the Government pretends to fear. Think of Cuba in alliance with England or Germany or France! Think of Cuba a naval station and ally of one of the great foreign powers, every one of whom is a rival of America! And so my answer to Mr. Bryan's comparison is that, if we have made a mistake in Cuba, we ought not to make the same mistake in the Philippines.

I *predict that within ten years we shall again be forced to assume the government of Cuba,* but only after our commerce has again been paralyzed by revolution, after internal dissension has again spilled Cuban blood, after the yellow fever has threatened our southern coast from its hot-bed in Havana harbor. Cuba independent! Impossible! I predict that at the very next session of Congress we shall pass some kind of law giving this Republic control of Cuba's destiny. If we do not we fail in our duty.*

* These passages on Cuba caused a sensation throughout the country, and Senator Beveridge was attacked and denounced as a dissenter from the Administration's policy — and this by Republican Senators, who publicly declared that we would have nothing more to do with Cuba. Yet at the next session of Congress, convening less than three months after this speech was delivered, we passed

Consider, now, the Opposition's proposed method of procedure in the Philippines: It is to establish a stable government there, turn that government over to the Filipinos, and protect them and their government from molestation by any other nation.

Suppose the Opposition's plan in operation. Suppose a satisfactory government is established, turned over to the Filipinos and American troops withdrawn. The new government must experience feuds, factions and revolution. This is the history of every new government. It was so even with the American people. Witness Shays' Rebellion against the National Government, almost shaking its foundations; witness the Whiskey Rebellion in Pennsylvania, which required the first exercise of armed national power to maintain order with a state of the Union. And we were of a self-governing race — at that period we were almost wholly Anglo-Saxon.

How can we expect the Philippine Malays to escape this common fate of all new governments? Remember that as a race they have not that civil cohesion which binds a people into a nation. Remember that every island is envious of every other one; and that in each island every officer is a " general," jealous of his dignity, intriguing for advancement.

How long would this stable government, which the Opposition asks us to " establish," *remain* " stable," if we withdrew our forces? And if resistance broke out in the Visayas, if revolt sprang into flame among the murderous Moros, what would be our duty? It would be to reënter where we had withdrawn and restore the stability of the

the Platt amendment giving us practical control over Cuba; and recent events have precisely fulfilled Senator Beveridge's prophecy made in this speech.

government which the Opposition declares that we shall establish before we withdraw. And so the Opposition program constantly defeats itself and compels us to do over and over again the work which we must perform at the beginning. And all this without benefit to the Philippine people, without improvement to their lands and with immeasurable loss to ourselves recouped not from a single source of profit. But the American flag floating there for ever means not only established liberty, but permanent stability.

Again governments must have money. That is their first necessity; money for salaries, money for the army, money for public buildings, money for improvements. Before the revenues are established, the government must have money. If the revenues are inadequate, nevertheless the government must have money. Therefore, all governments are borrowers. Even the government of the American people — the richest people of history — is a borrower. Even the government of the British people, who for centuries have been accumulating wealth, must borrow; its bonds are in our own bank vaults. Much more, then, must little governments borrow money.

If, then, we "establish a stable government," as the Opposition demands, and turn that government over to the Filipinos, they also must borrow money. But suppose the Philippine government can not pay its debt when it falls due, as has been the case in many instances on our own continent within the last quarter of a century; as is the case to-day with one of the governments of Central America. If that loan is an English loan, England would seize the revenues of the Philippines for the payment of her debt, as she has done before and is doing

now.   So would France or Germany or whoever was the
creditor nation.   Should we have a right to interfere?
Of course not, unless we were willing to guarantee the
Philippine debt.   If, then, the first purpose of the Opposition candidate is carried out, we must:

Keep " stable " the government which we first " establish," or the very purpose of the establishment of that
government is defeated.

If the second proposition of the Opposition is performed, we must:

First: Control the finances of the Philippines perpetually; or,

Second: Guarantee the loans the Philippine government makes with other nations; or,

Third: Go to war with those nations to defeat their
collection of their just debts.

Is this sound policy?   Is it profitable?   Is it moral?
Is it just to the Filipinos, to the world, to ourselves?
Is it humane to the masses of those children who need
first of all, and more than all, order, law and peace?   Is
it prudent, wise, far-seeing statesmanship?   And does
the adoption of a similar course in Cuba justify it in the
Philippines?

No.   Here is the program of reason and righteousness, and Time and Events will make it the program of
the Republic:

First: We have given Porto Rico such a civil government as her situation demands, under the Stars and
Stripes.

Second: We will put down the rebellion and then give
the Philippines such a civil government as the situation
demands, under the Stars and Stripes.

Third: We are regenerating Cuba, and when our preparatory work is done, we should have given Cuba such a civil government as her situation may demand, under the Stars and Stripes.

The sovereignty of the Stars and Stripes can be nothing but a blessing to any people and to any land.

I do not advocate this course for commercial reasons, though these have their weight. All men who understand production and exchange, understand the commercial advantage resulting from our ownership of these rich possessions. But I waive this large consideration as insignificant, compared with the master argument of the progress of civilization, which under God, the American people are henceforth to lead until our day is done. For henceforward in the trooping of the colors of the nations they shall cluster around and follow the Republic's banner.

The mercantile argument is mighty with Americans in merely mercantile times, and it should be so; but the argument of destiny is the master argument in the hour of destiny, and it should be so. The American people never yet entered on a great movement for merely mercantile reasons. Sentiment and duty have started and controlled every noble current of American history. And at this historic hour, destiny is the controlling consideration in the prophetic statesmanship which conditions require of the American people.

It is destiny that the world shall be rescued from its natural wilderness and from savage men. Civilization is no less an evolution than the changing forms of animal and vegetable life. Surely and steadily the reign of law, which is the very spirit of liberty, takes the place of arbitrary caprice. Surely and steadily the methods of social order are bringing the whole earth under their subjection. And to deny that this is right, is to deny that civilization should increase. In this great work the American people must have their part. They are fitted for the work as no people have ever been fitted; and their work lies before them.

If the Opposition say that they grant this, but that the higher considerations of abstract human rights demand that the Philippines shall have such a government as they wish, regardless of the remainder of the world, I answer that the desire of the Filipinos is not the only factor in determining their government, just as the desire of no individual man is the only factor determining his conduct. It is written in the moral law of individuals that " No man liveth to himself alone "; and it is no less written in the moral law of peoples that " No people liveth to itself alone."

The world is interested in the Philippines, and it has a right to be. The world is interested in India, and it has a right to be. Civilization is interested in China and its government, and that is the duty of civilization. You can not take the Philippines out of the operation of those forces which are binding all mankind into one vast and united intelligence. When Circumstance has raised our flag above them, we dare not turn these misguided children over to destruction by themselves or spoliation by others, and then make answer when the God of nations requires them at our hands, " Am I my brother's keeper? "

If you admit that it is the purpose of that Intelligence that rules the universe to civilize and unify mankind, how is this to be accomplished? If you say that it is by leaving each people to themselves to work out their own salvation, I answer that history shows that civilization has been preserved only by the most superior nations extending it. And the method of extending civilization is by colonization where the superior nation can establish itself among the inferior races; or in place of them, if the inferior races can not exist under civilization, as in New Zealand, Australia and the like. The method is by administration where the superior nation can not, because of climatic conditions, establish itself among or supplant the inferior races, as in Java, India, and the like. And finally that method is by creating and developing commerce among all the peoples of the world.

It is thus that America itself was discovered; thus that this Republic was builded; thus that South Africa was reclaimed; thus that Australia was recovered from the Bushman and made the home of civilization; thus that Ceylon was taken from wild men and tangled jungle and brought beneath the rule of religion, law and industry. It is thus that Egypt is being redeemed, her deserts fertilized, her starving millions fed, her fellahs made men and the blessings of just government bestowed upon the land of the Pharaohs. It is thus that the regeneration of India has progressed, her cities been cleansed, the reign of hygiene and health gradually established in the very kingdom of pestilence and disease; and the arbitrary and infamous tyranny of petty princes, holding power of life and death over miserable subjects, reduced to the orderly administration of equal and unpurchased justice under equal and impartial laws.

History establishes these propositions:

First: Every people who have become great, have become colonizers or administrators;

Second: Coincident with this colonization and administration, their material and political greatness develops;

Third: Their decline is coincident with the abandonment of the policy of possession and administration, or departure from the true principles thereof.

And as a corollary to these propositions is this self-evident and contemporaneous truth:

Every progressive nation of Europe to-day is seeking lands to colonize and governments to administer.

And can this common instinct of the most progressive peoples of the world — this common conclusion of the ablest statesmen of other nations — be baseless?

If the Opposition asks why this is the mission of the American people now more than heretofore, I answer that before any people assumes these great tasks it goes through a process of consolidation and unification, just as a man achieves maturity before he assumes the tasks of a man. Great Britain never became a colonizing and administering power until the separate peoples of England, Scotland, Ireland and Wales, welded into a single indivisible people, were ready to go forth as a national unit and do the great work to which the world was calling it.

The German people did not embark upon this natural policy until separate duchies, principalities and kingdoms were finally welded by a common war, common blood, and common interests into a great single and indivisible people ready to go forth as a national unit to the great work to which the world was calling it.

The French became colonizers of lands and adminis-

trators of governments only when her great statesmen,
from Richelieu to Colbert, had knit the separate and
divided French people into a national unit and sent it
forth to the work to which the world was calling it; and
France declined only when she abandoned that natural
law of national power and progress, and Napoleon diverted her energies to the internal strifes of Europe.
Then her decline began. She lost Canada. The Cor-
sican sold Louisiana to us. And to-day French statesmen at last realize the fatal operation of this law when
once disobeyed, and so again are seeking to become one
of the colonizing and administering powers of earth.

The American Republic has been going through the
process of fitting it for the execution of this natural law
of civilization. Hitherto we have had local divisions.
The proposition that we were a single people, a national
unit, and not a sum of segregated factions, was denied.
And it required war and commerce and time — the shed-
ding of blood, the uniting of communities by railroads
and telegraphs, the knitting together of the fabric of
Nationality by that wonderful loom of human intelligence
called the post; and finally, the common and united effort
of a foreign war, to bring us to a consciousness of our
power *as a people*. And there is never in nature a power
without a corresponding purpose. Shall we now stop
this process of nature?

We are this at last, a great national unit ready to carry
out that universal law of civilization which requires of
every people who have reached our high estate to become
colonizers of new lands, administrators of orderly government over savage and senile peoples. And being thus
prepared, the lands and peoples needing our administra-

tion are delivered to our keeping, not by our design, but by occurrence beyond our control. In the astronomy of Destiny, American Opportunity, American Duty and American Preparedness are in conjunction. Who shall oppose their progress?

These are the laws which history advises are the laws of civilization's growth. These, therefore, are the high ordinances of universal and racial morality which has for its ultimate object " that far-off divine event towards which civilization tends." And it is to this divine order of progress that I appeal in answer to the misapplied individual moralities that would give Australia back to its Bushmen, the United States to its Indians, Ceylon to its natives, and the whole world back to barbarism and night.

If the Opposition says that this program, written not in the statutes of man, but in the nature of things, will smother our institutions with a myriad of soldiers, I answer that the world to-day demonstrates that it will result in the reverse. If they point to Germany, and other nations with vast military establishments, to prove that colonization and administration over lands held as possessions and dependencies result in the supremacy of the soldiery over the common people, I answer that the examples do not sustain, but destroy the proposition.

Consider Germany. Her standing army in times of peace is 562,000 men. Does colonization cause or require them? No; because she maintained that mighty multitude before the present Emperor and his counsellors developed Germany's progressive colonial and administrative policy. No, again; because, of Germany's standing army of 562,000 men, less than 4,000 are in her possessions, the remainder of her mighty host being stationed within the Empire itself. No, again; because Austria, with no colonies at all, has a standing army in times of peace of over 361,000 men, none of whom is employed in the care of possessions. No, again; because France, a republic, has a standing army in times of peace of 616,000 men, of which less than 10,000 are employed in her colonies and possessions except in Algeria and Tunis, which are considered an immediate part of France. No, again; because Italy, with hardly a colonial possession, maintains a standing army in times of peace of nearly 325,000 men. No, again; because Spain, the world's second largest holder of possessions before we won them, maintained a standing army of less than 100,000 men, of whom less than 10,000 were kept in her misruled and oppressed possessions. No, again; because the greatest colonial power that the world has ever seen, the Empire of Great Britain, has a smaller standing army in times of peace than any power of Europe — less than half as many as Germany, almost two-thirds less than the soldiers of France, nearly one-third less than Italy, and one-third less than the soldiers maintained by Austria, an absolutely non-colonizing power.

Great Britain's entire standing army of English, Scotch, Welsh and Irish soldiers throughout the entire Empire is only 231,351, of which Ceylon, with a population of 3,500,000, has only one battalion of English infantry and two companies of English artillery. Egypt, with nearly 10,000,000, has less than 6,000 English officers and men; and India, with 300,000,000 population, has less than 75,000 English soldiers. The other soldiers upholding the English flag throughout England's possessions are native soldiers. England has learned the

statesmanship of sentiment; and so the people England
rules supply the soldiers who defend her flag.

What is it that establishes militarism in Germany?
On the west, the immediate proximity of France, her
hereditary foe; on the east, the immediate proximity
of Russia, her hereditary foe; on the south, the immediate proximity of an heterogenous empire. What is it
that establishes militarism in France? The immediate
proximity of Germany on the East, her hereditary foe;
the immediate proximity of England on the north, an
historic enemy; the immediate proximity of Italy on the
south, the third of the Anti-French Dreibund. These
are the things which establish militarism in Europe — not
colonization, not possessions, not obedience to the great
natural law of expansion and growth.

If France, Germany, Italy, Austria, would devote themselves to the world's great work of rescuing the wilderness, of planting civilization, of extending their institutions as England has done, as Germany is beginning to do,
as the American Republic, under God, is going to lead the
world in doing, the armaments of these European military
powers would necessarily dissolve, because there would
be no longer occasion for them; and because all their
energies would be required in the nobler work to which
they would thus set their hands.

To produce the same militarism in America that curses
Europe, it would be necessary for Canada on the north to
be an equal power with us, hostile with present rivalry
and centuries of inherited hatred; and for Mexico to be
the same thing on the south. And even then we should
have only half the conditions that produce militarism
in any European nation. Separate government in Cuba

is the only proposed step that creates conditions of militarism in America. Militarism in extending American authority! No! No! The wider the dominion of the Stars and Stripes, the broader the reign of peace.

If we do our duty in the Philippines, it is admitted that we ought not to govern the Filipinos as fellow-citizens of the Republic. The Platform of the Opposition says that " to make the Filipinos citizens would endanger our civilization." To force upon Malays, who three hundred years ago were savages and who since that time have been schooled only in oppression, that form of self-government exercised by the citizens of the United States, would be to clothe an infant in the apparel of a giant and require of it a giant's strength and tasks. If we govern them, we must govern them with common sense. They must first be made familiar with the simplest principles of liberty — equal obedience to equal laws, impartial justice by unpurchasable courts, protection of property and of the right to labor — in short, with the *substance* of liberty which civilized government will establish among them.

The Filipinos must begin at the beginning and grow in the knowledge of free institutions, and, if possible, into the ultimate practice of free government by observing the operation of those institutions among them and by experiencing their benefits. They have experienced unjust, unequal and arbitrary taxation; this is the result of the institutions of tyranny. They must experience equal, just and scientific taxation; this is the result of free institutions. They have experienced arrest without cause, imprisonment without a hearing, and beheld justice bought and sold; these are the results of the institutions of tyranny. They must experience arrest only for cause publicly made known, conviction only after trial publicly conducted and justice impartial, unpurchasable and speedily administered; these are the results of free institutions.

They have experienced the violation of the home and robbery by public officers; these are the results of the institutions of tyranny. They must experience the sanctity of the fireside, the separation of Church and State, the punishment of soldier or public official practising outrage or extortion upon them; these are the results of free institutions. And these are the results which they will experience under the government of the American Republic. For these are the results of American Institutions, and our *institutions* follow the flag.

The institutions of every nation follow its flag. German institutions follow the flag of the Fatherland. English institutions follow the banner of St. George. French institutions follow the tricolor of France. And just so, American institutions follow the emblem of the Republic. Nay! Our institutions not only follow the flag, *they accompany it*. They troop beneath its fold. Wherever an American citizen goes, he carries the spirit of our institutions. On whatever soil his blood is shed to establish the sovereignty of our flag, there are planted the imperishable seeds of the institutions of our Nation; and there those institutions flourish in proportion as the soil where they are planted is prepared for them.

Free institutions are as definite, certain and concrete as our Constitution itself. Free speech is an institution of liberty. Free schools are an institution of liberty. Freedom of worship is an institution of liberty. Any American school-boy can catalogue free institutions.

And as fast as the simplest of these institutions prepares these children Providence has given into our keeping for higher grades, just so fast more complex forms of our institutions will follow as naturally as childhood succeeds infancy, youth succeeds childhood and manhood crowns maturity. Our flag! Our institutions! Our Constitution! This is the immortal order in which American civilization marches.

And so the answer to the politician's battle-cry that " our Constitution follows the flag " is this great truth of popular liberty, OUR INSTITUTIONS FOLLOW THE FLAG.

We are a Nation. We can acquire territory. If we can acquire territory, we can govern it. If we can govern it, we can govern it as its situation may demand. If the Opposition says that power so broad is dangerous to the liberties of the American people, I answer that the American people's liberties can never be endangered at the hands of the American people; and, therefore, that their liberties can not be endangered by the exercise of this power, because this power is power exercised by the American people themselves.

> " *Congress* shall have power to dispose of and make all needful rules and regulations respecting territory belonging to the United States," says the Constitution.

And what is Congress? The agent of the American people. The Constitution created Congress. But who created the Constitution? " We, the people," declares the Constitution itself.

The American people created the Constitution; it is their method. The American people established Congress; it is their instrument. The American people elect the members of Congress; they are the people's servants.

Their laws are the people's laws. Their power is the people's power. And if you fear this power, you fear the people. If you want their power restricted, it is because you want the power of the people restricted; and a restriction of their power is a restriction of their liberty. So that the end of the logic of the Opposition is limitation upon the liberties of the American people, for fear that the liberties of the American people will suffer at the hands of the American people — which is absurd.

If the Opposition asserts that the powers which the Constitution gives to the legislative agents of the American people will not be exercised in righteousness, I answer that that can only be because the American people themselves are not righteous. It is the American people, through their agents, who exercise the power; and if those agents do not act as the people would have them, they will discharge those agents and annul their acts. The heart of the whole argument on the constitutional power of the government is faith in the wisdom and virtue of the people; and in that virtue and wisdom I believe, as every man must, who believes in a republic. In the end, the judgment of the masses is right. If this were not so, progress would be impossible, since only through the people is progress achieved.

* * * * * * * * * * * *

The Opposition says that American liberties will be lost if we administer the substance of liberty to those children. Does any man believe that the American institution of free schools will be destroyed or impaired because we plant free schools throughout the Philippines? Does any man believe that equal rights will be impaired here, because we establish equal rights there?

The individual rights of Englishmen have not declined since England became an administrator of external governments; on the contrary, as England has extended her colonies, the individual rights of individual Englishmen have increased. The rights of the Crown have not enlarged as England's empire has extended; on the contrary, they have diminished. The period of England's great activity in external government has been precisely the period of the extension of the suffrage in England itself, of the enactment of laws for the protection of labor and the amelioration of all the conditions of life among the common people of England.

The period of England's most active extension of empire has not been the period of her most violent oppression of Ireland; the contrary is true. Ireland's bitterest hour was in Cromwell's day and at Cromwell's hands; and yet England had no definite plan of empire then. Ireland's most progressive period has been within the last quarter of a century, when land laws were enacted by the British Parliament compelling Irish landlords to sell their lands to Irish tenants, and permitting the tenant to purchase his landlord's land by the payment of his rent at a price, fixed not by the landlord, but by the courts and commissions.

Ireland's brightest day has been within the last ten years, in which her people have deposited more money in savings banks than in a century before. And yet the last quarter of a century has been England's most imperial period. The last ten years have witnessed the most systematic work by England in empire building in all her history. And England's experience is not an isolated instance. It would not be isolated even if it were confined to England, since her sway is as wide as the world. But the experience of her people is the experience of every other people who have embarked upon the same great voyage.

This is no unprecedented struggle. It is the ever-old and yet the ever-new, because the ever-elemental contest between the forces of a growing nationality and those who resist it; between the forces of extending dominion and those who oppose it; between the forces that are making us the master people of the world and those who think that our activities should be confined to this continent for ever. It is the eternal duel between the forces of progress and reaction, of construction and disintegration, of growth and of decay.

Both sides are and always have been sincere. Washington was sincere when he advocated the adoption of the Constitution; Patrick Henry was sincere when he resisted it as the death-blow to our liberties. Jefferson was sincere when he acquired the empire of Louisiana; Josiah Quincy was sincere when he declared in Congress that the Louisiana acquisition meant the dissolution of the Union.

Webster was sincere when he asserted the sovereignty of the Nation, the indestructibility of the Union, and declared that the Constitution could not follow the flag until the American people so decreed; and Calhoun was sincere when he pronounced the doctrine of state sovereignty, the right of nullification, and announced that the Constitution, carrying slavery, followed the flag in spite of the will of the American people. Lincoln was sincere when he proclaimed that the Union was older than the Constitution, that nationality was the indestructible destiny of the American people, and that he would maintain that nationality by arms; and those mistaken ones were sincere who sought to divide the American people and on the field of battle poured out their blood fighting for their faith.

But their sincerity did not make them *right*. Their earnestness, ability, courage could not give them victory. They were struggling against the Fates. They were resisting the onward forces which were making of the American people the master Nation of the world — the forces that established us first as a separate political body, then welded us into a national unit, indivisible; then extended our dominion from ocean to ocean over unexplored wilderness; and now in the ripeness of time fling our authority and unfurl our flag almost around the globe. It is the " divine event " of American principles among the governments of men for which these forces have been working since the Pilgrims landed on the red man's soil. Men — patriotic, brave and wise — have sought to stay that tremendous purpose of destiny, but their opposition was as the feeble finger of a babe against the resistless pour of the Gulf Stream's mighty current.

For God's hand was in it all. His plans were working out their glorious results. And just as futile is resistance to the continuance to-day of the eternal movement of the American people toward the mastery of the world. This is a destiny neither vague nor undesirable. It is definite, splendid and holy.

When nations shall war no more without the consent of the American Republic: what American heart thrills not with pride at that prospect? And yet our interests are weaving themselves so rapidly around the world that that time is almost here.

When governments stay the slaughter of human beings, because the American Republic demands it: what American heart thrills not with pride at that prospect? And yet to-night there sits in Constantinople a sovereign who knows that time is nearly here.

When the commerce of the world on which the world's peace hangs, traveling every ocean highway of earth, shall pass beneath the guns of the great Republic: what American heart thrills not at that prospect? Yet that time will be here before the first quarter of the twentieth century closes.

When any changing of the map of earth requires a conference of the Powers, and when, at any Congress of the Nations, the American Republic will preside as the most powerful of powers and most righteous of judges: what American heart thrills not at that prospect? And yet, that prospect is in sight, even as I speak.

It is the high and holy destiny of the American people, and from that destiny the American bugles will never sound retreat. "Westward the Star of Empire takes its way!" AMERICAN INSTITUTIONS FOLLOW THE AMERICAN FLAG.

TRUSTS, A DEVELOPMENT

Speech opening the Republican Campaign in Nebraska, delivered at Columbus, Nebraska, September 28, 1900.

WHAT is a trust? It is a combination of capital, designed to simplify and unify business, or a combination of labor, designed to simplify and unify industry. It is easy to see, therefore, that there can be good trusts and bad trusts, just as there can be good men and bad men. A trust is a good trust when it performs the work for which it has been organized, and produces better goods at cheaper prices and delivers them to the consumer more conveniently than a dozen different concerns could do. The consumer is the sovereign factor. The well-being of the masses is the result of every industrial development that endures.

A trust is a bad trust when it raises prices dishonestly and without other reason than to satisfy the greed of its managers. A man is a bad man when he steals; and when he does that he ought to be put in jail. A trust is a bad trust when dishonestly it raises prices; and when it does that, its managers ought to be put in jail. But because one man steals is no reason why all men should be put in jail; and because one trust is dishonest is no reason why all trust managers should be put in jail. Mr. Bryan is in favor of destroying *all* combinations of capital. We are in favor of destroying only *such* combinations of capital as oppress the people, just as you are in

144

favor of putting in jail only such men as commit larceny, or murder or arson.

Let me give you Nebraska farmers a perfect illustration of a trust that every farmer in this country operates himself — the self-binding harvester. I got the job of driving the first self-binding harvester that was sent to central Illinois by the McCormicks. It was an old wire binder. It was a trust. It was the only trust with which I have ever had anything to do. It did what several machines and implements were required to do before. It enabled the farmer to harvest and market his grain at much less cost than he was able to do before. The first season the self-binding harvester appeared in central Illinois, the same arguments were advanced against it that are now advanced against trusts.

It was said that it threw labor out of employment. It was said it would result in each farmer's becoming independent of outside labor, and that he would not need any help from the day-laborers whom he had heretofore hired to do his harvesting. There was even talk of mobs to burn up the self-binders. But men who thought they were thrown out of employment by it, found that they were not; but that there were other, easier, better paid employments in other directions than the hard work that harvesting by hand afforded them; that the new conditions created by this very self-binder furnished them other and better employment.

Every labor-saving machine is a mechanical trust; yet more laboring men are employed to-day, and at higher wages and with shorter hours, than ever before.

The self-binder enabled the farmer to market his grain more cheaply than he was able to do before. So the trust enables the producers to produce more cheaply than they did before.   The self-binder therefore increases the farmer's profits because it enables him to market his grain more cheaply; and that is right.   The trust enables its managers to produce more cheaply than they did before; and increase in profits coming from that is legitimate, although they have no right to all such increase of profits.

Better products at cheaper prices to the consumer is the only justification for trusts.

If the farmers were able to force up the prices of grain dishonestly and still increase their profits, that would be wrong, and ought to be prevented.   Just so, when a trust dishonestly forces up the price of its products, that is wrong, and ought to be prevented.   And that is what we propose to do.   But because the self-binding harvester increases the farmer's profit by enabling him to produce cheaper grain, is no reason why the self-binder ought to be burned.   And just so, the fact that trusts cause cheaper production of products, but thereby also increases profits, is no reason why they should be destroyed.   Our idea is regulation and punishment.   The Opposition idea is simply destruction.

There is only one possible way of regulating trusts. That way is by the Nation controlling corporations.   This is one country now.   We have outgrown Calhoun " state rights."   There is no reason why a corporation organized in New Jersey should have greater privileges than one organized in Nebraska.   A trust, to succeed, must do business all over the country.   Therefore, it ought to be controlled, not by a state government, but by the Nation's government.   It is the old struggle between the

Nation and "state rights." If the Constitution does not permit national control at present, we should amend the Constitution so that the National Government may control trusts. But, through the interstate commerce clause, the Constitution does permit national regulation of all corporations doing interstate business.

Is the Opposition in favor of destroying the department store? Is there a woman in the United States who will refuse to trade with the department stores? If not, why? Because before the department store came she had to buy one thing in one little shop and another thing in another little shop, and all of poorer quality and higher price; whereas she now buys everything under one roof, at a cheaper price and of better quality, and has it quickly delivered. Under the old system, statistics show that more than 80 per cent. of the small stores failed. All of them had to sell poorer goods at a higher price in order to make their many profits, and even then they failed; whereas the department store sells at a lower price better goods in more convenient form, and the small dealer who before was waging a daily struggle with bankruptcy and failing in the end, is now the well-paid and prosperous head of a department of that great center of distribution for the masses, called the department store.

Yet that department store has not destroyed the small dealer who succeeded before. That small dealer still flourishes. The shops devoted to specialties, and where high individual skill is required, are more prosperous now than ever. The department store really furnishes the specialist his opportunity. It also makes the neighborhood stores more plentiful and prosperous to-day than formerly. They do the small and immediate business, just as small change does the small and immediate business required of money.

Because we have ten, twenty and fifty-dollar bills is no reason why we should dispense with the dollar, the quarter, the dime and the nickel. Each has its sphere of usefulness. Just so the trust and the small dealer, the department store, the specialist and the neighborhood store, have their respective spheres of usefulness. And the department store takes the place only of the stores which failed before and were constantly upsetting business. If the Opposition is logical, it is in favor of destroying the department store, because the department store is a trust in its most familiar form.

Mr. Bryan is in favor of trusts in reality as much as any man in the United States. He admits it himself. For he says that he is a great champion of labor organization. So am I. The labor organizations of my State supported me for the Senate; and when they did it, they knew just where I stood on every question then before the people. I am, and have been, since I was a boy, in favor of labor organization. It is the only way labor has of asserting its equal rights with the organization of capital, and in so doing is a public benefit; for the well-being of labor is of vital concern to the well-being of the entire Nation. It benefits labor in numberless ways. Over and over again Mr. Bryan has said that these organizations are a great blessing.

And yet labor organization is merely a form of trust. It is a labor trust, and it is a good thing. But even a labor trust sometimes does wrong. When it does, it loses the sympathy of the great mass of our people; and it ought to be resisted. Just so, the trusts of capital often do wrong. When they do, they ought to be punished. But because labor trusts are sometimes in the wrong is no reason why they should be destroyed. What both need when they do wrong is restraint and correction. But what Mr. Bryan proposes is destruction; and if he is logical, he must destroy the trust of labor as well as the trust of capital.

Let me give you another and simpler example of the trust. There is in this country a great railway system called the "Big Four Railroad." A great deal of it is in Indiana, and most of it is in that state and in Ohio. I remember the time when the railroads that formed what is now the Big Four Railroad system were short, separate lines. Service on each of these lines was poor. Cars were bad. Tracks and road-bed were far from safe.

The passenger who wanted to travel any considerable distance had to get off the cars at one end of a line and get on other cars of another line, and the longer he traveled the more he had to do this. He had to pay higher fare than now and to buy many separate tickets. The employees of those various lines were fewer in number than they now are and were paid smaller wages. Frequently the lines went into the hands of receivers and the working-men had trouble in getting their wages at all.

Finally a wise manager combined those lines into one system. What was the result? More trains, faster time, better cars, cheaper rates and through service. You can now get on one of that system's trains, and, without change, go to distant points which before required two or three changes and two or three tickets. The system employs many more men than the separate lines employed before the consolidation. The service is greatly improved. The convenience to the passenger is not a comparison, but a contrast with what it used to be. Therefore, there is more traveling, more business. You are carried more cheaply in palace cars; your grain is hauled at lower rates of freight, more safely and more speedily. 'And so it is that a miracle is wrought; better service and cheaper rates to the public on the one hand, and more employment and higher wages to the employees on the other hand; at the same time, more profit to the stock-holders who own the road. Dare the Opposition say that they would have that system broken up into the little companies from which it was formed? If they dare not, it is evident that they have abandoned their position on the trust.

It is said that the trusts prevent young men from rising in the business world. On the contrary, the active heads of most of these corporations are young men who have risen to their high position without influence or any other aid than their own ability. The president of the Carnegie Steel Company is still a young man, and he rose to his position from a boy in the works. What the trust is looking for — what any combination of capital is looking for — is fresh and vigorous ability. Unless they get that, they can not succeed. More than 95 per cent. of the active management of the great combinations of capital in this country, and the active management of each one of the departments of these great combinations of capital, is in the hands of young men without wealth, influence or position, but whose merit has been recognized by the directors of these great concerns.

If the trust does not have such ability constantly at its

command, it will break down, just as trusts often, and for exactly this reason, are breaking down. Keen, bold, daring minds see that a trust is not managed with ability, and they organize another trust which *is* managed with ability. A trust can exist only when each and every department of it, to the smallest detail of its business, is conducted with mathematical accuracy. The chief demand in this country to-day is for talented, industrious, honest and brave young men to aid the mighty work which this industrial development of our civilization requires.

As no woman would have the department store dissolve into the little, inconvenient, high-priced shops, selling poorer goods in a more inconvenient way; as not a man in this Republic would have any of our great railroad lines, which were formed out of a dozen small, poorly-operated, high-priced, miserably-equipped, inconvenient lines, broken up into those little roads again, just so, not a man in this country is against the industrial development of a trust, when it is honestly and righteously conducted. What we are all against is the dishonest operation of these trusts, just as we are all against the dishonest conduct of any man. But the sensible thing is not to destroy them — the sensible thing is to remedy them.

The right road is onward toward national control, and not backward toward the day when the farmer reaped his grain with a scythe, instead of with the self-binding harvester; not backward to the day when he threshed it with a flail, instead of with a vibrating thresher; not backward to the day when the stage-coach did the business of passenger transportation, instead of the travel of the country being carried at a fraction of the price the stage-coach charged, and in palace cars, with all the comforts and luxuries of this wonderful civilization.

So the elements that are required in our statesmen in dealing with this tremendous problem of human society, this natural industrial development, are moderation, earnest thought, thorough study and fearless justice, instead of violent and ignorant assertion, inflamed prejudice and mad resolutions, not to remedy, but to destroy. What we need is not sweeping declarations against the trusts of labor or the trusts of capital, but common sense and the spirit of justice. Common sense, in order that we may see what is just; and the spirit of justice, in order that we may do what is just.

CONSERVATISM; THE SPIRIT OF NATIONAL SELF-RESTRAINT

Address delivered in the Auditorium, at Chicago, on the afternoon of February 22, 1902, on the occasion of the celebration of Washington's birthday.

THE meaning of Washington in American history is discipline. The message of Washington's life to the American people is discipline. The need of American character is discipline.

Washington did not give patriotism to the American colonies. The people had that as abundantly as he. He did not give them courage. That quality was and is in the American blood. He did not even give them resource. There were intellects more productive than his. But Washington gave balance and direction to elemental forces. He was the genius of order. He was poise personified. He was the spirit of discipline. He was the first Great Conservative. It was this quality in him that made all other elements of the Revolution effective. It was this that organized our nebulous independence into a Nation of liberty. The parts of a machine are useless until assembled and fitted each to its appropriate place. Washington was the master mechanic of our Nation; so it is that we are a people.

But we are not yet a perfect people. We are still in the making. It is a glorious circumstance. Youth is the noblest of God's gifts. The youth of a Nation is like the youth of a man. The American people are young? Yes! Vital? Yes! Powerful? Yes! Disciplined? Not entirely. Moderate? Not yet, but growing in that grace. And therefore on this, his day, I bear you the message of Washington — he, whose sanity, orderliness and calm have reached through the century, steadying us, overcoming in us the untamed passions of riotous youth.

The American people have finally overcome every convulsion? True. The element of sobriety has never failed to master the maddest agitations? True again. But the cost of the struggle in every instance has been measured by the quality of the discipline resisting at the time. To-day we are calm, and are conscious of no need for self-restraint. Yes! But yesterday we were delirious, and the rumble of cannon on your streets and the rattle of musketry at your doors was hailed with feelings of security and relief.

The necessity of resorting to an armed force should never have occurred in your recent history. Many crises may be recalled by men not yet old. Popular reserve, the self-restraint of the people, the fireside conference, would have lessened every disturbing circumstance in our history, and prevented many or most of them. Reason is better than bayonets. Sober second thought is better than the destroying violence of a campaign over passion-born propositions.

In the daily press we read of a coöperative council of capitalists, clergy, workers and publicists to settle the conflicts between labor and productive wealth. We applaud it, and we should. But not because it will be effective — for it may not be effective. But we hail it as an evidence that the spirit of forbearance is spreading among the people. It is an expression of the instinct of order which must become the ruling element in American civilization.

This it is which, more and more, will settle strikes, and in the end prevent them. This it is which, more and more, will take wildness out of our politics, until reasonableness only remains. The remedy for friction between employer and employed is in the breasts of the men themselves and of their employers. The saving of the people is in the hands of the people themselves, and nowhere else. Better than councils and commissions and congresses is the self-discipline, the reasoning reserve, the regulated conscience of a free people. And congresses and councils are effective only as they are expressions of this.

Let us awaken to the fundamental fact that written laws are not everything, but that the people are everything. Back of our statutes stands our Constitution, and back of our Constitution stand our institutions, and back of our institutions stands our race. Let us remember that the people are the real foundation; not laws, not even constitutions. It is the people from whom statutes, constitutions and even institutions spring, who give these forms of civil method their meaning.

The Constitution of this Republic would be a different instrument as the fundamental law of a Latin nation even though that nation copied it word for word. It would be interpreted by their racial spirit, expounded in the light of their racial institutions. Every day since our Constitution was adopted we have been acting beyond the limits of its written word, but within the limits of its institutional meaning. If we had not done so we should not now be a nation.

More and more will this be so. The growth of modern industry; the gradual change of competition into coöperation; the manifold and infinitely interwoven activities of modern business; the steady knitting together of all the agencies of production, distribution and exchange until the whole Nation is well-nigh an industrial unit as it is a political unit; the extension of this process until international relations are so interlaced that no nation, even by war, can entirely cut the cords of commerce and culture that bind her to her sisters — the processes of civilization in short — bring into play national necessities and national powers as much greater and more complex than those exercised by the Fathers, as the Nation and its activities to-day are greater and more complex than they were a century ago.

We can not adopt new constitutions to meet these new conditions. They would be inadequate if we did adopt them; and each decade would make the constitution of the preceding decade obsolete if its *letter* alone were read. And so we rely on a law more permanent and more vital — the institutional law with its roots springing from the very soul of our race, by whose living meaning our written laws and constitutions are interpreted. Our hope is in ourselves. Our safety is in our racial customs and tendencies. Our salvation and supremacy is in the character of our people.

I do not mean that we should bind ourselves to custom. I am only a limited believer in the philosophy of precedent. Precedent becomes paralysis, if observed when customs no longer fit conditions. Conservatism does not mean adherence to existing order merely because it is existing order. Conservatism means the adaptation of means to ends naturally and without violence. Reason is the touchstone of conservatism.

And so it is that we must foster the element of conservatism in American character as we would fan the spark of life itself, for it is that vital spark. Let the American people write over the fireside of every American home those words of inspired direction: *Prove all things — hold fast to that which is good.* Time is the greater reasoner. Patience is the eternal method of accuracy and truth. Time and Patience, Patience and Time — these are the ancient counselors who never err. These are the sages to consult when perplexing situations seem insolvable.

There can be no instantaneous settlement of any large question. That is not the method of civilization's progress. Society is a growth — not a creation. And all social, industrial and political questions are related as a tree's branches to the common trunk. They are not, therefore, to be determined permanently by cure-all measures and put aside as settled, as you pack articles in a box and put it on the shelf, sealed and labeled.

Conditions undergo ceaseless change, and measures made for those conditions must also undergo ceaseless change. But if the change is wise it must be slow, and not sudden. The wrenching of the vast and delicate machinery of the Nation's business, the straining of the nerves of the whole people in unnecessary campaigns, have been due to impossible propositions instantly to enact felicity. This is not discipline, not sanity. It is not reason, but passion; not reserve, but rashness.

On the other hand, measures once enacted are not immortal. No economic statute can be perpetual. To say that it can never be bettered is to say that human conditions can never be bettered. But they can be bettered. Yesterday we lumbered in stages; to-day we fly in palaces. And the change from stage-coach to railway has required a new body of laws, which are themselves perpetually changing. Yesterday both capital and labor were individualized; to-day both are consolidated, systematized, coöperative. But these new conditions grew out of the old conditions — they were not suddenly created. And so we must let the new laws, regulating those new conditions, grow, and not suddenly create them. Good laws *grow;* bad laws are *made.*

Quick creations are ineffective. Conditions should establish laws, not laws conditions. And when this order is reversed both the law-made conditions and the law which makes them are unhealthy, irritating and dangerous. Events are the greatest law-makers. Deliberation, patience and the self-regulation of our activities are the surest of safe-guards.

Put not your faith in written word alone; put your faith in your own steady self-restraint. " The letter killeth but the spirit giveth life." As in your relations to morals, you remember the Master and strive to be like Him; so in your relations to the state and your attitude toward all questions that present themselves to you as one of a self-governing people, remember Washington and strive to be like him — reserved, considering, considerate and calm.

The national habit of self-control exercised in the current developments of each day, when times are not hot with friction, will act without effort in the hour when events flame with excitement. If the people will adopt this formula of conservative thought: *Everything is not bad because it is new, and everything is not good because it is old* — and upon that formula base conservative procedure, we shall always end with conservative results. Conservative results are safe results; safe progress is permanent progress. Beware of rebounds.

We are in a period of growth which is itself a proof of our youth and enlarging vitality. It is inevitable that each year, almost each day, shall behold unheard-of developments in our industrial, commercial, financial methods. Let us not be startled at them. They may be beneficent or they may be malevolent, but denunciation, hasty action, conclusions which are jumped at instead of being thought out, are no proper test. The habit of mind that leads us bitterly to denounce or unreservedly to praise, is not the temper which a free people should foster.

For a free people must depend upon themselves and not upon some separate power which attempts to solve every problem for them, as is the case in autocracies. We are fond of saying that in a republic each citizen is a king. But saying so does not make it so. Each of us can be king, and therefore the Nation itself clothed with majesty as no people ever were arrayed; but only by each citizen acting as a king should act; thinking as a king should think, steadily, calmly, with balanced judgment and well-considered action.

The developments in the combinations of capital call for just such treatment; the developments in combinations of labor call for just such treatment. We behold millions of money which yesterday were acting separately, to-day massed in mighty organizations for the production, their transportation, their distribution of national products. Let us not be alarmed at their magnitude. Let us not be thrown into a panic by their novelty.

It is not helpful to toss on the statute books hasty screeds and call them laws. It will throw no light upon the real question for excited meetings to grow frenzied over excited appeals. No great problem was ever illuminated by the torch of a mob; and between the conflagrations of the Commune and fiery talk of agitators who feel they must carry the next election at any cost, there is little difference. Both may be useful in revolution; both may be useful in the bloody overthrow of tyranny; but neither is the method of a free people, who hold their own destiny in their own hands.

It is apparent to the shallowest observer and certain to the profoundest, that the great combinations of capital recently developed are based upon some of the fundamental principles of progress. It is equally apparent and certain that in their development, evils and crudities have attended them. But this is true of everything. It is even true of the development of a child into a boy, of a boy into a man; and constant care is exercised in the training of the infant mind and character.

As violence, hot words, stormy conduct spoil the vision of the parent; so will the same savage methods spoil the vision and make foolish the action of the people in the regulation of the development of capital and labor. The combinations of capital devoted to the production of steel, flour, meats or oil, systematize the industry, reduce the expense of production, simplify and make easy distribution, invade and conquer foreign markets. The organizations of wealth devoted to the preparation of meats and other food stuffs sell their products abroad as well as here.

Their vast resources enable them to put refrigerating ships upon the sea and furnish the breakfast-tables of London and Berlin. And to supply that foreign demand the farmers of Illinois, Dakota and Kansas are called upon at profitable prices for cattle which otherwise they could not sell at all. So we see that this golden shuttle of modern enterprise, shooting backward and forward, not only through our own land, but across the seas into Europe and Asia, too, weaves occupation and prosperity for our citizens in its ministry to the wants of our fellow-men abroad.

These are a few of the benefits visible to all. On the other hand, the arbitrary raising and lowering of prices, the unjust exaction of unfair profits from our own consumers, are the evils. But the benefits are fundamental, and the evils incidental. And you can not shear away the good from the bad by some measure evolved over night from an excited brain and adopted next day as a party measure to carry an election the day after. The whole field of national and even international industry and trade must be considered. When you reflect that you can not do the simplest thing wthout involving every activity of industrial civilization all over the world, you can appreciate how dangerous makeshift measures are.

I repeat — the simplest act of civilized life affects all human industry. Take, for example, your journey home this afternoon in the cab or railway or street-car. It involves the growing and felling of forests.   It calls into play the energies of miners searching out the ore from which are made the wheels that carry you.   It involves the cattle from whose hides are made the harness of your horses, or the leather used in cars.   It involves the activities, the lives and the livelihood of ten thousand men immediately at hand; and broadening from this center of focused activity, it circles out to the remotest confines of the world's industry.

If so simple an act as your journey home this afternoon, to which you give no heed, so commonplace has it become, is thus far-reaching, how infinite in consequence are measures controlling these industries, and how vastly greater even is the policy of a people with reference to them.   Do I say, therefore, that no measures should be taken; no policy be formed?   No, I say the reverse.   But I say with greater earnestness, caused by the danger of unthoughtful and undisciplined action, that those measures and that policy should be well considered, and executed with sanity and judgment.

On the other hand, this development is having its beneficial effect upon the capitalists themselves.   Responsibility always brings a broader understanding and a gentler consideration of others.   And dealing, as the managers of these vast agencies of production and exchange do, with all the people of the Nation, and well-nigh with all the world, a new comprehension of those people is forced upon the capitalist, whether he will or no.   The financier of the twentieth century has got to be more than a financier.   *The modern financier must be a statesman.*

To-day the wise capitalist no longer indulges in the legerdemain of mere stock speculation.   He must build machinery; he must erect mills; he must construct railroads; he must buy steamship lines. Therefore he must understand the people, he must consider the people. The financial rashness of the Black Fridays of our history was as much a manifestation of our undisciplined and undeveloped state as was the burning of railroad properties at Pittsburgh in the red days now almost forgotten.

And so we see that capitalists must understand that the opinion of the people is as definite a factor in their great plans as the quantity of coal remaining in the mine or the producing capacity of a mill. As much a factor? Yes, more of a factor. For, after all, it is the consuming and producing capacity of the people upon which all industries are built. It is the thought and settled resolve of the people which is the most important element in our national economy.

The constructive capitalists of America have come to understand that public opinion must be taken into account as much as the amount of cash on hand or bills receivable. They have been forced to this, let us say, or they have learned it. No matter, they have come to understand it; and so we see that, voluntarily, the greatest corporation of the world — the United States Steel Corporation — has published to all the people a statement of its business and its operations, of its assets and its liabilities, of its products and its sales, of its history and its prospects. That is a thing which the financier of ten years ago would have called foolish, the unwise pandering of the theorist to the curiosity of the crowd.

But the financier of the twentieth century no longer calls it so. He *knows* it is not so. He knows that it is a necessity of his business — a thing essential to the popular support of his enterprise. Another great corporation of Illinois whose managing mind appears to be a statesman's as well as a financier's, began some three or four years ago to distribute the stock of his railroad among its employees, and to sell shares at lowest terms to the people living along its line.

Ten years ago that would have been called socialism — to-day it is business. It is conservatism. It is the realization of things as they are and the adjustment of the measures of wisdom and humanity to existing conditions, in order that the best of existing conditions may be preserved, and from them still better conditions may be evolved. All this is sanity; all this is calm and gentle and considerate thought; all this is the beginning of that discipline which comes from self-restraint and the respect for the rights and opinions of our fellows.

Organizations of labor are cognate to the organizations of capital. Each is the outgrowth of that principle of coöperation which is the very spirit of civilized society. The family is coöperation; a partnership is coöperation; the simplest form of a state is coöperation; and as the state grows more perfect, its citizens more and more coöperate each with all and all with each. Neither labor organizations, therefore, nor those of capital are unnatural or harmful. But the tyranny of greed may pervert the one; the tyranny of passion may ruin the other. Moderation should be the watchword of both; and if each were to adopt it, it would bring safety and glory as well.

If capital will not be reasonable, if labor will not be reasonable, the people will be reasonable for them.

There is no place in this country for the absolutist of capital. There is no place in this country for the absolutist of riot. The bully of wealth is wealth's worst enemy. The bully of labor is labor's worst enemy. Let the wise laborer elbow from his company him of the flaming utterance and untruthful tongue. Let the wiser capitalists suppress their would-be Czars. Out with the element of unreason in both camps, and the divided hosts will be one! Out with unreason everywhere in the Republic! Let the spirit of Washington be monarch of the hearts and minds of men everywhere beneath the flag which Washington established.

As the twentieth century financier must be a statesman, so the twentieth century labor-leader must be a statesman, too. He, too, must consider the people's thought. He, too, must measure popular tendencies. He, too, must counsel no act without weighing the effect that act will have throughout the whole complicated machinery of related and interdependent industries. And such statesmanship is being evolved. A man can not long remain the head of one of the great armies of organized workers without developing conservatism. Necessity teaches him the value of moderation.

When he feels his hand upon the lever that directs the movements of a hundred thousand toilers, his awful responsibility instructs him in self-restraint. The events of the last two years have proved that the directing heads of two of the greatest labor trusts are conservative counselors. Their number will increase. More and more the organizations of labor will insist that their leaders shall be men of thought, slow to wrath, steady in action.

More and more, they will come to appreciate that a leader is none the less loyal because he is wise.

How majestic is the majesty of moderation!

To the aggressive tendencies of the times the calm of Washington counsels prudence, self-restraint, the holding well in hand of the people's thought and action by the people themselves. And there are retrogressive tendencies as well which the spirit of Washington equally rebukes. It is as unreasoning to say that an outgrown law shall not be modified as it is to say that immature statutes shall be enacted. One is the hysteria of precedent; the other is the hysteria of alarm.

Men say " Down with the tariff! " Men say " Maintain the tariff," or " Lift it higher still." Conservatism says, " You both are wrong — adjust the tariff to conditions. Tariff merely for protection is no fetish; tariff for mere revenue is no god. No system of taxation is sacred. It is merely a means to an end or many ends. It is not an end in itself." This is the voice of Conservatism and it is the voice of truth and soberness.

Even self-government is not an end in itself. It is a means to an end. With Anglo-Saxon peoples self-government is the means to the end of individual and collective human happiness. And all the laws of self-governing peoples are just that and nothing more. Tariff laws are no exception. If they are wise, they grow out of conditions; and so they become unwise when the conditions out of which they have grown, have themselves outgrown the laws. When this becomes true, such laws need readjustment, for the very same reason that called for their original enactment.

We have entered upon an era of production that over-

whelms our understanding. It was not so yesterday.
Yesterday we made little we did not want ourselves, and
so the " Home market " was then the word of economic
truth; and that word called into life a system of protection as perfectly fitted for its purpose as ever the mind
of man devised. Mills, factories, railroads, farms, mines
— a thousand forms of productive industry developed
magically; and over all the busy genius of invention
brooded, making one hand do that which thousands
toiled to do before, fertilizing fields, abbreviating space,
extracting gold from hopeless rocks, discovering wealth
and human uses in the very refuse of a cruder day.

And so it came to pass that our home market is supplied and the overflowing surplus threatens to choke the
very machinery that produces it unless we find a place to
sell that surplus. And so it is that to-day Progress
speaks a new word of economic truth as needful now as
was the old word then. As the " Home market " was
the word of wisdom in its season, so " Foreign markets " is the word of wisdom now.

We have more coal, more iron, more skill in work-
manship, more ability and experience in organizing capital for productive uses than any other portion of the
globe. And so we sell abroad our girders, beams and
plates of steel, and the many forms into which wealth
and work and genius have fashioned the useful metals.
We *must* sell them abroad. Otherwise, idle over his
accumulated products, will sit the laborer; lifeless will
be the throbbing mill; deserted the producing mine;
chained to the rotting docks the ships of export.

We must sell our fabrics of cotton and of wool abroad;
our meats, our flour, and all the stuffs that feed and

clothe the human race.   For other nations have factories, too.   Other nations spin and weave, and plant and sow and reap.   They will not always permit us to supply their people.   The word " Home market," which yesterday was our talisman, to-morrow will be theirs, and for the same reason that it was once ours.

Conditions have turned the tables; and where yesterday we asked protection from them, to-day they are demanding protection from us.   They will erect tariff walls against us as we once erected tariff walls against them.   Where, then, shall we turn with our ships of merchandise?   What, then, will be the destination of our weighted trains of freight?   Not the home market, for it is already supplied, and it is our surplus that fills those ships and burdens those countless cars of commerce.   We can not turn entirely to the Orient, for that market is not yet sufficiently understood, although it will be; it is not yet sufficiently exploited, although it will be.   When the oriental market is open and occupied by us, it will be our commercial and financial salvation.

Meanwhile our own consuming capacity will increase. But while it is increasing, our surplus can not wait.   It must be disposed of as it is produced.   And, always, there will be a surplus.   The capacity of a people for production beyond their own needs is the measure of their increasing wealth.   And so, while the increase of our own consuming capacity is important, the development of our foreign markets is indispensable.   Both are necessary to the consumption of our ever-increasing production.   And of foreign markets, the oriental field is virgin soil and awaits our intelligent cultivation.

But that is a question for to-morrow. We must consider the requirements of to-day. We must turn to "the instant need of things." We must make those common-sense arrangements with our neighbors among the nations by which our surplus of American products may be taken across the seas. This is the statesmanship of common sense. The eye of Blaine perceived it in the distance, and too soon announced its principle. The even more prophetic mind of Grant, whose elemental statesmanship will be better appreciated a hundred years from now than it is to-day, perceived it even before Blaine saw it. And even if both had failed to grasp its meaning, that meaning would be unmistakable at this hour. For, gradually, foreign statesmen are closing their markets to us. They will do it more swiftly in the future than they have done it in the past, or else they will fail in their duty to their peoples.

It is not a situation that calls for fanaticism in favor of any law; it is not a situation that calls for fanaticism in favor of the destruction of any law. It is a situation that calls for the patient, intelligent adjustment of means to ends. It is a situation that calls for the counsels of conservatism. Out upon the selfish interest that would enrich itself at the expense of the permanent prosperity of the Nation! Out upon the passionate demand for the destruction of all protection! Up with the standard of moderation and let all the forces of American conservatism rally around it! So shall employment continue to wait on labor. So shall investment continue to plead with capital. So shall this marvelous American civilization, whose far meaning even the most prophetic mind can not grasp to-day, continue to evolve out of the play of our free and unfettered activities.

It was a wisdom higher than our own that drove us into the markets of the world. You may say that it was the wisdom of events. You may say it was the wisdom that springs from the wealth of our resources and the ingenuity of our brains and the skill of our fingers. I prefer to believe and I do believe that it was a loftier wisdom still — the universal wisdom of the Father. And it was His wisdom, too, that placed in our guardianship new peoples and alien races. You may say that a blunder did that. I shall not quarrel with you. You may say that it was a conjunction of circumstances. I shall not argue the point. Whatever the compelling cause, the fact exists and the duty is ours.

Call it circumstances, call it events, call it blunder, or call it the decree of destiny — other peoples are our wards and we must not desert them. Their lands are our trust and we must not betray it. All will admit that if we could succeed in discharging this trust so that these dependent peoples would be happier, our Nation better and the civilization of the world thereby advanced, it would be a noble conclusion for which the most doubtful heart might yearn. All this we may accomplish. All this we will accomplish.

We daily hear dogmatic demands for the independence of our Malay wards, demands which ignore concrete conditions. Is this moderation? Is this the method of calm reason? Is it not better to fit our acts to whatever the actual facts may be? Adaptability is the American characteristic. We are told that self-government is the American characteristic. We are told that this and that is the American characteristic. We are asked to frame our action upon this tradition or that, regardless of changed situations, of absolutely different facts. But adaptability is *the* American characteristic. The fitting of means to ends, the adjustment of measures to conditions — this is the heart of Americanism.

The secret of American success has been that we have looked the facts squarely in the face and then made our measures fit those facts. We have done this regardless of maxims, indifferent to theories and even over the letter of our Constitution itself when it stood in the way. President Madison thought that the Federal Government had no power to build a national highway. The power to make internal improvements was not conferred on Congress by the Constitution, he said. This was the view of the Fathers.

Rivers, roads and harbors were matters of local concern, they thought. Their theory of local self-government, of the sovereignty of the state, of the independence of the community, required that the National Government should not better local conditions. If a river was non-navigable at a point within a state through which it ran, it was not the mission of the National Government to dredge it. Its care was in the keeping of the people who lived upon its banks. Local self-government, they said, was an end and not a means.

But Progress said that the prosperity of the people is the end, and local self-government, general government, or any other kind of government nothing but a means. Progress said, " The logic of strict construction is built on words; I demand logic built on facts." And so into the written Constitution, the necessities of national intercourse read the power of the National Government to make internal improvements. And to-day that power is so much a matter of course that not one man in ten thousand knows that that power was originally denied. Thus it was that the spirit of American adaptability triumphed even over the letter of the Constitution.

Business is the great expounder of our fundamental law. Conditions construe our Constitution more completely than all the lawyers who ever lived. Geography, invention, exploration, are continuous interpreters of that great instrument. Mountains, rivers, plains and lakes, railways, telegraphs, the planting of new communities, the discovery of new resources, the interchange of thought and products — to these great human facts the spirit of 'American adaptability has conformed ancient customs, honored traditions, written constitutions. There is no written power in the Constitution for the National Government to charter banks, but a man would be considered mad to-day who denied that power. The list of instances where the practical genius of the American people has adapted the Constitution to their needs is the most striking circumstance of our history and the profoundest proof of our vitality.

From that saving wisdom of adaptability we will not now depart. If Philippine conditions require Filipino self-government, self-government we will give the Filipinos because it is wise. If legislative participation in their government is permitted by Porto Rican conditions, we will give the Porto Ricans that because it is wise. If Cuban conditions require American suzerainty, we will maintain that because it is wise; if annexation, we will accomplish that because it is wise; if utter separation, that shall be done because it is wise. If facts demand that we administer government in our far-Eastern possessions without the participation of an incompetent people, that government we will, ourselves, administer, because it is wise. We are wedded to no theory; we are chained to no catchword; our hand is not fettered by any unchangeable method.

If on that Christmas Day Washington thought that drunken Hessians and all the elements of surprise existed, he crossed the Delaware and attacked like another Attila. When he thought that overwhelming British forces discouraged American troops and all the elements of weakness in his own ranks required avoidance of conflict, he retreated like another Fabius. That is the American spirit. And so with our new and world-wide duties. If facts demand autonomy for our possessions, autonomy it shall be. If facts demand guardianship at our hands, guardianship it shall be. Over the American mind and heart and directing American action, the genius of the practical presides. We are no China cursed with custom, drugged and dead with precedent. We are Americans — the people of the appropriate and the adaptable.

The treatment of our dependencies is the issue now confronting us. Let us then plant ourselves on the fundamental certainties. And the first of these certainties is that not one single foot of soil over which American civil authority is established will be abandoned. " What we have, we hold! " — this is the voice of our race. People of our blood seldom leave land they have occupied. No master people ever yields while it remains a master people.

Emerson declares that when the powers of a man decline he draws in his enterprise; he quits business; he prepares for the inevitable end. The same is true of a people. But the American people are not on the decline. The American people are not ready to go out of business. The American people are stronger for the world's work now than any people ever were before. And our portion of the world's work, which Destiny has laid upon us in common with the younger and the growing races, is the duty and labor of guardianship.

We are the executors of a trust estate in Porto Rico, in Cuba, in the Philippines. That trust we shall execute as thoroughly as Americans do everything. And so American government in the Philippines will be permanent. The American flag in Porto Rico will float there as long as the Republic's government itself shall stand. American suzerainty over Cuba will remain until time laces that island more closely to us with more enduring bonds. Events call for the conservatism of adaptability. Conditions demand the moderation of the free hand. The radicalism of ancient methods has no place among new conditions. Remember the parable of new wine in old bottles.

What should we say if the Ancient Mariner, stepping from his vessel of wood and sail and spars and ropes to the bridge of a twentieth century ocean liner, should declare that the steam which drove it, the electricity which lighted it, the steel plates, the copper bottoms and all the methods of modern ship-building are sacrilege, because such methods and such accomplishment were not known in his day? This hoary representative of a day that is dead would not be considered conservative. The board of directors that would place him in command of a modern liner would not be considered conservative.

Moderation means the progress of facts — not the daring of dreams on the one hand nor yet the cowardice of reminiscence on the other. And so with the dependencies of the American Republic, American statesmen must deal as practical thought directed to actual conditions demands that they should deal. They must not deal spasmodically. They must not deal retrogressively. They must deal practically, steadily. The free hand must be the steady hand if it is to be the hand of the master; and the free hand can be the steady hand only when its action is governed by actual, and not imaginary conditions.

But in this great problem of our dependencies, more even than in the surprising developments of our internal economy, patience is the word of power and of success. A race can not be transformed overnight. The methods of three centuries can not be remedied between sunrise and sunset. The character of a people is not to be altered even by the school-teacher in a season or a year. Let us not be in haste.

We are dealing with an elemental problem, a racial problem. We must act, therefore, with a deliberation as large and a patience as steady as the problem is vast and historic. We must employ no magic but time, no legerdemain but that of steady and continuous effort unvarying and undismayed. There must be no spasms of extravagance, no spasms of retrenchment, no panic of retreat, no fury of advance. Let us not pine for the fruit before the seed is planted.

So, fellow-citizens, we shall go on in the spirit and

method of Washington, practically, steadily, calmly, without prejudice and without fear. Whatever the future may hold for the American people in internal development or foreign dominion, that future will be met with that thoughtful moderation which adapts means to ends. If old methods suffice, those old methods we shall use because they are approved. If present methods suffice, present methods we shall use because they are at hand. If new methods are necessary, new methods we shall invent because the case demands them. Fanatical reverence for the old will not influence the American people. Fanatical adoration of the new will not influence the American people.

The conservatism of adaptability, the patience necessary for the doing of the work in hand whatever that work may be — these are the saving influences which will govern American action now and hereafter. The discipline of the day's work, the balanced judgment that clears the vision, the steady sanity essential to the settlement of actual situations — these are the counselors which now and henceforth the American people will consult. Neither passion nor fear, neither theory nor precedent, neither imagination nor impulse, shall corrupt in the American character that orderly adaptability which has been the very soul of American progress. And before these influences of light every cloud that fear discerns on our horizon will dissolve; every impassable ocean which imagination sees in our pathway will be safely crossed; every foe which foresight beholds in the distance will be vanquished, and the flag which Washington unfurled will float over ever-broadening horizons brightening every hour with the increasing glories of actual achievement.

THE ORGANIZATION OF AMERICAN BUSINESS

Speech opening the Republican campaign in Colorado, delivered at Denver, September, 1902.

IS the destruction of those twentieth century organizations of commerce and industry known as trusts, possible, wise or right? What are trusts? What causes them? What is their part in the Nation's development? Denunciation answers nothing. Passion darkens understanding. Reason and Fact — these are the only handmaidens of Truth.

Trusts are a development of the principle of coöperation — among savages it is each man for himself. In civilization all men more and more depend upon their fellows. Take a simple illustration — the supply of food in the form of meat. Only in a savage or sequestered state does each man provide his own meat. When settled communities develop, occupations are divided. Some are farmers, some shoemakers, some carpenters, some butchers. The butcher supplies the village with meat; surrounding farmers furnish the cattle. This was our own condition in the early days. Each community was cut off from the rest because roads were few and poor.

But population increased; cities grew; railways running through town and village converged into the great centers of population; trunk lines connected these with ocean ports; ship lines connected these, in turn, with every harbor of the world. Telegraph and telephone put every village in communication with the Nation's uttermost boundaries.

Thus demand for the farmer's cattle was no longer confined to his little town. Railroads brought the world's markets to his very doors. It was necessary to prepare this meat daily for millions of people. The village butcher could no longer do this work. Ten thousand — a hundred thousand — butchers, acting separately, could not purchase, prepare and ship the daily food of the Nation.

Thus the people's necessities developed immense organizations of capital for the preparation and shipment of meats. Nothing but these organizations could do that work. Nothing but these organizations could invade and supply foreign markets with American meat. Not one or ten thousand or a hundred thousand individual butchers, acting separately, could buy the cattle raised on the farms and plains of Colorado, Dakota, Nebraska or Montana. Thus, organization of meat-supply was caused by the needs of the masses. And yet the number of men employed in the industry has not decreased; on the contrary, more men, even taking into consideration our growing population, are earning greater wages in this occupation than ever before.

Another example — the manufacture and sale of plows. Here are the steps: First, every man his own plowmaker; then, the making of awkward, heavy, high-priced plows at village blacksmith shops; then, as the world's markets call for farmers' products, the demand for more plows; then, answering that demand, combinations of capital for their manufacture. And here is the result — to-day plows are furnished to our farmers fifty per cent. cheaper and one hundred per cent. better than they were twenty-five years ago.

Why do prices fall? Because high prices prevent great profits. Railroads reduce freights because the lower their rates the more freight they carry and the greater the total profit; the higher their rates the less freight is shipped and the lower their total profits. When I was a boy, twenty-five cents bought only a small can of poor coal-oil. To-day it tires your boy to carry home from the grocery store the quantity of oil he can buy for a quarter of a dollar. The price of sugar has steadily fallen and its quality has steadily improved. The same is true of iron and steel, of boots and shoes, of clothing and of every article of manufacture.

Prices now and then temporarily rise, but the scale for a series of years shows their steady fall. Still, prices and railroad rates are too high. The chief cause of this is overcapitalization upon which charges are made, not for real values, but to pay dividends on watered stocks. So overcapitalization and all the evils of trusts must be remedied.

But you do not burn a house because the roof leaks; you do not abolish state government because a state treasurer is a defaulter. You simply correct the abuse. When a trust unjustly raises prices, it robs the people; but the robber is as foolish as he is criminal, because the people cease to buy in proportion as he lifts the price, and his total profits fall. Yet, though the crime of unjust prices punishes itself, the would-be plunderer of the people must be made powerless to attempt it. And we will never cease till we have manacled the hands of the pirates of capital.

Unjust prices must be made impossible. And unjust lowering of the wages of labor merely to feed the greed of some sordid director of organized industry is even baser theft than raising the prices of the necessities of the people. But this practice is disappearing before the might of organized labor and before the increasing wisdom and human kindness of the employer. The employer has learned that honest wages mean honest work; that ill-fed labor means shiftless labor; that discontented toil means the lowest quality of production. But not all industrial management is wise and honest; and the foolish and criminal must be suppressed.

True that the managers of modern industrial organizations are forced to justice to their men from motives of merest greed; true, too, that more and more the modern employer of modern labor desires the welfare of his men as much as the success of his enterprise; true, too, that all over the land we hear daily of the voluntary advance of wages.

After the last election employers issued notice of increased wage in every city of the Republic; and only last month the Steel Trust without request from its workingmen voluntarily advanced their wages ten per cent. But sometimes the reverse is done; and when that occurs unjustly, the power of the Government should interfere if it can.

Watering stocks and selling worthless securities to the innocent can best be prevented by publicity. True, the greatest of all trusts has begun this policy itself; true that the vast labor organizations are developing statesmen of industry. But this will never cease until every

national corporation is compelled to publish its condition
to the people.

How may this be done? Legislation can give no solution except that of national control. And already we
are beginning the work which will end in the control of
every corporation that does business throughout the Republic. The Department of Commerce is the seed from
which will grow a national supervision of national industries that in the end will prevent most corporate
wrongs. There is no organization so great as the Government. There is no unrighteous power within the
Republic that must not yield to the power of the people.

But no evil can be remedied by the torch. The incen-
diary is never a statesman. If the tree needs pruning the
hurricane is not the agent for that delicate task. And
these are the methods of the Opposition: they propose
to remedy evils by destroying a development; to cure
defects by reversing evolution. No method of moderation for the Opposition. Their demand is for annihilation of the whole scheme of organized industry. Between the sane, moderate, sober, earnest effort of the
Government, and the revolutionary violence of the Opposition, let the American people choose.

See how this development compels the people to study
the Nation's industry, as before they neglected it, and
how this reacts upon the policy of these great combinations. The little producer of former days attracted no
attention; his books were closed to the public. What he
did was none of the public's business. But on these modern organizations the eyes of the Nation and the world
are fixed. What they do is everybody's business. They

are at the mercy of the people. Therefore the good will of the public is their first security.

Note the result — the voluntary publication to the people of the complete state of its business by the greatest trust ever formed. And this policy of publicity thus begun by the Steel Trust will become necessary to every other similar organization. Why? Because with the thought of the Nation upon them, they are forced to take the Nation into their confidence. Fix the thought of the American people on business and it benefits the people and the business alike.

The magnitude and universal operations of tremendous combinations of capital are subject to the constant critical thought of student, statesmen and people; their very size makes them the object of popular suspicion, the subject of every demagogue's inflaming attack. Out of all this grows the weakening of corporate influence on legislation and also the tendency toward national control of these corporations. Along this line of national control of trusts we are now proceeding.

These modern organizations of capital and labor are gradually destroying the ancient inequality of employer and employee. In the old days the employer said to the working-man: " I will pay you so much in wages,"— and the working-man accepted or starved. He could not argue with the million small employers of a generation ago. He could not strike against the million individuals, partnerships and little corporations that hired labor then. To-day the representatives of organized labor meet the representatives of organized capital, discuss profits and markets, and agree upon a scale of wages. Thus, little by little consolidated labor is becoming a partner with consolidated capital.

If a great corporation to-day reduces unjustly the wages of labor, it is confronted with a strike; and where that strike is just it is supported by the public opinion of the Nation. Not only is consolidated labor becoming a partner of consolidated capital, but the whole American people is taken into the confidence of both partners; the Nation's sense of justice is becoming the arbiter whose decision no body of laboring men however violent, no body of capitalists however arrogant, dare defy.

Not only this but also out of the conference of employer and employee and the submission of the whole argument to the great court of American public opinion there is growing coöperation of effort, mutual sympathy, mutual understanding, mutual confidence. Thus is modern industrial organization evolving a practical brotherhood of man. The American people! — Leave them alone and they will achieve fraternity. The demagogue! — Let him have his way and class hatred will rend the Republic asunder.

What is the effect of this universal tendency on individual and national well-being? The last four years have witnessed the greatest organization of industry in the history of the world. And yet more men are employed, higher wages are paid, the great masses of the people have more comforts than ever before.

What shipper would dissolve the great railroad lines of the country into the little lines of which they were composed? What railroad laborer prefers employment by a little line constantly threatened with bankruptcy to employment by a great and solvent line serving vast areas of territory and millions of shippers and consumers? What working-man employed in any manufacturing industry would prefer instead, service in a little shop whose market and prosperity is uncertain? Yet, this is what the Opposition proposes. Destroy the country's great successes because you hate them, even though you are crushed in the ruins you bring down — this is the advice the Opposition gives to the common people of the Republic.

What working-man favors the dissolution of labor organizations? And yet the Opposition demands the destruction of labor trusts as well as of manufacturing and transportation trusts. If the Opposition candidate denies this, ask him why he is in favor of the destruction of one and not in favor of the destruction of the other. Both are the development of the same principle; both are fundamentally right, but have incidental evils. And we propose to remedy those evils as fast as practical methods show they can be remedied; but annihilation is the Opposition's only plan.

Within the last five years greater organization of productive industry has occurred in the American Republic than in the combined history of all the world before; and in that same period our exports have exceeded our imports by six hundred per cent. more than in the entire history of the Republic put together. And at the same time more labor has been employed in America and we have consumed more within the Nation itself than in any quarter of a century of our history.

Foreign statesmanship knows this; and therefore the Russian Minister of Finance has proposed that the nations of the world shall join in an agreement to suppress industrial organizations known as trusts. Why that Russian proposal? Because American commerce is invading and capturing foreign markets. And yet the salvation of American prosperity demands larger and even larger foreign markets. This alone will keep American labor employed. Produce all you can; sell all you produce; feed your commerce with foreign markets — this solves, forms the labor problem. For the pressing labor problem is chiefly the problem of employment and wages.

Suppose these organizations were destroyed; suppose we were hurled back fifty years to the individual and disconnected enterprises of that day, how many agricultural implements would the little blacksmith shop sell in Europe or Africa or Asia? How much steel would the little individual steel mills of fifty years ago sell in competition with England, Germany and France? How much of any American product would be sent across the seas under the conditions of half a century ago? And if those foreign markets are lost to us what becomes of the millions of American laborers now employed?

Constantly America is producing a surplus. The prosperity of any establishment depends upon the sale of its surplus. If that surplus is unsold a certain number of working-men must be discharged. These idle working-men cease to buy products of farm and ranch. Thus the ability of the farmer and the cattle-raiser to purchase what the factory makes is decreased. And then the factory must discharge more men; and thus action and reaction continue until we have worked out the syllogism of ruin.

Hold what foreign markets we have; capture new foreign markets every year; push the advance of American commerce — that is one insistent task of American statesmanship at the beginning of the twentieth century. Where may we sell another barrel of American meat, another car of American flour, another shipload of American machinery? These are the questions upon whose successful answer American well-being depends.

Will the destruction of industrial organizations give us a single new market? Will not their destruction surrender to our rivals those foreign markets already ours? And yet the destruction of American industrial organization is what the Opposition demands. Will a universal reduction of the tariff, without first securing reciprocal trade advantages from foreign nations, give us a single foreign market? On the contrary, if trusts are destroyed, and a revenue tariff adopted, every little American producer will be brought into competition with every big foreign producer; and not only will our foreign market decline, but our home market itself will be lost; and yet just that is what the Opposition demands. Will retreat from our possessions in the Orient or the Gulf give us new markets? On the contrary, the getting of territorial footholds all over the world is one method by which every other commercial nation secures new markets with undeveloped lands and peoples. Yet surrender of America's outposts of commerce is what the Opposition demands.

What then will give us new foreign markets for our ever increasing surplus produced by the American factory and American farm? First of all, intelligent tariff arrangements with other nations. Twenty years ago James G. Blaine saw and advocated that policy of commercial common sense.   In his last utterance to the American people McKinley summed up the wisdom of a life's experience and thought by declaring that " the period of exclusiveness is passed."   But reciprocity does not mean reduction of tariff regardless of what other nations may do.   It means that where a market can be opened to American products in a foreign country by granting to that country special privileges here, we will grant those privileges only in return for that market.

And thus, for every dollar we reduce our tariff we shall get in exchange a foreign market which will absorb many dollars of American products.   It is the simple principle upon which rests all trade from primeval barter up to international commerce.   It is merely getting something for what we give.   The Opposition to the Government demands destruction of the tariff without exacting a single advantage to American commerce from those foreign nations which free trade with us would benefit.

American business and labor must plan for the future. To preserve for to-morrow the prosperity of to-day — that is wisdom's task.   To keep our mills and factories busy, to keep our working-men employed, to open markets for every ounce of wool, pound of meat, bushel of grain our farmers produce — this is the statesmanship the hour demands.   Accomplish this, and gradually most of our social and economic problems will solve themselves.   Time and employment is what the American people need.   Add to American intellect, American energy and American tolerance, the elements of time and employment and America's future is secure.   Idleness and hasty methods go hand in hand.

THE COMMAND OF THE PACIFIC

Speech opening the Republican campaign for the Pacific slope, delivered at San Francisco, California, September 15, 1902. This speech was made their campaign document by the Republicans of the Pacific slope.

Fellow Americans of California and the Pacific Slope:

THE Pacific is the ocean of the future; and the Pacific is yours. The markets of the Orient are the Republic's future commercial salvation; and the Orient's commercial future is yours. Important as other questions are, the one great question that covers seas, and islands, and continents; that will last when other questions have been answered and forgotten; that will determine your present prosperity and the greatness of your children's children in their day, is the mastery of the Pacific and the commercial conquest of the eastern world.

That question is peculiarly your question, people of the Pacific slope. If your wealth is to increase you must produce a surplus; and if you produce a surplus, you must sell it. And where will you sell it, people of the Pacific slope, save over the seas of sunset? If your laboringmen are to be employed, you must have commerce; and where will commerce great enough for your ever increasing population be found, save in your supply of the ever increasing demands of the millions of the Orient?

And yet when events have given this future into your keeping, the Opposition asks you to surrender it for an unsound sentiment; to give up your position of power for a phrase; to sell your birthright for politicians' advantage. And therefore to-night let us consider which side of this elemental argument is wise and right and beneficial to the people of the Pacific slope. Let us weigh the case of the statesmanship of the Government and the indictment of that statesmanship by the Opposition to the Government.

The only statesmanship that develops a nation is the statesmanship of events. A people grows; it is not made. And public policies are wise only as they express a people's development. This is why most of the plans of reformers fail, why most of the theories of dreamers are idle. They are born of some individual's thought and not of the common thought of the Nation, not of the real situation of the country and the world. No public man can leave his work a landmark of his people's progress, unless he becomes the voice of his day's development. And he who stands against the natural progress of his people is, in the eyes of history, like a little child trying to change the seasons according to his infant and foolish will.

So in German history, Bismarck, notwithstanding his autocratic and oppressive policy, yet stood for the unification of the German Empire for which the German people were prepared; and the world has even now forgotten the names of those who opposed him. So in French history, Napoleon, with all his mountainous evils, yet stood for modern methods and against systems which the world had outlived; and his work looms larger as it recedes.

So in our own history Washington stood for our separate existence as a people, for which our situation and a century and a half of self-development had fitted us. Then, the hour struck for our closer consolidation as a nation; and Lincoln was the living expression of that historic need. Then came the time when the American people were prepared to do their part in shaping upward the destiny of neglected races; and Theodore Roosevelt is the expression of that day.

Mark now the historic conjunction of the elements of national growth, national duty and national necessity. First, the time had come when the Republic was prepared to do its part in governing peoples and lands not ready to govern themselves. Second, at this hour of our preparation for this duty, war gave us the Philippines and our possessions in the Gulf. And, third, at that very time our commerce was crying aloud for new markets where we might sell the surplus products of our factories and farms — and the only remaining markets on the globe were those surrounding the lands which war had given us. American duty, American preparedness, American commercial necessity came in the same great hour of fate.

Let us consider the argument of advantage to ourselves, flowing from the Philippines, the Orient and from American mastery of the Pacific. What is the great commercial necessity of the Republic? It is markets.— foreign markets. At one time we needed to build up our industries here and for that purpose to save for them our home markets. Protection did that; and to-day our home market is supplied. Now we have invaded the markets of Europe and filled them almost to their capacity with American goods. Our great combinations of capital devoted to manufacturing and transportation compete successfully with foreign manufacturers in their own countries.

But still we have a surplus; and an unsold surplus is commercial peril. Every unsold bushel of wheat reduces the price of every other one of the millions of bushels of wheat produced. If our manufacturers produce more than they can sell, that surplus product causes the mills to shut down until they produce no more than they can sell. And after we supply our own market, after we sell all we can to the markets of Europe, we still have an unsold surplus. If our prosperity continues this must be sold.

Where shall the Republic sell its surplus? Where shall the Pacific coast sell its surplus? And your surplus unsold means your commerce paralyzed, your laboringmen starving. Expansion answers that question.

[Senator Beveridge here presented at length the statistics of trade with our possessions, the Orient, etc.; and the statistics of England and German trade with England and German possessions and the far East.]

If it is not true that her possessions help England's commerce, why does not England give them up? Why does not Germany give up her possession in Northern China? Why is she spending tens of millions of dollars there, building German railways, German docks and vast plants for future German commerce? Why does Russia spend a hundred million dollars of Russian gold building Russian railways through Manchuria and binding that territory, vast in extent as all the states of the Pacific slope combined, to the Russian empire with bands of steel? Why is Japan now preparing to take Manchuria from Russia as she has already taken Formosa from China?

The Philippines not help us in Oriental commerce! They have helped us even now by making the American name known throughout the East, and our commerce with the islands and countries influenced by the Philippines has in two short years leaped from $43,000,000 to $120,000,000.

If an American manufacturer established a great storehouse in London believing that it would help his business and then found his sales in London increasing 300 per cent. in less than three years, would he give away that branch establishment because some theorist told him that branch houses did not help trade and that he could sell as much and more if he shipped direct from his factory to the English purchaser?

And yet this practically is what the Opposition asks the American people to believe about and do with the Philippines. From every English and German possession in the East English and German goods are shipped in bulk and then reshipped as quick orders near at hand call for them. And these possessions influence the entire population of the countries where they are located.

If this is true of English and German possessions, will it not be true of America's possessions at the very door of this mighty market? If it is not true, it will be because American energy, American sagacity, American enterprise are not equal to the commercial opportunity which the Philippines give us in the Orient. Americans never yet found an obstacle which they did not overcome, an opportunity they did not make their own.

Has the decay of American energy begun with

you, men of the West? Who says so is infidel to American character. Answer these slanders of your energy and power, people of the Pacific states — answer them with your ballots! Tell the world that, of all this masterful Nation, none more vital than the men and women who hold aloft the Republic's flag on our Pacific shores!

If we need this Oriental market — and we can not dispose of our surplus without it — what American farmer is willing for us to give the Philippines to America's competitors? What American manufacturer is willing to surrender this permanent commercial advantage to the nations who are striving for those very markets? Yet, that is what the Opposition asks you to do. For if we quit them certainly Germany or England or Japan will take them.

And these markets, great as they are, are hardly yet opened to the modern world. They are like a gold mine worked by ancient methods and yielding only a fraction of its wealth. Apply to that gold mine modern machinery, modern science, modern methods and its stream of gold swells in volume. This illustration applies to Oriental markets. For example, China buys from all the world at the present time $250,000,000 worth of foreign products. These are consumed by less than 75,-000,000 of the Chinese people. The reason of this is that foreign goods can not penetrate the interior. There are no railways, no roads; merchandise must be transported on human backs, and corrupt officials lay heavy transportation taxes at every stage. But now all this begins to change. All over China railroads are projected, surveyed and even now are building.

And wherever they have gone Chinese commerce has

increased, just as our own commerce increases here wherever a railroad goes. And wherever railways go wagon roads branch from them. Thus the methods of modern civilization are weaving a network of modern conditions among this most ancient of peoples. And if China now buys $250,000,000 worth of products from the rest of the world, what will she buy when all this change that now is taking place brings her 400,000,000 as purchasers to the markets of the world? The most conservative experts estimate that China alone will buy at least one thousand million dollars worth of the products of other countries every year.

Half of that vast commerce ought to be American. Half of that must and will be American. The Pacific is the highway to these markets, and the Pacific is yours. California, Oregon, Washington, bordering the Pacific; American Hawaii in its center, the American Philippines on its farthest shores, give the Republic the mastery of this greatest of the oceans. And its mastery means the mastery of the markets of its shores. Considering this, is half of China's future markets an unreasonable American prospect? Let Chinese labor develop China; American labor will develop America; let China supply us with what China produces and America needs, and America will supply China with what America produces and China needs — that is the right relation between the Chinese empire and the American Republic.

And without these markets, what will you do, people of the Pacific slope? More and more the factories of the rest of the Republic supply the Nation's home market and invade the market of Europe. The factories and farms east of the Rocky Mountains have an advantage over you

in the markets of England, Germany and France, because
they are nearer; but you have an advantage over them in
the markets of the Orient, because you are nearer.   You
have factories; you ought to have more.   You have
fruits; but you can not live by fruit alone.   You must
have industries as diversified as your resources, as many
and as vigorous as the talents and energies of your citizens.   The more complex your activities, the safer your
prosperity, the surer your happiness.

But increased industries require greater commerce;
and commerce depends on markets; and these illimitable
markets are at your door.   And yet the Opposition demands that Hawaii and the Philippines, which give us
the mastery of the Pacific and the command of the markets of the East, shall be handed over to the Republic's
commercial rivals.   That demand of the Opposition, disgraceful to the country as a whole, is almost treasonable
to the Pacific slope.

The Philippines and the Orient are your commercial
opportunity.   Does our duty as a Nation forbid you to
accept it?   Does our fitness for the work prevent us from
doing it?   Or does the Nation's preparedness, the Republic's duty and the commercial necessity of the American
people unite in demanding of American statesmanship the
holding of the Philippines and the commercial conquest
of the Oriental world?

Do they say that it is a wrong to any people to govern
them without their consent?   Consider Hayti and read
in her awful decline since French government there was
overthrown the answer to that theory.   Remember that
English administration in Egypt has in less than twenty
years made fertile her fields and redeemed her people,

debased by a thousand years of decline, and read in that miracle the answer to that theory.

Examine every example of administration of government in the Orient or Africa by a superior power and find the answer to that theory. Come nearer home. Analyze the three years of American administration in Porto Rico — American schools for the humblest, just laws, honest government, prosperous commerce. Now sail for less than a day to the sister island of San Domingo and behold commerce extinguished, justice unknown, government and law a whim, religion degenerated to voodoo rites, and answer whether American administration in Porto Rico, even if it had been without the consent of the governed, is not better for that people than San Domingo's independent savagery.

Let us trust the American people! The most fervent belief in their purity, their power and their destiny is feeble, after all, compared with the reality on which that faith is founded. Great as our fathers were, the citizens of this Republic, on the whole, are greater still to-day, with broader education, loftier outlook. And if this were not so, we should not be worthy of our fathers; for, to do as well as they we must do better. Over the entire Republic the people's common schools increase, churches multiply, culture spreads, the poorest have privileges impossible to the wealthiest fifty years ago.

When any man fears the decay of American institutions, he ignores the elemental forces around him which are building future generations of Americans, stronger, nobler than ourselves. And those who ask you to believe that administration of orderly government in the Philippines will poison the fountain of Americanism here at home, ask you to believe that your children are a mockery, your schools a myth, your churches a dream.

American soldiers, American teachers, American administrators — all are the instruments of the Nation in discharging the Nation's high duty to the ancient and yet infant people which circumstance has placed in our keeping. If it is said that our duty is to teach the world by example, I ask if our duty ends with that? Does any man's duty to his children end with mere example? Does organized society owe no duty to the orphan and the abandoned save that of example? Why, then, are our schools, our asylums, our benevolent institutions, which force physical and mental training upon the neglected youth of the Republic? And does the parent or does organized society refrain from discharging this duty if the child resists?

And just so nations can not escape the larger duties to senile or infant peoples. Nations can not escape the charge laid upon them to develop the world's neglected resources, to make the wilderness, the fields, the mines and countries inhabited by barbarous peoples useful to civilized man. No nation lives to itself alone. It can not if it would. Even the great powers influence one another, not only by example, but by tariffs, by trade arrangements, by armies, by navies. How much greater should be this influence when circumstance gives to the keeping of a great power the destiny of an undeveloped race and the fortunes of an undeveloped country?

* * * * * * * * * * * *

People of the Pacific coast, it is chiefly through you the ancient East must be made modern; and chiefly through you the maritime empire of the world must be brought from the Atlantic to your Western seas. Chiefly yours the wealth that shall ever swell in volume from Oriental trade; and chiefly yours shall be the world's acclaim for this vast enterprise.

This splendid prospect opening before you is no dream. It is a reality at hand. It is no imagination; it is the fulfilment of prophecy.

Humboldt, the scientist of statesmanship as well as of nature, saw in the Pacific the great commercial ocean of the future and upon its shores the theater of the crowning efforts of human enterprise. He saw the Pacific slope, an empire in itself whose cities undreamed of save by him, should be the focus of the commerce of the ancient Eastern world. He saw tremendous lines of mighty ships carrying our trade and our civilization to newly opened Asia. He saw that the tidal wave of human enlightenment would not end at the Golden Gate, but that it would sweep on till the paralyzing institutions of the far East should be swept away and its unnumbered millions made modern. He saw that the power which must dominate this historic drama for which continents, islands and oceans serve as the stage, peoples and races as the characters, must inevitably be the American Republic. And he saw that the section whose mission it should be to master this great situation for the whole American people necessarily is the Republic's Pacific slope.

It is an opportunity so elemental and so rare that the favor of Providence alone explains it; and that opportunity is yours. You will not neglect and despise it. That future whose greatness requires great men to meet and master it, you will not fail to appreciate and rise to its far heights — you, the sons of a magic soil and clime;

you, born beneath the shade of forests miraculous, reared with the world's greatest mountains behind you and the world's greatest ocean before you; you, children of imperial circumstances that mark you as the guardians of universal situations and the solvers of elemental problems. The people of the Pacific slope can not belong to the feeble company of little Americans, doubters of the righteousness, wisdom and power of the American people, infidels to American destiny, opposers of American progress.

No, you are the descendants of men who proved their belief in the expanding powers of our race by crossing deserts and scaling mountains to reach this land of promise. You are the children of the fearless ones in whose minds burnt the fire of prophecy and in whose breasts beat the heart of faith in their race and in themselves. And now when the dream of statesmen and philosophers concerning you is being realized, you will turn to the graves of your heroic sires and, gathering from their great faith new faith for your work, move forward to the achievement of your duty as unquestioningly and courageously as they moved forward to the doing of their vast duty in their day. So shall you carry the Republic's banner in the advance over the oceans which henceforth shall be hers. So shall the mastery of the Pacific be the Nation's large achievement and the regeneration of the Pacific's peoples the Republic's high hope and heavy work. Thus, people of the Pacific slope, have nature and events made you the advance guard of the Republic's onward march and given into your hands the keys which unlock the doors of the Republic's future and your own.

POSITIVE AND NEGATIVE IN POLITICS

Speech closing the Republican compaign of 1902 in Ohio, delivered in Music Hall, Cincinnati.

THE day of passion in politics is past. The day when prejudice controls elections is gone. The day when the demagogue can influence American voters is no more. At the end of the argument, the American people never have decided any question upon any other basis than that of reason and righteousness. But the time was when, for a brief season, waves of unrighteous agitation could sway masses of voters for a period and menace the well-being of the Republic. In the end these have always been overcome; and with greater ease and in shorter space as time wore on.

It was a bitter battle and a long one against the agitation for repudiation; but the sound cause won. It was a sharp fight and an earnest one against fiat money; but the sound cause won. It was a desperate struggle and a dangerous against free silver — but, after all, the real battle lasted only three months; and the sound cause won. The storm of fear against imperialism dissolved almost before it formed; and just so to-day the crusade of the Opposition against American organized industry has ended almost before its banner was unfurled.

It ended because honest men and thinking men met that proposition of industrial annihilation with reason and facts. A campaign of abandoned issues — that is how history will describe the political conflict of 1902 — a campaign of abandoned issues because a campaign of false issues. The real and only sovereigns of the world are Truth and Reason.

Why is it that the power of the demagogue in American politics has declined and is declining now with accelerating speed? Why is it that appeals to passion are daily becoming more powerless at the ballot-box? It is because of the growth of American intelligence — because the facts on any question get to the voters more quickly. Only a few years ago weeks were required to place before the citizen facts on any question; and error, misrepresentation and all the craft of designing men based thereon had time to take root and flourish. Imperfect communication among the people was the demagogue's opportunity.

But to-day the facts on any question proposed at sunrise, are laid before the whole people before nightfall. In the cities an extra edition of a newspaper, except where such papers are " owned " or " controlled," dissolves a falsehood in an hour. Rural free delivery places before every farmer the truth of every situation at each day's set of the sun. The telegraph brings the mind of Los Angeles and that of Boston together quicker than the speed of daylight. Communication between New York and Cincinnati is instantaneous. Railways put every citizen of the Republic in personal contact with every other citizen. Electric roads have abolished the seclusion of every farm-house.

Eighty millions of people are in closer touch to-day than the inhabitants of Cincinnati alone were thirty years ago. What one man knows all men may know. And, knowing the facts, the people reason on them; and reasoning on them, the people reach just conclusions; and reaching just conclusions they act, they vote. And so it is that the influence of passion on the American mind has passed. So it is that the day of the demagogue is done.

But they would not be without an issue had any proposition they advanced been true and sound. They are without an issue now because every proposition they advanced is false in fact and wrong in reason. And therefore, while we can not to-night discuss a single living question on which this campaign began, we can examine as curiosities of history those propositions which the enemy have deserted. A political speech can now be nothing but a lecture on antiquities.

Let us take them in their order. Last Spring the Opposition to the Government declared that imperialism was ruining the Republic; American soldiers were dishonoring the American flag and disgracing the American name; an ocean voyage had changed the nature of American officers; tropic skies had transformed gentlemen into savages; havoc, pillage, outrage were American methods in the Republic's advance across the seas.

Where now is this campaign of slander? Abandoned before the charge of facts led by reason! Who dares now ask the support of American voters upon the ground that their soldiers have shamed their country? And, yet, that was the battle-cry of the Opposition to the Government only four months ago. How many votes would any candidate get to-day upon the issue that Lawton, MacArthur, Chaffee, Wheaton or Bell were officers of infamy? Yet, that was the slogan of the Opposition to the Government only four months ago.

Who now denounces Governor Taft as a man who perjured himself to hide a policy of oppression? And yet that was the charge of the Opposition to the Government only four months ago. These were the weapons with which politicians, driven to desperation, proposed to wage a war of vilification before the American people. These were the charges with which the Opposition newspapers were black for weeks and months. What Opposition newspaper that would not now withdraw if it could its issues maligning the conduct of the American army, the work of American administrators, the high purpose of the American people in our dependencies?

Why this abandonment of an issue chosen by themselves? Merely because the facts compelled it. And facts compelled it because those facts reached the people; and those facts reached the people because this is the twentieth century and this people so closely knit together into a brotherhood of mutual intelligence that every man among them gets the whole truth on any question whether he will or no. No American can be ignorant to-day, save on the theory of his predestination to error.

The people found that humanity was introduced in oriental warfare for the first time in history by American soldiers; that in all the military chronicles of the world such forbearance was never shown as that shown by American soldiers to insurgents against our flag; that the sternest measures which American officers took to stamp out brigandage in our possessions were mildness itself compared with the horrors of our Civil War; that the record of our arms in the Philippines is as beautiful in the kindness shown by American soldiers to the people in peace as it is brilliant with the courage shown by the American soldiers to the enemy in battle.

The people know that where American soldiers went peace followed; that justice followed peace; that industry followed justice; and that education kept step with both. The people know that the sentinels America has posted all over the islands are American teachers; the fortresses America has erected are American school-houses; the military roads America has constructed are American highways of commerce. Not England alone, but the world, is proud of Cromer's work in Egypt; yet, Taft has wrought in the Philippines work still more amazing.

Indeed, our only error has been our haste. Our national vice is impatience. We ask for the bread in the baker's oven before the seed wheat has been sown in the field. We are giving Malays in a moment what we ourselves wrought out in a century. And for the error of forcing the development of decades into years and of generations into decades we shall surely suffer. But aside from that, our work in its large plan and historic perspective is noble and fine and of benefit to us not yet to be measured even by imagination's scope. And while we do not yet adequately see we are already beginning to discern dimly as we recede from it the Himalayan proportions of that statesmanship which gave to the Republic the mastery of the Pacific and the commercial empire of the Oriental world. And so, " Imperialism " is dead at the hand of Truth.

And just so and for the same reason the annihilation of organized industry is preached now with diminishing fervor. Consider the debate which drove the Opposition from their issue of industrial iconoclasm.

"Organizations of industry are ruining you," cried the Opposition to the American farmer four months ago. "That is so," answered the farmer. "For last week I paid off the mortgage on my farm executed during the last Opposition administration." (In the last six years the American farmers paid off $300,000,000 of mortgages on their farms.)

"Organizations of industry are ruining you," the Opposition declared to the American working-man. "That is so," answered the American working-man, "for I am steadily employed at higher wages than ever were heard of in this or any other country in any period of human history; my home is full of comforts; my children are at school." (In the last five years the average wage of the American working-man has increased nearly fifteen per cent., the average wages of skilled working-men nearly thirty per cent.; and the number of men employed has increased by the million.)

"Yes, I am being ruined by organizations of industry," admits the American working-man, "because five years ago I was forced to take my savings out of the savings-banks of the country in order to live; to-day I am putting my savings into the savings-banks of the country against the day of possible Democratic disaster in the future." (In five years American working-men have increased their deposits in savings-banks over a thousand million dollars.)

"You are slaves of organized industry; go back to the early days when American labor was free and unoppressed," the Opposition cried to the American working-man four months ago. "I agree with you," answered the American working-man, "and I find as evidence of

my slavery and of the industrial liberty of American toilers in the old days, that in 1850, with a population of
23,000,000 the working-men of the Republic had on deposit in savings institutions $44,000,000; whereas to-day,
with a population of nearly 80,000,000, the working-men
of the Republic have on deposit in savings-banks over
2,500,000,000 — I find that with only three times the
population the Nation had in 1850, American working-
men have on deposit in savings-banks alone *sixty times as
much* ready cash as their free and prosperous brothers
had fifty years ago." Thus the books of savings-banks
confound the Opposition's oratory. Figures are fatal
to falsehoods.

" Organizations of industry are destroying you," cried
the Opposition to the American manufacturer only four
months ago. " That is clear," answered the American
manufacturer, " because during the last six years I have
added only 200,000 new factories to the old ones and
increased the capacity of the old ones nearly one hundred
per cent. It is true because I am running my works by
night as well as by day; whereas, five years ago I ran
them only a few hours in day time and sometimes not at
all. It is true because five years ago banks would not
loan me money on any security, and now they send solici-
tors to get my custom."

" Consolidations of railroads are making you worse
than serfs and peons," cried the Opposition to the railroad men of the Republic four months ago. " That is
true," said the American railway man, " because 200,000
more of us are employed now than were employed in
1896; true, because in 1896 more than 29,000 miles of
railways went into receivers' hands with liabilities

amounting to more than $1,500,000,000, and this year only one line fifty-two miles long went into the hands of a receiver and remained there less than ninety days; true, because in the period of bankruptcies and receiverships, wages were held back two, three and six months and sometimes lost altogether; whereas, to-day they are paid the moment they are due and I do not lose a cent."

And so, the farmer, the business man, the laborer answered, with the figures and the facts, the attack of the Opposition upon twentieth century organization of industry.

The figures and the facts answered the Opposition's frightened imagination. Imagination is an engine of progress when Reason is the engineer and Faith the fireman — an engine of disaster when Despair reverses the lever and Ignorance puts out the fires. Remember that every development of the Republic has been denounced as the Republic's doom; remember that, in the end, every development of the Republic has ultimately been for the Republic's righteousness and power; and, therefore, heartily know that the developments around us will finally flower into a glory and goodness undreamed of to-day. Belief in American character and American mind, and in America's destiny based on these — let that be our political religion.

" Modern organization of industry destroys the chances of young men," cried the Opposition to the youth of the Republic only four months ago. And the young man answered: " That is clearly so, because I find that the great personages in twentieth century commerce are young men who were the favorites of Poverty, spoiled children of Tireless Industry; that all over the Republic most of the Nation's industries are actively managed by men under fifty years of age; and I find that not one of them was advanced through favor, not a single one of them is the son of a millionaire, not a single one of them succeeded to the inheritance of some mighty father's mastery."

I see that to-day more than ever before in human history, Fortune says to the young men of the American Republic: " My favors are for him who can win them." I hear Fortune saying to young Americans to-day: " Come not to me with flabby muscle and untrained mind; my gifts are not for such as you.   But come to me from farm, office, factory, all you whose muscles are steel, whose hearts beat steady and true, whose brain is firm, whose mind is clear.   Come unto me, all you who are *men* in every meaning of that word.   Come unto me, you young Americans whose wills have written on your foreheads the imperial words 'I will not be denied.'   For every one of that quality of manhood I have rewards richer than those of which your fathers ever dreamed." With these words of Fortune ringing in their ears the young men of the Republic answer the Opposition to the Government.

And so the American farmer, the American workingman, the American manufacturer, the American people laughed out of the court of public opinion the proposition of the Opposition to destroy organized industry.   The farmer saw more clearly than anybody else the profound reason for the growth of organizations of industry.   The farmer has cattle, hogs and sheep to sell.   Thirty years ago his market was confined to the nearest country town, because his farm and his village were cut off from the

rest of the world for want of railways; but to-day a
great network of quick despatch brings Cincinnati, Chicago, New York as close to the farmer's pasture as his
village was a generation ago.

And so he sees that changed conditions which put him
in instant touch with the markets of the Nation and the
world require organizations of industry great enough to
prepare and distribute the food necessities of the Nation
and the world.   He sees that the capture of European
markets for American meats absolutely demands organizations of capital great enough to do this stupendous
work; and that without them he would be helpless.   The
farmer sees that this illustration runs through the entire
field of his production; and that his prosperity and the
prosperity of those organizations which purchase and
handle his product, are mutual and rest upon the same
solid basis of the changed conditions wrought by railways and telegraphs and telephones and the whole progress of the age.

And what the farmer sees the working-man sees also,
and the business man and every man who thinks.   Organization of industry, broadly speaking, is the outgrowth
of the increasing interdependence of man on man.   The
cities have great buildings; these are a form of " trust."
They displace the little buildings of a former generation
and business men desert their separate offices and flock
beneath a single roof where conveniences are better and
communication more speedy.   The modern hotel is a
form of the " trust "; each room has a long-distance telephone by which the guest can speak to any point, not
only in the city but in the country itself.   The linotype
machine in newspaper offices is a form of the trust — it

enables one man to do more quickly and accurately what ten men did fifteen years ago.

From the labor-saving machine to the modern office building, from labor union to steel combine, the whole tendency of modern times is toward organization of industry. All the politicians in the world could not prevent it; the people themselves could not destroy it; because at the bottom and in the final analysis this tendency is based on human progress itself — based on human invention, on the infinitely important fact that our eighty millions of people are in perfect and systematic communication with one another. You can not stay progress with a political platform — for progress is the large reasoning of a Higher Intelligence working through the deeds of men; and only history reveals its syllogisms.

Evils of trusts there are; who denies them? Evils of every human institution there are; who denies them? Evils in individual character there are; who denies them? The evils of human character gradually correct themselves; yet we, by law, hasten the process. The evils of every human institution remedy themselves; yet we by law hasten the process. And just so the evils of trusts are remedying themselves; but we will by law hasten the process.

[Here Senator Beveridge gave a résumé of laws passed and proposed on trusts.]

Such correction and remedy will repair defects without halting progress. All industrial development is not good — what human development is perfect? Men there are who are bad; partnerships there are which are bad; trusts there are which are bad. But the Opposition proposes the utter overthrow of the entire modern organization of industry, because a few such organizations are bad; just as the Opposition denounced the whole American army because out of 130,000 soldiers a dozen had proved derelict. There are barnacles on the ship? Yes. But the Opposition proposes to scuttle the ship because of the barnacles. We propose to remove the barnacles and let the ship sail on.

In four months then, the issue of "imperialism" has become a relic and the issue of the destruction of organized industry has become another example of short-lived political extravagances, like that of repudiation, of fiat money, of free-silver. And now in the closing days of this campaign the Opposition harks back to the ancient issue of the tariff. They ask you to let them revise the tariff. But tariff revision by the men who constitute the Opposition would be tariff mangling. If tariff revision by an honest but mistaken Opposition in 1893 wrought ruin to American industry, what would tariff revision by their present-day successors mean?

Are the forces which control the Opposition to-day as moderate and sane as those which produced the Wilson Bill ten years ago? And if the Wilson Bill shattered American prosperity, what would a tariff bill drawn by the men who are to-day in Opposition do for American prosperity? If the former was a storm, the latter would be a hurricane. If the former was a fire whose ravages were quickly repaired, the latter would be a holocaust whose ruin a decade of American energy could not rebuild. Is there anything engaging to the conservative mind in the proposal to make the present Opposition the custodians of our tariff and of the Nation's business? Does that appeal to the good sense of American voters?

Has the band of iconoclasts now constituting the Opposition done anything to win from the thoughtful greater approval than they gave to the company whom Mr. Cleveland led?

Suppose the alternative was offered each one of you whether to hand the tariff over to exactly the same men who in 1893 so wrecked it, or to let it remain in the keeping of the party which restored it to its usefulness — what answer would you make? And in the light of that answer, can you even tolerate the suggestion that the tariff should be delivered into the hands of the men who are not tariff revisionists but tariff revolutionists? And yet these are the men to whom you are now asked to surrender a tariff system that has been a hundred years in the building.

The people will have little patience with those in any party who propose the abandonment of those tariff principles to which the business of the Nation is adjusted, which required years of time and the toil and thought of the best minds in the land to construct.

Consider that American protection is a growth and not a creation — the growth of more than a century. Alexander Hamilton planted its seed. Its reason lay deep in the necessity of the American people to become a nation industrially independent of every other nation, so far as products are concerned. Henry Clay defended from the vandals that growing plant with that vivid eloquence which men called "logic on fire." James G. Blaine defended it from the assaults of the spoilers. William McKinley was the successor of Hamilton, Clay and Blaine in the care of American protection.

And now when the American people are gathering the

fruit of that tree, let us not lay the ax to its roots at the bidding of the unskilled who here and there discern an overgrown branch; for the branches of that tree are tariff schedules and the pruning of a schedule requires not the felling of the tree. If that tree needs pruning, is it not more reasonable to intrust that delicate work to those who have attended it from seed to sapling and from sapling to fruitage, rather than to those who resisted its very planting, who " barked " it once and who have sought every opportunity to destroy it utterly?

For pruning it may need. Blaine saw that; McKinley saw it. And both have told us how that pruning should be done. Blaine said in substance: When the tariff can safely be reduced on any schedule without injuring an American industry, use that proposed reduction as a basis for getting from another nation advantages in its markets for American products. And Blaine called that " reciprocity." McKinley said: " If, perchance, some of our tariffs are no longer needed for revenue or to encourage and protect our industries at home, why should they not be employed to extend and promote our markets abroad? " and McKinley called that " reciprocity." Reciprocity is the profitable method of tariff readjustment. It purchases with the reduction of every schedule a new market for American products. The Opposition to the Government proposes the destruction of the tariff without exacting from foreign nations thus benefited a single advantage to the American producer in return.

It is as if a wholesale house which needed to dispose of its old stock should say to the retail store: " I have certain last year's goods which I must get rid of and I will give them to you, not even at cost, not even in exchange for your permanent custom; but I will give them to you unconditionally and for nothing; I will make you a present of every yard of last year's calico regardless of what you do for me in return." Any wholesale merchant who would do that would be bankrupt in a year. And yet this is the way the Opposition asks you to dispose of our tariff to other nations. Beware of the physician who persuades you that your health is really illness and whose medicines make his diagnosis true.

We are in favor of modifying any schedule no longer needed to protect an American industry; but the modification of any schedule gives foreign nations an advantage in our market. And so we say that as a condition of that reduction foreign nations, or such of them as we can deal with, shall first give us equal advantage by reducing their tariff on our goods. That is the method by which we propose to make every reduction of our tariff open a foreign market to the surplus products of the American factory and farm.

But how will the Opposition's method of tariff destruction, without thereby securing a single new market for our surplus, help American commerce and continue American prosperity? For, be it remembered the continuance of our prosperity depends chiefly on the sale of our surplus; and the sale of our surplus depends chiefly on ever broadening foreign markets; and ever broadening foreign markets depend chiefly upon three great policies.

The first of these is the policy of reciprocity; and the Opposition is opposed to reciprocity. The second policy for securing foreign markets is expansion; and the Opposition is opposed to expansion. (We now sell every year nearly $40,000,000 to our dependencies alone which bought of us before we took them hardly $5,000,000 annually — and our colonial trade has hardly begun.)

The third policy for securing foreign markets is made up of practical methods for capturing Oriental trade; and the Opposition is against every practical method of securing Oriental trade. And so we see that the little puff of agitation for unconditional tariff reduction is born of unreason and nurtured by a thoughtless disregard of the sale of our surplus upon which our whole prosperity absolutely depends.

From first to last, therefore, one note dominates each separate clamor raised by the Opposition; and that note is destruction. In " imperialism," destruction; in organized industry, destruction; in the protective tariff, destruction. What would the Opposition do with the rising structure of American civilization and American power in our dependencies? They tell you themselves that they would destroy it. What would the Opposition do with the whole development of organized industry? They tell you themselves that they would destroy it. What would the Opposition do with the entire protective tariff system? They tell you themselves that they would destroy it.

What do we propose to do with these great developments?

In our dependencies, we tell you frankly, we will continue the tedious and weighty work of enlightenment and uplift which we have so well begun and which the noisy impatience of a few of the impractical is causing us to hasten all too rapidly. We tell you frankly that the flag shall stay where our soldiers placed it and that every day we will add a new support to the staff from which it floats. We tell you frankly that gradually, making many a mistake through haste, but nevertheless with sure progress, we will build up the world's ideal system of the administration of dependencies. We tell you frankly that we will broaden American sovereignty wherever Circumstance compels that duty; and that American sovereignty once established shall never be dethroned.

In the fundamental question of development and organization of American industry we tell you frankly that we will not try to tear up by the roots the progress of a century; but that, as careful and thoughtful men, we will patiently correct every evil of industrial organization wherever practical thought can find some practical method of doing so. We bear in mind the Master's parable of the wheat and the tares; and we know that the wheat is the general well-being which to-day blesses the American people; and that the tares are those evils which, throughout the entire range of human activities from the development of the individual man to the development of nations, unfailingly appear. As to the protective tariff we tell you frankly that we will deny all demands for the destruction of that system of American industrial development, but that we will modify antiquated schedules and will purchase with every such modification a new outlet for American surplus.

Broadly these are our propositions on the one hand, and those of the Opposition on the other hand. One party employs the method of the torch; the other the method of the trowel. One is the ax of the reckless woodman; the other the plane, the level and the square of the instructed craftsman.

When we reduce the items of these policies to a broad generalization we find that the question is one of building against burning, of construction against conflagration, of the remedy of ills against their ending by the death of the patient. We find that the fundamental difference between the two political forces in America is the difference between belief and disbelief in the progressive wisdom and righteousness of the American people.

THE VOICE OF THE NORTH TO THE SOUL OF THE SOUTH

Address of Senator Beveridge representing Indiana, the Indiana Shiloh National Park Commission and Indiana's Union soldiers, at the dedication of Indiana's monuments on the battle-field of Shiloh, Tennessee, April 6, 1903.

SINCE all must die, how fortunate to die for an undying cause and under the approving eye of history.

So fell those who fell on this field. For they gave their lives to save the life of the Nation, and history recites no nobler story than the story of their sacrifice.

Thus they are the subject not only of our pride and love, but of our envy. For it is not given to us so to close the volume of our years; and if it were, we dare not say that we should meet that opportunity as they met it.

That the ground on which they stood and fought may be marked and that our children may be worthy of the heroes sleeping here, Indiana builds these monuments. Not that she would rear warriors — we pray for peace — but that she would have her sons develop souls so great that the giving of their lives for a worthy cause will be to them a welcome thing.

And such were the souls of our fathers and brothers, who, on this field, on this spot, paid that price for our Nation's immortality.

For their blood was shed to make of the American people a single Nation, and not for any lesser purpose.
Other results of our Civil War were incident to that.
And so they died no less for the people of the South than
for the people of the North — for the American people
undivided, indivisible. Their martyrdom was to establish for ever the brotherhood of the flag — a relation-
ship so lofty that it can not recognize sections within the
boundaries of the Republic.

That purpose they accomplished. Devotion to the
Nation is to-day the first principle of all Americans. In
our recent war the proudest to wear the Nation's uniform
were the sons of those who on this field met in arms their
Northern brothers; the first to die beneath the flag was
a son of Carolina. And the giving of one's life is the
highest proof of loyalty. Exhausted in arms but by
arms unconquered, the Southern people have yielded to a
great and true idea. That idea is American nationality.

To me the thought of a people, a nation, a master nation devoted to ideals, is so vast and fine that even the
simplest words are not strong enough to state it. And
that was the thought our heroes died for. And that
ideal fought on for them. It is now the ideal of us all,
men and women of North and South alike.

How little these words — Southern and Northern!
Let us forget them. How much grander the single
word, American! Let us think of that, and only that.
Let us who live be worthy of our dead.

And let us who live be tolerant of the views of the
heroes of the other side. Only the years can tell what
elements of just opinion were confused and tangled in
that cataclysmal conflict. For us it is enough to know

that our central thought of nationality was true and that our brothers of the other side assert it now even as we ourselves assert it.   Tolerance, then, and loving kindness, and charitable forgiveness on both sides; and through all the land sweet reasonableness!   Nothing but these are important; for in these abides Truth — and Truth is the only sovereign.

War is awful.   Yet this word can be said even for war — it reveals elemental and eternal things.   In peace, men consider action, plan and purpose from the central point of selfish interest.   War comes, and the same men are conscious of a thing which can not be measured by yardstick, nor weighed in scales, nor listed in stock-markets; and yet a thing for which they go to the grave — glad, grand, masterful in a savage unselfishness.

That wonderful thing which makes men welcome death is principle.   In war's light they see it.   Our heroes who sleep here saw it.   God grant us their joy of seeing, without their agony of battle.   Not that they found it hard to die — they did not — but horrible to slay.

For the moment, at least, standing with their graves around us, we may measure the height of their outlook — the breadth of their thought.   And, as we measure, how little, transient, foolish seem men's plots for power, plans for place, schemes for self-aggrandizement!   How they dissolve into nothingness and only the true, the beautiful and the good remain!

I speak for Indiana soldiers.   Therefore I submit no statistics of comparative carnage.   Whether more men were killed here, or there, in Cæsar's conquests, or Napoleon's wars, or Alexander's battles, or on our own sad, red fields is not important. History shows that mankind in all ages and in all lands has been physically courageous. The cause, the thought, the principle, the ideal for which they fought, is the real thing. That is what Indiana's soldiers think. That is how I interpret Indiana's mind.

In the presence of our heroes dead, surrounded by our heroes living, how dare I interpret their supreme sentiment otherwise?

For Indiana's veterans, in common with all the people of our state, believe that nothing is worth fighting for that is not worth dying for; and that nothing is worth dying for but Truth.

Such is our Indiana view of peace and war.

For Indiana's people are neither rich nor poor, neither covetous, nor envious, nor cringing, nor brawlers, nor afraid.

They are sturdy, gentle people, living simply, eager for noble teaching; and knowing, when called on in righteousness, how to give battle and how to die.

And in this we take no peculiar pride. We take pride only in that we share this view with all Americans. For we Indiana people are national above all else.

I said I spoke for Indiana soldiers. But you who live and these who died were not Indiana soldiers — you and they were Union soldiers — the Nation's soldiers *from* Indiana. We have no state flag. Not many of Indiana's three million people would know what it was if we did have one. But every one of Indiana's people knows the Stars and Stripes. Every one of them would die for it. It is the Nation's flag — it is our flag, our only flag.

Let it similarly be the only flag of every state. Let others be forgotten.

When thinking of the Nation let Carolina forget her Palmetto banner, dear though it be with memories, and remember only the banner of the Nation! Let Texas forget her Lone Star ensign, sacred though it be with tradition, and remember only the flag of our common country! Let Maine forget her pine tree device and remember only the colors of the Republic!

States are invaluable for local government; but with this battle-field before us we can not see state lines — our eyes are too full of tears. We forget that ever there were sections; and, whether we will or no, our very souls cry out two words —" Nation!"—" American!"

Yes, that is it!— the American Nation! We have " found ourselves " at last. And it is because our heroes died here that we have come to the consciousness of that fact — the American people, a Nation, one, indivisible, everlasting. And you, and I, and all of us are parts of that Nation. That is enough. If those who rest here know that we have comprehended that thought — and they do know it — they are glad. It is enough for any man to *die* for. How blessed of the Father, therefore, are we who may *live* for that thought!

And we do not live worthily of it, if we do not consecrate our Nation to righteousness. But how shall we tell what is righteous and what is unrighteous? We believe differently and sincerely. To one it seems God's work to give order and law, and, by slow processes, so that they may see and understand, liberty and civilization to alien and inferior peoples. To another, such a course seems wrong. To one, a certain internal policy seems best; to another, it appears indefensible. Honest opinion daily divides us on both principle and expediency.

How shall we tell which is right? Who is to decide? Patience! God will decide. No harsh words! No denunciation! Trust the common thought and conscience. Trust the people. *Vox populi, vox Dei.* If, in the long run, that maxim is not true, republican government, democratic institutions, the rule of the people is a mistake. And the people's government is not a mistake.

With this thought, then, we meet all problems, troubles, dangers, doubts, serene and brave. Conflict of capital and labor, foreign wars, domestic broils, agitation and unrest, vexed questions and situations so grave that no key to them seems possible — all will yield to the master key made of the combined sense and conscience of the American people. To doors so solidly shut that opening appears hopeless, Time will fit and turn that master key.

Time and the people — they will make all plain and right at last in this Republic of ours. Time and the people, and, over all, the Father — who can doubt our outcome, remembering them? Who, remembering them, can cherish hate? Who, remembering them, can be bigoted or despairing? " With malice toward none, with charity for all "— these are the best American words. Let us live up to them and be patient! Let us live up to them and be hopeful! Let us live up to them, and realize our brotherhood! Thus, and only thus, shall we be worthy of him who spoke them and of these fallen ones.

On behalf of Indiana and of Indiana's Shiloh Monument Commission, I salute Indiana's heroes, dead and living — all and every one, from private to commander.

And in the name of Indiana soldiers — the Nation's soldiers — voicing a fraternity as noble as their courage, I salute, too, their former foes in arms, but now their comrades — comrades in the comradeship of this new day which has dawned for the Republic.

THE WORLD'S DEBT TO METHODISM

Response to a toast at the Wesley Bi-Centenary Banquet, Indianapolis, May 23, 1903.

AMONG the items of the world's debt to Methodism is that charity which " vaunteth not itself, is not puffed up " and cheerfully concedes to all other Christian churches full credit for equally devoted work for Christ. In speaking to the toast you assign me, I voice no vainglory of sect or creed; for Methodism knows no egotism of religious cult, no narrowness of spiritual clan. Methodism is as broad as charity, as tolerant as the Master's love. If this is not true the world owes us no debt, but we owe the world an apology for our existence.

We come before mankind, then, merely as one of the workers in the vineyard and not as the sole and only laborer in the regeneration of the world. We look upon our work with pride, but with the pride of Christians who will rejoice if any sister church makes better showing. For " in honor preferring one another " is the chivalry of our religion.

This tolerance of others, this grace and poetry of our faith is a part of the world's indebtedness to Methodism. For Methodism came in the hour of mingled religious bigotry and spiritual stupefaction. On the one hand, Wesley was charged with being a Jesuit; and, on the other hand, with designing the revival of Puritan fanaticism. Rowland Hill declared that he could not tell from Wesley's sermons " whether he was a Jew, a Papist, a pagan or a Turk "— and this because of the breadth of his view in an age of coffin-like narrowness. For against the bigotry of non-essentials Methodism opposed simple faith in the Saviour; against the doctrine of unavoidable damnation Methodism asserted free salvation to all who ask it. It was Charles Wesley who wrote " The Hymn of Universal Redemption."

When Methodism came, England was spiritually debased, religiously sodden. Greene's *History of the English People* tells us that " of the prominent statesmen of the times the greater part were unbelievers in any form of Christianity and distinguished for the grossness and immorality of their lives. At the other end of the social scale, the masses of the poor were ignorant and brutal to a degree hard to conceive." Montesquieu said that " in England every one laughs if one talks of religion." Macaulay described moral conditions in unsparing words. Catholicism was suppressed, Puritanism sleeping, the Church of England in a drunken coma. England was in the dark ages of morals and religion; and England was the heart of the modern world.

At this hour came Methodism and revived the souls of men. And Methodism's fervor was no fitful fire, extinguished in the hour of its blazing. It was a steady and increasing light. What Methodism gained, it held. It put method and performance in its work. As Loyola organized for Catholicism, Wesley organized for Protestantism. Many admiring critics call Wesley the Loyola of England's religious awakening — Loyola, for whom Wesley himself had such great admiration. Methodism was the renaissance of religion and morals; and the historians of the Church of England to-day admit that Methodism aroused again in that noble organization the spirit its clergy had smothered even in their own hearts.

Lecky says that that splendid institution, the Church of England, owes its new life to Methodism. And so it is that the evangelization of Protestant peoples is the world's first debt to our church. That revival which Methodism worked in the masses spread to every English cathedral, to every Protestant house of worship, and, gathering force and increase with the years, it has rolled on, like the stone cut by hands unseen from the mountain side, till the twentieth century is filled with the coming glory of man's universal Lord.

Equilibrium of enthusiasm and form is the condition of conservative progress. And progress that is not conservative is merely impulse. Enthusiasm creates; form preserves. Methodism was the realization of this necessary balance. The orderliness of the sect was the origin of their name; their fervor quickened a failing faith. Zeal for human rescue, systematized for practical ends, is a debt the world owes to Methodism — though the debt is forgotten in the universal adoption long ago of the spirit of Wesley's method by every Protestant creed.

Let no man undervalue authority, order and form. Without it liberty is mere caprice, religion spasmodic and fruitless emotion. Even ocean waves are rhythmic. Diffused electricity lights no lamps, drives no wheels, cures no ills. Early Methodism insisted that it was of the Church of England, only vitalized and made potential by the Spirit's visitation — so great was Methodism's appreciation of custom, law and form. Wesley speaks of the " exquisite decency "' of the Episcopal service.

This love of law, this reverence for government made loyalty a secular principle of Methodism. The storms of wrath against ancient wrongs which the French Revolution loosed, seemed like to overthrow all human institutions, good and bad. God was dethroned in France and a spurious " Reason " crowned. Hurricanes of chaos, sweeping out of this center of chaos, threatened other lands and calmer peoples. Had they devastated, also, the Anglo-Saxon world, no mind can measure the effect on civilization and the destiny of man. History tells us that Methodism stilled this tempest among the English speaking race.

Burke fulminated — but the *masses* never knew. Wordsworth, Coleridge, Southey sang — but the *millions* heard them not. But in street and lane, in shop and field and mine, Methodism spoke and the *people* heeded. And so it is that the myriads of the tongue of Shakespeare remained and still remain the hosts of law-regulated liberty, sane, calm, believing — their history defaced by no excess, the flags of their nations unstained by frenzy-shed blood. Is that no benefaction to mankind? If it is, profane history, coldly writing, says that mankind's debt for that is due to Methodism.

Methodism and loyalty! In 1789, our Bishops, formally on behalf of our church, addressed George Washington in words of loyal devotion to the new Constitution and the infánt government which, in that hour, needed every friend. And here is the answer of the Father of His Country to Asbury and Coke — Asbury, the father of American Methodism:

"To the Bishops of the Methodist Church in the United States of
America:

"Gentlemen — I return to you individually, and through you to
your society collectively in the United States, my thanks for the
demonstration of affection, and the expressions of joy offered, in
their behalf, on my late appointment. It shall be my endeavor to
manifest the purity of my inclinations for promoting the happiness
of mankind, as well as the sincerity of my desires to contribute
whatever may be in my power toward the civil and religious liberties of the American people. In pursuing this line of conduct, I
hope, by the assistance of Divine Providence, not altogether to dis-
appoint the confidence which you have been pleased to repose in me.

"It always affords me satisfaction when I find a concurrence of
sentiment and practice between all conscientious men, in acknow-
ledgments of homage to the great Governor of the Universe, and
in professions of support to a just civil government. After men-
tioning that I trust the people of every denomination who demean
themselves as good citizens will have occasion to be convinced that
I shall always strive to prove a faithful and impartial patron of
genuine, vital religion, I must assure you in particular that I take
in the kindest part the promise you make of presenting your prayers
at the throne of grace for me, and that I likewise implore the divine
benediction on yourselves and your religious community.

" GEORGE WASHINGTON."

Every Union soldier learned to love the very name of
Methodism. On the Bishops of our church Lincoln
leaned as on a second cabinet. And in 1864 this savior
of the Republic sent the following letter through our
General Conference to the million Methodist firesides
where loyalty to the flag was taught in the same lesson
with devotion to the Cross:

"Gentlemen — In response to your address, allow me to attest
the accuracy of its historical statements, indorse the sentiments it
expresses, and thank you in the Nation's name for the sure promise
it gives.

"Nobly sustained as the government has been by all the churches,
I would utter nothing which might in the least appear invidious

against any. Yet, without this, it may fairly be said that the Methodist Episcopal Church, not less devoted than the rest, is by its
greater numbers the most important of all.

   " It is no fault in others that *the Methodist Church sends more
soldiers to the field, more nurses to the hospitals,* and more prayers to Heaven than any. GOD BLESS THE METHODIST CHURCH!
Bless all the churches! And blessed be God, who, in this our great
trial, giveth us the churches.

   " (Signed)   A. LINCOLN."

   " More soldiers to the field, more nurses to the hospitals "— from the first, that was Methodism's way. It
reached the *people*. Denied in the cathedrals, it sought
the fields. Repelled from the sanctuary, it set up the
altar amid the grime of factory and mine. It knew
neither wealth nor poverty and cared for neither as such
— it knew and cared only for the hearts and souls of
men.

   Read Thackeray's tribute to our founders and our
method, and know anew that, to Methodism's mind, the
people only are important; that the people's purity is the
highest work; and that the people respond to the noblest
and best when honest appeal is made to them direct.
Hear Thackeray speak: " Whitfield cried out in the
wilderness. Wesley quitted the insulted temples to pray
on the hillside. I look with reverence on these men."
Such was Thackeray's feeling for the earthly founders
of our church.

   Slavery has vanished from the civilized world; the
Methodist Church was the first formally to declare
against it —and Lincoln tells us that what Methodist
preachers taught and Methodist mothers prayed for,
Methodist sons died for.

   Bible societies have carried the gospel's written words

over all the world.   But know that it was in Methodism's
mind that these organizations for publishing the Scrip-
tures to all mankind had their origin; and that it was in
Methodism's heart that was found their most determined
promotion.

Methodism brought practical philanthropy into religion.   Greene tells us that the humanitarian movement
in England flowed out of Methodism's evangelization of
the British nation.   Hospitals and every method of human amelioration were, from the first, a part of Methodism's work.   Succor for the suffering was, from the first,
a part of Methodism's mission.   All this is universal now
and commonplace, but in the Protestant world, it began
with Methodism's practical purposes.   For if Methodism
can be condensed into a phrase it would be this: The
union of the spiritual and the human, of the theoretical
and the practical, of faith and of works.

While Methodism first sang its psalms, it took thought
for education.   Its faith feared not knowledge.   Wesley
organized schools before he formulated the machinery of
church administration.   He wrote text-books while he
penned the articles of Methodist confession.   And to
this day the mind of Methodism is fertile in devising new
and modern methods for educating the masses.

Our whole church is a propaganda of enlightenment.
The Chautauqua movement, which makes every home a
school, is a Methodist invention; and the beautiful Chautauqua salute, every time it is given, is a white and waving praise to Methodism's practical masterfulness in lifting up the minds of otherwise neglected millions.

Secular instruction Methodism considers the handmaid of moral teaching.   Its founders were men of

learning, Oxford-bred; and the college and the cathedral, the school-house and the meeting-house, in Methodism's thought, stand side by side. And to-day, two hundred and thirty universities and schools, with $30,000,000 of property and endowments and nearly 50,000 students proclaim the world's educational debt to Methodism.

Methodism is powerful now and rich. Its membership reaches nearly 10,000,000. And yet its activity is not abated; and its activity is the activity of the times. Always the Protestant church of high and careful organization, its organization to-day is akin to that perfect machinery of the industrial and commercial world of the twentieth century. Witness the Epworth League — as perfect a recruiting force as ever was perfected among the young. Methodism organizes the enthusiasms of youth; the Epworth League marches forward in ordered companies, regiments and battalions — an army of good will, a force for peace and righteousness.

Organization, conservatism, enthusiasms made practical, ideals made real — this idea and practice are a part of the world's indebtedness to Methodism. And the spirit of the practical manifested in religious activity is invaluable to a Republic where every theory, however wild, every scheme, however fantastic, is urged upon the people with all the allurement of novelty, with all the dangerous power of inflaming speech. Methodism has stood clear-eyed and calm against all spurious agitation.

Already I have spoken much too long; but the theme is inexhaustible. No one address can enumerate the items of the world's indebtedness to our church. But humanity owes an obligation, not to Methodism alone, but to every church whose work has been to carry forward the Cross to an all-redeeming conquest. The world's debt to us is to a single company merely of the mighty and ever increasing army moving ever forward under our divine Captain, for the betterment of man and the salvation of the world. With all who acknowledge the Saviour as their Master we claim fellowship; over none do we assert our precedence.

The minds of men behold differently the details of dogma; and denominations, especially among English-speaking peoples, serve the invaluable purpose of meeting all views and enlisting all classes to a great and common end; but on the eternal things — on God, on immortality and on Christ — there is perfect concord and agreement.

Methodism says to every sister church: " Surpass us in zeal if you can; excel us in disciplined energy if you can; but we defy you to excel us in the cheers of approval with which we shall be the first to greet your noblest effort."

To every company of Christians, by whatever name it may be known — whether Catholic or Protestant — Methodism exclaims: " Come, brothers, we are with you! Your glory is our glory; our triumph is your victory."

To every member of every Christian church Methodism exclaims as to its own members:

> "Onward, Christian soldier,
> Marching as to war,
> With the cross of Jesus
> Going on before."

And in this spirit will be found, after all, the world's chief debt to Methodism.

SCHOOL AND NATION

Inauguration address at the installation of the Reverend Edwin Holt Hughes, S. T. P., as President of De Pauw University, Greencastle, Indiana, December 9, 1903.

THE glory of all American colleges should be that they produce citizenship as well as culture. And of these, citizenship is more valuable than culture. Culture is important; citizenship is indispensable. Upon the installation of a new president of this institution of learning we naturally turn to the purpose of education in a Republic — for the school is the most active influence among our American millions except the influence of the American home. From the council that gathers daily around the American fireside radiate those streams of wisdom and purity which keep the civic life of our country sane and wholesome. But next to the American family, the school is plainly the strongest force molding our destiny. So what the school does is of vital concern to the Nation. The word "school" is used as the broadest term for all educational institutions.

It is said "the school is a corner-stone of the Republic." That is true if the office of the school in our national life be accurately understood and performed. But in our hurried way we have taken education to mean mere instruction in definite subjects — the learning of facts, rather than training in wisdom. Our general

234

thought has come to be, "Let us teach American youth geography, history, chemistry, and the country is safe. Let American youth learn Latin, and the Republic is safe. Let us raise up a race of Euclids, and the Nation is secure."

But is this a true conception of the relation of the school to the Nation? There were few schools among the people when our Nation was founded. Yet the national spirit was strong in their hearts. Many apostles of nationality all through our history have been men not of the highest culture. The best and greatest of them have not been men of finished education. Consider Washington, Lincoln, Jackson. The same is true of leaders of the people in other lands.

Of course, some of them have been the finest products of university training. But this one truth is common to all of them. They were inspired by faith in their people, by a passion for national solidarity, by devotion to high ideals of their country's destiny. Each of them in every land believed in the mission of his own people, and that, in some form, that mission was and is to work righteousness in the world.

Mere learning, then, does not necessarily make citizenship. Knowledge of dead and living languages, mastery of the physical sciences, instruction in higher mathematics — none of these in itself produces the civic sense. And an educated man who disregards the common welfare is more dangerous to a Republic than an ignorant man because he has more resources with which to take from the common good for his own advantage.

Even if such a man is not active against the State, and merely contents himself by leaving public affairs alone, his neutral example is a negative influence for evil. His less fortunate neighbors will say: " If this man, with all his education, does not care for the public good, why should I bother myself about it? " And this means the beginning of the decay of the civic sense — that profound personal interest which every citizen must have in the Nation if the Republic is to work out its theory and purpose.

It is plain, then, that the American school must produce something more than book culture. The soul of our American instruction must be American nationality; or, rather, fundamental civic righteousness expressed through the activities of the American Republic.

Your professor of chemistry will tell you that science has been able to reconstruct a grain of wheat, with all of the chemical properties in the exact proportion in which they are found in the natural grain of wheat. So far as science can tell, absolutely nothing has been left out. Yet this grain of wheat which the chemist constructs will not grow. So in a Republic, the school which does not produce the spirit of nationality is a dead thing. It is the chemist's grain of wheat, not God's grain of wheat.

In a Republic, then, the great mission of the school is to create the national spirit. The fruit of public instruction in governments like ours must be patriotism. You may produce your man of culture, and yet if you have made him too dainty for the duties of citizenship, you have not only wasted your work, you have actually wrought evil. The most highly cultured man of loftiest mind who yet has not the political spirit is not as useful to a free government as the humblest country lad, if the latter has the civic sense that makes him take a hand in politics. For he is a good citizen, and the educated exquisite is not a good citizen.

Your man of culture may march to the Republic's battle-fields and *die* for the Nation; but that is not enough. He must *live* for the Nation. If his education has lifted him above the common duties of citizenship it has robbed him of his civic manhood. And civic manhood is the life of republican institutions.

Let us reduce this to the simplest terms. Citizenship means suffrage. So if the Republic is to endure, every citizen must not only be willing to vote; he must be willing to sacrifice business, convenience, comfort, and every other thing, rather than fail to vote. We read with tears in our eyes the heroic tales of the men who died to give us the right to vote; yet, as we read, we too often neglect that right. Unfortunately, this is true of many college men, and increasingly true. It must cease to be true of any college man. His very equipment commands him to do more for the Nation than men less cultured.

That equipment should mean activity in politics; for politics is the method through which our form of government works. And politics means the machinery of elections as much as the formulation of policies which the citizen must pass upon at the polls. So the farmer who answers to his political committee for his precinct is performing a duty to the Nation. But the person whose civic sense has been drugged by the refinements of a soulless education until he disdains such work is a deserter from the noblest duties and dearest rights ever bestowed on man. The one defends the pillars of the Republic;

the other applies to those pillars the acid of neglect which rots their strength.

Excepting in emergencies or when the political fortune of some great public man is at stake, many people do not attend to our republican government, even to the extent of voting. And our republican form of government requires the same attention that the fields of the farmer require, or the business of the merchant, or the shafts of the miner, or the tracks and engine of the railroad man, or the practical conduct of this university. If even a considerable body of our people fail to vote, we have a Republic in name, but not in fact. And so, if the spirit of citizenship is growing dim, the holy flame must be rekindled.

This is the business of the school when considered in its relation to the Nation. The teacher in a Republic must be the high priest of our republican nationality. What says Emerson:

> "For what avail the plough or sail,
> Or land, or life, if freedom fail?"

And doubt not that freedom will fail if all of us do not give to her our best devotion. Our fathers gave their blood for her; we are degenerate sons indeed if we do not give at least a little portion of our daily energy and interest for her. Liberty is no indifferent goddess. She will not abide where she is not appreciated. She is not to be courted by neglect. She will not tarry where she is not loved. And the love of words is nothing to her. She must have the love of deeds.

So our institutions of learning, from the humblest country school-house to the greatest university, ought to give some portion of an hour each day to the teaching of nationality, to instruction in the pricelessness of our institutions, to exhortation that the highest duty of every boy and girl is to live and die for the Republic. The method of doing this is the business of the teacher. But whatever the method, it must be done. Woe to us if our appreciation of free institutions fails.

We expect to lead this world; and America will lead the world, but not unless the sense of civic duty is kept as keen as instinct, as exalted as faith. And to keep it so is the duty of every teacher. In a Republic, in short, civic education is the soul of the school. With that the school is God's grain of wheat feeding the world and multiplying itself from this principle of life within it. Without it the school is the chemist's grain of wheat, a mere lifeless imitation.

And patriotism can be taught. Other nations are teaching it. Education is the finest thing in the world if it increases interest in the Nation — if it produces pure, brave and effective citizens. What is so noble as the trained intellect and high character serving the Republic, whether in obscure ward or President's chair — for the Republic must be served in the one as well as in the other. And to produce such service is the office of the school in the Nation. But education is a baneful thing if it destroys interest in citizenship.

I say the national spirit can be taught in the school. Take an humble example. One day in a certain city in the interior of Japan the words of a song filled the air. There were hundreds of voices. Even in the distance one could tell that they were the voices of youth. The musical sounds drew nearer. Soon the head of a column of school-children appeared. Scores, hundreds of little boys marched by, singing with all their might a song of their dear Japan, caroling of their flag of the crimson sun. They were voicing in music the ambition of their lives to serve their country and their heart's hope some day to die for their beloved land. Their notes were militant, but full of soul. Japan is without religion as we understand that term; but her statesmen have made devotion to the empire the religion of its multiplying millions.

So we see that even little Japan has its lesson for us. There can be no substitute for religion; but the next highest phase of human thought and feeling is that devotion to one's land which we call patriotism. Real education does not destroy pride in the Nation or weaken our conception of the duty of the citizen. But in a Republic real education means that the sense of citizenship must be the beginning and the end of it. I can think of nothing so admirable as the product of the American school whose practical devotion to the Republic has been intensified by his culture; of nothing so glorious as the American refined by education, and yet whose national spirit has been strengthened by his learning.

So the American school must be the great nourisher of the Nation. The Nation, the Nation, always the Nation! The school for the Nation! All education for the Nation! Everything for the Nation! When you write beneath your calculation in higher mathematics *quod erat demonstrandum,* it must be our Nation of which those words are written. When you prepare an historical thesis, it must be our Nation for which your studies tell you that God has been preparing through all the ages.

The test tube must reveal something more than the mysteries of force and matter; through all the gases of the laboratory you must see our Nation — God's great agent of righteousness in the world.

In a Republic, too, the school must teach conservatism. In monarchies the university has always been the generator of radicalism. In a Republic the reverse must be true, because the Republic is the reverse of the monarchy. No government can be good unless it is steady, moderate, sane. The ballast of a monarchy is the unchanging form of its administration; and so, despite its defects, it sails steadily. But the ballast of a Republic must be the sober second thought of its citizens. We shall end in confusion if we are swept off our feet every now and then by unsound agitations, by gusts of passion, by storms of prejudice.

On shipboard I never tire of hearing the command from the bridge, " Steady as she goes." That is the word for our Republic. Let us see to it that our national policies are right, and then " steady as she goes." Let our course as a Nation be determined by the fixed stars of the highest ideals, and then " steady as she goes." Yield not to the selfish purposes of any man or class of men, but consider only the good of the whole American people, and by that high national wisdom keep the ship " steady as she goes." Conservatism, then, instruction in the spirit of moderation, is the second great duty of the school as an agency of our national life, " steady as she goes."

Yet these will not suffice. Education is nothing if the spirit of nationality is extinguished. And even the spirit of nationality can not save us if we are a variable and eccentric people. Therefore, conservatism. But even something more than this is needed, and that something is righteousness. There is the final word in all education. And the highest formula of righteousness which the world has ever produced is that philosophy of life and death which we call the Gospel of Christ. That statement is not accurate, for the world did not produce Christianity. It has a higher origin. It is God's word to the world. He who understands it has the secret of good thinking and good doing. And so in the last analysis, considering the school merely as an influence in national life, we rise on the steps of reasoning to the eternal throne of all real power.

The old mother who has had neither time nor opportunity for learning, and yet knows by a higher evidence than learning can afford that God reigns and rules the world and all the worlds, is wiser than the most cultured professor who sits in the seats of knowledge, but who questions that greatest fact in the universe. Speaking of the mission of the school in the Nation, we may paraphrase the sacred word and say, " And now abide patriotism, conservatism, righteousness, but the greatest of these is righteousness."

This has a definite connection with the duty of the school to teach nationality; for history tells us that, in spite of occasional exceptions to the contrary, the highest expression of the national spirit, the strongest manifestation of civic ideals has been among peoples whose faith has been simple, pure, profound. There is no time for analysis of this tremendous fact. I merely point you to the fact. And whatever you do, do not fight a fact. Truth is the one unconquerable thing in all the universe.

So, considered merely as a factor in free institutions, the school must foster the religious spirit.

It is appropriate that these words be spoken here. For this institution, from its youth as a college to its maturity as a university, has been true to these ideals. It sprang from the people. It looked for inspiration to the great Source of all life and light. It considered itself the Republic's servant. Heroic has been its history. Its faculty in early days suffered hardship. Its students were drawn from farm and shop — children of men who feared God and loved the Nation and ate their bread by the sweat of their faces. Unpoisoned by luxury, unweakened by doubt, they were, teacher and student, the stuff of which righteous and unconquerable nations are builded. Many of its professors refused chairs in famous universities and gave their lives to this college of the people — missionaries of Christian education. Many of its students, burdened by poverty — or blessed by it — suffered physical hunger that their minds and souls might grow strong and noble under such teaching. And so DePauw has been a mother of citizenship as well as of culture.

Now that we are in the day of material prosperity, fail not to remember DePauw's heroic past. Fail not in stern devotion to these ideals. Fail not to justify the faith of those plain people whose hard-won earnings sustained Asbury, or of those splendid men who poured their wealth into DePauw, chief of whom was that great layman whose name we are proud to bear.

MARCUS A. HANNA — THE BUSINESS MAN IN STATESMANSHIP

Remarks in the United States Senate, April 7, 1904.

Mr. President:

SINCE to all earthly work an end must come, our words of farewell to a fellow-workman should not alone be those of grief that man's common lot has come to him; but of pride and joy that his task has been done worthily. Powerful men so weave themselves into their hour that, for the moment, it all but seems the world must stop when they depart. Yet, it does not stop nor even pause. Undisturbed Time still wings his endless and unwearied flight; and the progress of the race goes on and up toward the light, realizing at every step, more and more of the true, the beautiful and the good.

So it is not important that any of us should long remain; the Master Builder lacks not craftsmen to take our place. But it is important to the uttermost that while we are here, we should do our duty to the perfection of our powers, fearlessly and faithfully, with clean hands, and hearts ever full of kindness, forbearance, charity.

These are the outline thoughts that the absence of our friend compels. With his whole strength he did his work from boyhood to the place of rest. He was no miser of his life — he poured it into discharge of duty, keeping with Nature no account of heart-beats.

The things he did were real things. He was the very spirit of the practical. Yet the practical did not kill nor even impair the human in him. He never lost the gift of lovableness. His sense of human touch and fellowship was not dulled, but made more delicate by Time and the World. The years made him wiser, but they made him mellower, too.

And so he won the people's affection as well as their applause. And affection is worth more than applause. There is no greater glory than this — to make a nation your friend. Senator Hanna did that. For, when the angel of peace, which men call Death, took him to his well-earned rest, the people knew that a friend had left them. And the people were sad that he had gone away.

This human quality in him made all he did a living thing, all he said a living word. He was the man of affairs in statesmanship; yet his personality gave to propositions of mere national business something of the warmth and vitality of principles. He was the personification of our commercial age — the age of building, planting, reaping; of ships on ocean, and on land steel highways and the rolling wheels of trade; of that movement of the times which knits together with something more than verbal ties all the children of men, weaves tangible civilization around the globe and will, in time, make of all peoples neighbors, brothers, friends.

Thus he was, unwittingly no doubt, one of the agents of God's great purpose of the unification of the race. We are all such agents, small or great. If this is not so — if we are not, ignorantly perhaps and blindly, but still surely, spinning our lives into the Master's design, whose pattern He alone can comprehend — if we and all things are not working together for good — if life is but a breath exhaled and then for ever lost — our work means less and is worth less than that of coral insects, which, from the depths, build ever toward the light until islands stand above the waves, permanent monuments of an intelligent architecture.

Work with real things — real earth, real ocean, real mountains, real men — made him conservative. And his conservatism was real. Much that is accepted as conservatism is spurious, mere make-believe. Conservatism does not mean doubt or indecision. It does not mean wise looks masking vacuity, nor pompous phrase as meaningless as it is solemn.

Conservatism means clear common sense, which equally rejects the fanaticism of precedent and the fanaticism of change. It would not have midnight last just because it exists; and yet it knows that dawn comes not in a flash, but gradually. So the conservative is the real statesman. He brings things to pass in a way that lasts and does good.

Working with real things among real men also kept fresh his faith and hope. No sailor of the seas, no delver in the earth, no builder of roof-trees can be a pessimist. He who plants doubts not our common mother's generosity, nor fails to see in the brown furrow the certainty of coming harvests. He who sinks a well and witnesses the waters rise understands that the eternal fountains will never cease to flow.

Only the man whose hands never touch the realities of life despairs of human progress or doubts the providence of God. The fable of Antaeus is truth for body, mind and soul. And so, Senator Hanna, dealing with living men and the actualities of existence, had all the virile hope of youth, all the unquestioning faith of prophecy. These are the qualities of effective leadership of men.

He is gone from us — gone before us. Strength and frailty, kindness and wrath, wisdom and folly, laughter and frown, all the elements of life and his living of it have ceased their visible play and action. "Where," said despairing Villon, "where are the snows of yesteryear?" Vanished, he would have us believe. Yes, but vanished only in form.

"The snows of yesteryear" are in the stream, in cloud and rain, in sap of tree and bloom of flower, in heart and brain of talent and of beauty. Nothing is lost even here on our ancient and kindly earth. So the energies of our friend, and those of all men, have touched into activity forces that, influencing still others, will move on for ever.

As to the other life, we know not fully what it is; but that it is, we know. Knowing this, we who are left behind go on about our daily tasks, assured that in another and truer existence our friend is now established, weakness cast aside as a cloak when Winter has passed, vision clear as when at dawn we wake from dreams, heart happy as when, the victory won, we cease from effort and from care. For him the night is done, and it is written that " joy cometh in the morning."

FRANCES E. WILLARD

A Tribute To The American Woman

Remarks in the United States Senate, February 17, 1905, on the occasion of the unveiling of the Willard statue in the United States Capitol.

'Mr. President:

FROM the beginning woman has personified the world's ideals. When history began its record it found her already the chosen bride of Art. The things that minister to mankind's good have, from the very first, by the general judgment, been made feminine — the ships that bear us through storm to port; the seasons that bring variety, surcease of toil and life's renewal; the earth itself, which, through all time and in all speech, has been the universal mother. The Graces were women, and the Muses, too. Always her influence has glorified the world, until her beatitude becomes divine in Mary, mother of God.

Mark how the noblest conceptions of the human mind have always been presented in form of woman. Take Liberty; take Justice; take all the holy aspirations, all the sacred realities! Each glorious ideal has, to the common thought, been feminine. The sculptors of the olden time made every immortal idea a daughter of the gods. Even Wisdom was a woman in the early concept of the race, and that unknown genius of the youthful world

248

wrought Triumph itself into woman's form in that masterpiece of all the ages — the Winged Victory. Over the lives and destinies of men the ancients placed Clotho, Lachesis, and Atropos for ever spinning, twisting, severing the strands of human fate.

In literature of all time woman has been Mercy's messenger, handmaid of tenderness, creator and preserver of human happiness. Name Shakespeare — Miranda and Imogen, Rosalind, Perdita and Cordelia appear; name Burns — the prayer *To Mary in Heaven* wakens in the heart of all that touch of nature which makes the whole world kin; name the Book of Books — Rachel and the women of the Bible, in beauty, walk before us, and in the words of Ruth we hear the ultimate formula of woman's eternal fidelity and faith.

So we see that through all time woman has typified the true, the beautiful, and the good on earth. And now Illinois, near the very heart of the world's great Republic and at the dawn of the twentieth century, chooses woman herself as the ideal of that Commonwealth and of this period; for the character of Frances E. Willard is womanhood's apotheosis.

She was an American. She was the child of our American prairies, daughter of an American home. And so she had strength and gentleness, simplicity and vision. Not from the complex lives that wealth and luxury force upon their unfortunate children; not from the sharpening and hardening process of the city's social and business grind; not from any of civilization's artificialities, come those whom God appoints to lead mankind toward the light.

Moses dwelt alone on the summit of mystery and human solitude. The Master abode in the wilderness, and there the power descended on Him with which He put aside the tempter. In the forests the father of our country learned liberty's lessons from Nature, liberty's mother; and from the valleys and the heights, the fields and pouring streams, got understanding of the possibilities of this land, a knowledge of its uses, a perception of its people's destiny. We can not imagine Abraham Lincoln coming to us from a palace. No! We can understand him only as he really was — a man of the people and the soil, thinking with the people's mind the grand and simple truths, feeling with the people's heart an infinite compassion for and fellowship with all the race.

So, Mr. President, all the saints and heroes of this world have come fresh and strong from the source of things, unspoiled by abuses and unweakened by false refinements. And so came Frances E. Willard, the American woman. The wide, free fields were the playgrounds of her childhood. The great primeval woods impressed her unfolding soul with their vast and vital calmness. Association with her neighbors was scant and difficult, and home meant to her all that the poets have sung of it, and more. It was a refuge and a shrine, a dwelling and a place of joy, a spot where peace and love and safety and all unselfishness reigned with a sovereignty unchallenged. And so this child of our forests and our plains, this daughter of that finest of civilization's advance guard — the American pioneers — early received into her very soul that conception of the home to which, as the apostle of universal womanhood, her whole life was dedicated.

To make the homes of the millions pure, to render

sweet and strong those human relations which constitute the family — this was her mission and her work. And there can not be a wiser method of mankind's upliftment than this, no better way to make a nation noble and enduring; for the hearthstone is the foundation whereon the state is built. The family is the social and natural unit. And so by the deep reasoning of nature itself Frances Willard's work was justified.

But hers was no philosopher's creed. She gained her inspiration from a higher source than human thinking. In her life's work we see restored to earth that faith which, whenever man has let it work its miracle, has wrought victory here and immortality hereafter. Such was the faith of Joan, the inspired Maid of France; such that of Columbus, sailing westward through the dark; such the exalted belief of those good missionaries who first invaded our American wilderness to light with their own lives on civilization's altar the sacred fire that never dies. The story of Frances Willard's faith in the conquest of evil by the good seems incredible to us who demand a map of all our future before we take a step.

For Frances E. Willard knew no questioning. The Master's message was at once her guaranty and her command. The Bible was to her, in very truth, divine. What immeasurable and increasing influence that one book has wielded over the minds of men and the destiny of the world! If it be the word of God, as we profoundly believe, surely it comes to human ears with all the dignity and peace and power that His word should command. If it be the word of man, then even the doubter must admit that the ancient Hebrews had miraculous skill to cast a spell which, strengthening with the years, spreads wider to-day than ever and embraces the future as far as even the eye of imagination can behold. Not all invention or all statesmanship or all of literature has so touched and bettered human life as this one book. And it was the Bible that gave Frances E. Willard her mission, her strength, her hope, her argument and her inspiration.

Thus prepared and thus equipped she went out into the world and to her work. No method can measure what she did. The half-million of women whom she brought into organized coöperation in the Woman's Christian Temperance Union is but a suggestion of the real results of her activities. Indeed, the highest benefits her life bestowed were as intangible as air and as full of life. She made purer the moral atmosphere of a continent — almost of a world. She rendered the life of a nation cleaner, the mind of a people saner. Millions of homes to-day are happier for her; millions of wives and mothers bless her; and countless children have grown into strong, upright and beautiful maturity, who, but for the work of Frances E. Willard, might have been for ever soiled and weakened.

Mother of all mothers, sister of all wives, to every child the lover, Frances E. Willard sacrificed her own life to the happiness of others. But it was needful that she should so consecrate her strength and length of years. For how shall the service of utter unselfishness be achieved save in the utter sacrifice of self? So Frances E. Willard gave up her life and all the rights and glories of it that all of her sisters might lead fuller, richer, happier, sweeter lives themselves.

So, Mr. President, by placing her statue in the hall of

our national immortals, a great commonwealth to-day for ever commemorates the services of this American woman to all humanity. And the representatives of the American people, in Congress formally assembled to-day, are paying tribute to the little frontier American maid who heard and heeded the voices that came to her from the unseen world, and, obeying their counsels, became the first woman of her generation, the most beloved character of her time, and, under God, a benefactress of her race.

JAMES WHITCOMB RILEY — POET OF THE PEOPLE

Address as President of a meeting of the Indiana State Teachers' Association in honor of James Whitcomb Riley, in Tomlinson Hall, Indianapolis, December 28, 1905.

IT would seem that Indiana and the Middle West, the center of the Republic geographically, the center of the Republic numerically, is becoming the center of the Republic intellectually. Only in America could the center of culture follow close on the heels of the moving center of population; because only in America is learning equally distributed among the people, so that where the center of population is, the center of intelligence must be.

At any rate Indiana at this hour is giving more creative literature to the English-speaking world than any single portion of the Republic. Charles Major, the American Dumas; Meredith Nicholson, our latter-day Hawthorne; George Ade and Nesbit and McCutcheon, whose true humor sets the land aglee; Booth Tarkington, whose genius expresses itself in the most finished art of any contemporaneous novelist; David Graham Phillips, whose savage force and masterfulness are elemental and epochal — all these and more are children of Indiana.

And dean of all, first of all and dearest of all is that American Burns, whom Indiana has given to the Nation — James Whitcomb Riley. I say given by Indiana to the Nation; for all that Indiana has and is belongs to the Republic as a whole. And, besides, our joy and pride in

this master singer of the people is too great to be provincial.   Only the heart of the Nation is great enough to
share and hold it.

Dearer to the universal man than its soldiers, statesmen or scholars are the world's poets; for the poet interprets the soul of man to itself and makes immortal the
wisdom of the common mind.   After all, the source of
all poetry is in the hearts of the people.   In the consciousness of the masses is that intelligence concerning
the higher truths of the universe, of which this life is
but a reflection; and it is this intelligence, uttered in
words of music, that constitutes real poetry.

So he who knows not the people nor loves them can
not sing that song to which their very natures are at-
tuned.   The aristocrat of letters may make verses whose
perfect art, like that of Horace, renders them immortal,
or state high truths in austere beauty, like that of Arnold.
But only the brother of the common man can tell what
the common heart longs for and feels, and only he lives in
the understanding and affection of the millions.   Only
the man who is close to the earth and, therefore, close to
the skies, knows the mysteries and beauties of both.   Only
he who is close to humanity is close to humanity's God.

This double kinship to God and man of the true poet is
what makes him so dear to the man in the furrow and
the street — he listens and hears a voice of beauty singing
the very thoughts his locked lips have not uttered and
the yearnings that have filled him always.   The poet is
our soul's interpreter, voice of our spirit, evangel of our
higher and our real life, utterer of the prophecy which
God has planted in our breasts.

The poet of the people is a part of the people, and their

better part; and that is why the people love him.   That is why we love James Whitcomb Riley.   He has understood us — understood us because he is of us; and, understanding us, has told us of ourselves, of our ideal selves, and therefore of our truly real selves.   For only that is real in the soul of man which to the mind of man is ideal.

That is why the poet of the people becomes the poet universal.   He supplies that touch of nature that makes the whole world kin.   Everybody knows Burns.   His verse has gone into our common speech.   We quote him without knowing it.   Burns is human and says things we understand and things we need.   Omar Khayyam's song of poise and resignation rises above the clattering footfalls of the centuries, and the modern world is listening to him now.

Riley is of this universal quality.   He voices the sentiment and wisdom of the common man, and states these in terms of our own dear land.   There is something in him of Burns and something of the Tentmaker and a dash of Villon, and yet all Riley, all original, all born of our own home soil — every atom pure American.

What I like most in Riley is his sympathy with everybody and everything that needs or deserves it.   The best things in Burns are his songs to a homeless mouse and a mountain daisy crushed beneath his plow.   Riley is full of that same charity.   He sympathizes with an old horse turned out to pasture.

Sympathy is the divinest faculty of man.   It is a suggestion of Heaven.   It sweetens misfortune and makes adversity smile.   Toil turns to play beneath sympathy's touch, and the thorns of difficulty bear roses.   There is nothing so fine as a friendliness of soul that knows and understands the sorrows, troubles, temptations, joys, hopes, aspirations and all the emotions of other souls.

Love, like this, is the greatest of gifts. Such friendliness is understood by the common people and in quiet hours. These are qualities growing out of the soil, and so out of the heart of God.

Take all your fine statements of high truths, but leave me the living speech of human sympathy. That is Riley's kind of speech. He is so full of it that it masters him and makes him write it out in poetry. That is how we have *Griggsby's Station* and *Nothin' to Say* and *The Old Band* and *Lockerbie Street,* and that very tenderest of all his lines expressing a new idea in literature — the sorrow of a childless one, who at heart and in longing and in loving capacity is a parent, for the real parent over the loss of a real child:

> Let me come in where you sit weeping,— aye,
> Let me, who have not any child to die,
> Weep with you for the little one whose love
> I have known nothing of.

We have these and a hundred others like them, and thank God for them, and so thank God for Jim Riley.

Riley is more the poet of the people than Burns was in this: he is the poet of the children. The plain people love children more than all things else. Only God and country are dearer to the common heart than the infant race growing up to take our place when, like old trees, we shall fall at last. Children are visible immortality. The beauty of youth is the loveliest thing in human life; and in the heart of childhood abides the future.

The common people know children and understand them; and so does Riley. Shelley's genius arranged

brilliant words and amazing thoughts, but he never got
as near to the human heart as the man who wrote *Fool
Youngens* and *Old Man Whiskery-Whee-Kum-Wheeze*
or *The Raggedy Man.* I should rather be the interpreter
of childhood than to be the author of *Manfred.* What
said the sacred Word — *Except ye become as little children ye shall not enter into the kingdom of heaven.*

Riley speaks our tongue. His words are the language
of the people. He is the interpreter of the common
heart. That is why he is so full of that sane fatalism
called resignation — submission to the eternal forces of
whom he would make friends, not enemies.

> When God sorts out the weather and sends rain,
> W'y, rain's my choice,

— says Riley, echoing the man of the fields, who, like
Riley, would a good deal rather be *Knee Deep in June.*

But this voice of our ordinary American millions utters
the depths of our soul and searches the heights of our
faith when he tells of our trust in and reliance on the
good God who, we know, with the wisdom of the heart,
surely exists and surely cares for us.

There are some of us who owe more *personally* to
James Whitcomb Riley for that priceless thing — an
unquestioning faith in God and Christ and immortality
— that can well be put in words. The people who have
not abandoned that wisest of wisdoms, the wisdom of
the heart, do not argue about or question these infinite
truths. And Riley, the people's voice, asserts them.
The poet does not syllogize about these eternal realities
— the poet knows.

It is these people — these millions of common people

— who pay the tribute of their love and admiration to James Whitcomb Riley to-day. For this meeting is held by the State Teachers' Association, and no body of men and women represents so truly the people as the teachers. Walking along a country lane in Germany one day, a German statesman said to me, pointing to a modest-appearing man, " There goes the German people — there walks the soul of the German nation."

And in answer to my look of inquiry he said:

" That is a typical German teacher; he is the bulwark of the fatherland."

This is truer of the American Republic than of the German Empire. A republican form of government rests on the citizen, and the teacher ought to be and is the maker of the citizen. So the teacher is the truest representative of the people; and thus it is that when the teachers of Indiana greet James Whitcomb Riley, the people greet their poet. " May he live long and prosper," and his true song be sung for many a year to come, and its music echo for ever in the souls of the people!

PROGRESSIVE LIBERTY

Speech before the Indiana Republican State Convention, April 11, 1906.

AS the Republican party has won all its victories in the past, so it must win its victories in the future as the champion of progressive liberty. We do not deserve to win by reciting the deeds of our fathers, or even our own deeds, however large and righteous, but which have yet passed into history. We deserve to win only by what we are doing right now, this hour, this minute; and by what our present performance promises for the morrow. The Republican party must always be the here-and-now party, the up-to-date party, the party of conservative advance.

Nor can we depend upon the weakness of the Opposition.

There is no glory, no honor, no service to the people in beating men merely because they are called Democrats — no, nor in electing men merely because they are called Republicans. No battle is worth fighting whose purpose is to keep one crowd in office and another crowd out of office. The happiness of men and women and children living in this Republic — that should be a party's only conception of duty at home; the spread of American commerce, the broadening of the Republic's power for good — this should be a party's only conception of duty abroad.

A new era has opened upon this world. The growth of cities; the crystallization of industry into organizations so vast that they are almost governments to themselves; the increase and perfect connection of railroads and all modern facilities for travel; the multiplied methods of production; the million forms into which human effort and industry have been directed in the last two decades — all these are new conditions at home demanding new thought to solve the new problems they involve.

The building of the Panama Canal, the greatest task ever undertaken by human hands; the administration of the American government over millions of people in Porto Rico, Hawaii and the Philippines, each of these acquisitions treated differently according to the wisdom of the situation; the establishment over Cuba of the Republic's suzerainty, more complete than any in the world — all these and others are new conditions abroad demanding new thought to solve the new problems they involve.

And so it is that, at home and abroad, it is a new world in which we live — a world of new methods, new ideas, new men; for let us not forget that since the Civil War one generation has been born and passed away and another generation is half spent already.

These problems of the hour we are solving on the hour. We are placing on the statute books a law which begins the Nation's control of the charges of those mighty railway systems that transport the Nation's citizens and wealth. And whether that law remedies all the evils it is meant to cure, whether it wholly satisfies the people or partly disappoints them, a beginning will have been made; and in the solution of those questions which have grown out of modern corporate development the principle of the Nation's authority over business transacted throughout the Nation will once more have been asserted. When that principle shall be exercised further, the common sense and conscience of the American people will determine.

To-day nearly seven million women and children are at physical labor in factories, mines, farms and stores. Once our chief concern was that the people should have employment at all. To-day another duty has grown out of our successful answer to the problem of keeping the people employed, and this new duty is to keep the people healthfully and happily employed. As our factories and mills are power houses of prosperity they must also be made training schools for citizenship. And so the Administration is seeking to safeguard the health, education and morals of the working-women and children of the Republic. When it ceases to seek that it should cease to exist.

After all, the purpose of this Republic is to produce manhood and womanhood. After all, the whole object of civilization is character. After all, human life from the beginning of time until now has been a tragedy unless day by day the happiness of the average man and woman has become greater, sweeter, truer. And so it is such problems as honest business between man and man; the charging of just rates by railroads for carrying the Nation's people and merchandise; the regulation of the labor of children and women in all our material industries so that the future American citizen may be physically, mentally, morally better even than their parents; rigid economy in handling the people's money and daily accounting for every expenditure — it is social and economic problems like these which we must rightly solve if as a party we would live or should live.

For these are the problems that touch the people's very bodies and well-nigh touch their souls. And it is for the people that our party lives, and not merely to get votes for the party organization; it is for the great, splendid, true-hearted, toiling millions of Americans unmatched in high and honest purpose among all the peoples of the earth — it is for these that our party lives, and not merely that colossal national wealth of and for itself shall be created.

Yes, we must march onward. For half a century we have been answering the great questions which the welfare of the American people demanded — the Union saved, slaves freed, free homes bestowed upon millions, factories and mills builded from ocean to ocean by the policy of protection, the financial miracle of resumption worked, the gold standard established, Spain driven from Cuba and the Philippines, American civilization begun in the Orient — these are but some of the problems which the American people, through our party, have solved.

And now we must not stop. We must turn to these new social and economic questions which have to do with the daily lives and happiness of human beings and which press for answer; questions that involve the righteousness of American business, a juster distribution of wealth by preventing dishonest accumulation of gain; questions that look to the physical, mental, moral upbuilding of all the workers in factory and on farm throughout the entire Republic; to the public control of great public

businesses, like insurance and banking institutions, so
that the people may know the condition of their savings
— the solving of questions such as these is our present
duty.

We believe in property and the rights of property; but
we also believe that the just rights of capital and the real
welfare of the people are one and the same. We believe
that all honest interests of the few are wrapped up in the
prosperity of the many; and so we stand as the defender
of all honest capital on the one hand, the protector of all
peaceful labor on the other hand. And, therefore, we
are enemies to the death of those modern Catilines who
set at each other's throats the laborer and the man who
employs him.

A class is forming swiftly which proposes to solve the
great social-industrial problems of the times by impossible measures. Now and then even the counsel of
violence is heard. Against those extremists and their
doctrines we set a face like flint. We must always be
progressive — he who loses but a step in this swift and
systematic march of our modern days is lost. But we
must also be practical, for the people demand not only
that our principles shall be right, our purposes uplifting
to the masses, but that our plans and policies shall work
out practical results.

How strangely crowded are certain periods in the lives
of nations with the gravest conditions at home and
abroad. On the one hand, our domestic problems growing out of the changed industrial conditions are the most
important since the Civil War; on the other hand, the
very progress of civilization itself has brought us face
to face with problems outside our immediate bound-

aries, whose solution will affect the destiny of the Republic and the world.

In San Domingo chaos, murder and pillage reigned until a year ago; government was practically dissolved, debts unpaid and foreign nations were about to seize the country. All this was occurring within physical sight of our flag. All this American statesmanship must permanently stop. We can not permit any foreign nation to seize territory anywhere on the Western Hemisphere. We can not permit foreign guns to command the entrance to the Gulf, the Mississippi River and the Panama Canal.

And we can not permit anarchy within sight of our shores any more than we will permit it upon our soil. We can not permit civilization to relapse into savagery beneath our eyes and ask of the world and history the criminal question, "Am I my brother's keeper?" And to prevent this is the purpose of the treaty which the President has submitted to the American Senate.

Against this treaty the Opposition has arrayed itself. But the Treaty will in the end prevail. And when it does, civilization and commercial honor will have been vindicated and vitalized not in San Domingo alone, but in every island and in every country from Cuba southward to the Antarctic seas; and another day's march will have been taken toward the premiership of the Republic over the Western Hemisphere.

Think of another great task which we are this moment doing — the building of a canal which will float the maritime commerce of mankind. It is a wonderful thing to know that in our day this dream of the centuries is being realized — a wonderful thing to understand that, as we sit here, the traditional policy, the inherited hope of the American people steadily held through two long centuries, is being brought to pass. It is a circumstance so vast that we who are living while it occurs do not appreciate nor even comprehend the magnitude of this tremendous enterprise.

But right now in this first decade of the twentieth century — a century destined to be the greatest of all history — this mightiest work of human hands is actually being performed. And it is being done by the American people, who, in doing it, have made us their agent. When the American people want something done they always come to the party that knows how. Ours is the party that stands for the right things and gets those right things done. When we cease to be such a party, we shall meet and deserve defeat.

To-day the United States is the first power in the Pacific; and we are there not only for commerce, not only for the preservation of the world's peace; but chiefly for the working out of righteousness. One hundred years from now history will say that, in the first decade of the twentieth century, the greatest progress made among all the peoples of this world was made by the wards of the American Republic in the Pacific and Caribbean seas, under the authority and the helpfulness of American administration and under the inspiration of the American flag. Fortune follows the flag; blessings fall wherever it floats.

The historian will call our times the beginning of the "American period." Already the nations are submitting for settlement their world questions to the American Republic. Yesterday a war which brought to conflict the most numerous armies of modern history was lighting up the world with its flames. That war threatened to spread all around the globe. But the hand of American statesmanship appeared and confined the struggle to the green fields of Manchuria, whose streams soon ran blood-reddened to the sea.

And then when Japan and Russia were locked in a death struggle, that hand again reached forth, stayed their tragedy and a master's voice said, "Let there be peace," and there was peace. It was your Government and mine that did these things, and you and I live in this wonderful and beneficent day. There never was a time when an American could be so proud of his country as now; never a time when the flag meant so much.

* * * * * * * * * * * * *

How noble the deeds the American people have wrought, how seemingly impossible the heights they have scaled! I have cited them only to show you that the broadest vision is narrow, the loftiest conception is low compared with the destiny which events are working out for this humanity-helping Nation. I would have you go forth understanding that the problems of to-day are not the result of political plans or the schemes of parties, but questions of humanity and civilization which fate is addressing to her chosen children. I would have you go to your homes understanding that we must think of and care for the welfare of human beings right here at home and of civilization wherever its cause is intrusted to us throughout the world.

BUSINESS AND GOVERNMENT

Speech opening the Republican campaign for the Middle West, delivered at Chicago, September 22, 1906, in answer to Mr. Bryan's proposition of government ownership made in his Madison Square Garden speech in New York.

THE people's government should do no business that the people can do better themselves; the people's government should own no business that the people can better own themselves.

But the people's government should control and regulate industries owned by some of the people and of a magnitude so great as to affect the welfare of all of the people.

The people, through their government, should not permit individuals or associated individuals to practise business methods that will be unjust to all. But the people's government should not own any industry which private enterprise can efficiently manage and whose abuses government regulation can prevent.

Government ownership of nation-wide business is the European theory of industry. Government regulation of nation-wide business is the American theory of industry. I am for the American theory and against the European theory. Government control of railways, but not government ownership of railways.

The great organizations of industry came because they

were necessary; so it follows that on principle they are good. It is in their practice that they are sometimes bad, and it is that they shall be as good in practice as in theory that the principle of government control comes into play.

So long as the managers of these mighty corporations manage them as trustees of the people whom they serve and whose money is invested in them, government control is not needed; but when these managers treat their trusts as their private affairs to be conducted for their individual profit alone and not also for the welfare of the people, government regulation is needed — government regulation, but not government destruction; government regulation, but not government ownership unless government regulation fails.

And government regulation will not fail if these captains of industry do their duty. Government regulation will never be felt by the managers of great business enterprises who conduct business as trustees of the people, just as criminal laws are not felt by the citizen who attends to the duties of citizenship.

Liberty is realized only by him who obeys those common rules of action called laws by which alone liberty lives.

I repeat that the modern development of organized industry is not only necessary but that it is good. Take as a single illustration the railways. Without them Chicago would still be a frontier town; the farmers of Iowa could not get their cattle and grain to market; merchants would be without either customers or stock; the daily newspaper could not be served to the country districts. Without them the Nation would fall asunder.

They make the man who lives on the Atlantic the

neighbor of him who lives on the Pacific and all Americans brothers. They are the greatest element in creating that common Americanism which makes the Republic's eighty millions a compact, homogeneous people. They are highways of commerce, avenues of intelligence, agencies of patriotism — they are all this and more if managed, not as a private business, but as a public trust.

Or take the Beef Trust. Without the organization of the meat industry the food requirements of the American people could not be satisfied. If the Beef Trust would act not exclusively as a machine for private profits alone, but also as the trustee of the people which it serves and from which it gets its profits it would be one of the most beneficent forces in the industrial world.

Just as the organization of American industry developed out of changed conditions, so the principle of government regulation develops out of the action of these organizations themselves. Just as the old methods of private business are utterly inadequate in the new conditions, so the old principle of arbitrary private management is utterly inapplicable to the new methods. And so it is that the new principle of regulation by the government of all the people, over business so great that it affects all the people, has developed from the very same causes that produced those great businesses themselves.

For example, railway rates are in the last analysis a tax on every human being in the Republic. They affect the prices of all commodities. They directly touch every variety of business in the Nation — that of every farmer who ships a bushel of grain, of every wholesale merchant who ships goods and every retail merchant who receives them, of every factory that ships its products, of every mine that ships its ore. They touch every man, woman and child who travels from town to town.

It is necessary that these rates shall be just; and the justice of those rates can not be left exclusively to the managers of the railways whose immediate purpose is the greatest possible profits. If those profits were disposed of for the equal good of all stock-holders, it might be different; but they are often juggled for the advantage of a few stock-holders, as witness the recent surprise in Union and Southern Pacific dividends and the results that followed. *" Open and above-board " must henceforth be the motto of American business.*

The throat of one shipper should not be cut and his blood given to another shipper; and this can not be left to the railroad manager alone, because his immediate purpose is the largest profits and he might find greater profits in treating one shipper better than others; as witness the facts disclosed by the investigation of the Pennsylvania Railroad, some of whose officers were found to be stock-holders in shipping companies which therefore got cars denied to other shippers of the same products.

It ought not to be left to the railroad managers exclusively, because they might be coerced by powerful shippers to treat unfairly less powerful shippers; as witness the coercion of railways by the Standard Oil Company, the Beef Trust and other powerful concerns which conducted their business not as a public trust for the public good, but solely as a private system for private gain alone.

Therefore it becomes necessary that the people whose savings are invested in these very railways; the people from whom the railways derive their revenues; the people whom the railways serve and who serve the railways, should have a voice in their management. So it is necessary that the railways whose rates are a tax upon all the people, whose operation directly affects all the people, should be controlled and regulated by the government of all the people.

This is the reason for the railway rate law passed by the present congress.

That law may not be very effective at the beginning; and that is not greatly important, for it will be effective in the end. I think it crude and expect little from it as it stands. But the important thing is that for the first time in our history the railway rate law puts into practical operation the principle of government control of railways.

Where experience shows that that law is defective it will be amended until finally the law will grow into a statute of perfect regulation, railway abuses will be ended, railways managed with an honest profit to their owners and faithful and impartial service to the people.

And that is the only way laws should develop. Laws that are mere creations are not beneficent — seldom workable. But laws that are developments from changing conditions, laws that are written by the wisdom of experience, are always beneficial. Laws that are enacted as creations are usually the products of an enthusiast's brain — laws that are growths of a principle from the soil of every-day practice are the developments of a people's instructed wisdom.

It was thus our financial system grew; thus our industrial system developed; thus our Constitution itself was evolved, and thus that it has been growing ever since and will continue to grow as long as the American people grow.

Such is the philosophy of the principle of the government's control and supervision of railways. We have begun the application of that principle, begun it because the American people demanded it. And they demanded it because they needed it. And now that we have begun it, let us give it an exhaustive trial.

Why talk of government ownership when government regulation has only begun? Why fly to the European theory, born of European conditions, when the American theory has just been born of American conditions?

American theories have suited American conditions in the past. Let us trust American theories in the future. Let us Americans go on building our own free institutions on our own models and teach mankind that law-regulated liberty is not only best for government but best for business and best for life.

Government ownership violates the American principle that government enterprise ought not to own and manage what individual enterprise can own and manage.

Government supervision is a recognition of that American principle and the application of its corollary that a business which affects all the people should be regulated by the government of all the people.

Government supervision leaves business in individual hands, but requires that individual to act as a trustee for the people and thus prevents abuses hurtful to the people.

Government ownership takes business out of the hands of the people and substitutes for private abuses of railway management, which government supervision cures, bureaucratic abuses of railway management, which nothing can cure.

Government supervision leaves the making of rates, local and general, over our maze of 250,000 miles of railways, in the hands of men who are familiar with local and general conditions and have individual interest in the successful management of particular roads; and yet government supervision corrects those rates when they are unjust or oppressive.

Government ownership puts the making of rates in the hands of an enormous crowd of government officials unfamiliar with local and general conditions and without individual interest in the management of particular roads.

Government supervision leaves the system of individual management, under which the country has been developed, but requires that management to act as a trustee for the people; government ownership creates a vast machine so complicated that its workings would be cumbersome, a machine so great as to be endangered by its own weight.

Government supervision means the intelligence and conscience of the people acting as restraining agencies upon the wrongs of railway management; government ownership means an American bureaucracy as much greater than any other bureaucracy on earth as the American railway system is greater than any other railway system on earth.

Those who advocate govenment ownership admit that private management is more efficient, admit that American railway service is the best railway service in the world. But they say that the government ownership is the only way of keeping the railways out of politics.

It is true that the railways meddle too much in politics. When they meddle at all they meddle too much, and they meddle a great deal. But government ownership is not the way to stop such meddling.

Criminal laws must stop it. Prison bars for corrupt railroad lobbyists; prison bars for corrupt railway agents in primaries and conventions; prison bars for corrupt railway representatives and all other such men who try to influence the nomination and election of Senator, Congressman, Judge or any other public officer — that is the way.

Let the railways attend to their own business just as you are expected to attend to your own business, and no man will speak of government ownership. And their business is not to nominate and elect any public officer; their business is not to purchase, coerce or influence his action. Their business is to haul passengers and freight and nothing else.

And it is that they shall attend to that business as trustees of the people that the railroad rate law was passed, the anti-rebate law was passed, the Sherman act was passed; and generally the foundation of that system of government regulation laid of which these laws are illustrations.

I have no fear that railway evils will continue; for even if these laws we have passed shall not prove effective, the organized and intelligent conscience of the people shall prove effective. *Every man who, by railroad influence, is nominated to any office, from constable to President, ought to be defeated, no matter to what party he belongs.*

The people have already begun to defeat such men, and will hereafter defeat them increasingly as time goes on until the absolute uselessness of trying to control politics will dawn on railway managers, who will finally see that they have squandered the money paid out to accomplish plans that an aroused and instructed people wreck and destroy.

The principle of government supervision applies to any other business so great that, like the railway business, it affects all the people. That is why we passed not only a law to compel the railways to give the people just service, but also a law to compel manufacturers to give the people pure food. The government exists for the people, and not the people for the government. The people established the government to do their work; the government did not establish the people to do its work.

And therefore when manufacturers sought to make money by poisoning the people, there was only one way by which the people could protect their health and lives, and that was by requiring their government to inspect the food and medicine which manufacturers were selling them.

When the maker of food and medicines conducts business not with individuals, but with great masses of individuals, his business is no longer private but public. He is no longer an individual; he is a trustee — and his trust is rendered sacred because it directly affects human life.

And so we passed a law requiring the products of every manufacturer of medicine and food sold to the people to be inspected by the government of the people. But that does not mean that the factories which make the people's food and medicine should be owned by the people's government.

And yet if the making of people's food and medicine, a matter which concerns the health and life of the people, ought not to be owned by the people's government, railroads, which affect only the business of the people, should not be owned by the people's government.

Government supervision naturally applies to all great industries affecting all the people; government ownership could not possibly apply to all great business which affects all the people.

If it could we should, in a hundred years, behold the government doing everything and the individual doing nothing. Instead of individual initiative we should have government inertia.

Instead of doing business under government supervision we should be doing business under government employ.

Instead of making profits as the owners and operators of legitimate industry, we should be earning salaries as the employees of government industry.

Instead of the government being our servant, we should be the government's servants.

Government supervision is the principle vital to the preservation of individual enterprise, to the preservation of the private element in business and, at the same time, to the best protection of the people's interest in that business.

It was this principle of government supervision of all business affecting all the people that inspired the historic law regulating the American meat industry and requiring American packers to sell to the American people as healthful meat as they sell to foreign people. That law does nothing more than to put into effect the great idea which modern civilization has developed that when business becomes so great that it affects all the people it is a trust that should be administered for the benefit of all the people.

One man has a right to sell a blind horse to another man because the other man has the opportunity to examine the horse. *Caveat emptor,* says the law —" Let the purchaser beware." But the Beef Trust has no right to sell unhealthful meats to the millions because the millions can not know whether the meat is wholesome or diseased.

The sale of a single horse is a private transaction. The sale of millions of pounds of meat to millions of people becomes a public transaction.

The seller of the horse need not look out for the interests of the buyer of the horse; the buyer must look out for his own interests. But the seller of enormous quantities of food to enormous numbers of people must look out for the welfare of the people who buy because the people can not look out for their own welfare.

And so without anger, or malice, or passion, I drew the law which requires every packing establishment to be conducted by sanitary regulations prescribed and enforced by the government and every pound of meat and every can of food product sold to the people to be inspected by the people's agents; and, without anger, malice or passion, Congress passed it.

That law requires no more than would be done voluntarily by private individuals making money for themselves, but also acting as trustees managing a great in-

dustry in the interests of humanity as well as of their
pocketbook.

If that law had provided less than that, the people's
representatives would have been unfaithful to the people.
It was not a blow at the meat industry; it was merely
another ray of light from that new day that has dawned
for civilization; only a modern statement of that ancient
doctrine that *no man liveth to himself alone;* only another step in the making of this American people a
nation of the strongest and healthiest men and women
beneath the sun.

But because the government should regulate the packing industries of the country it does not follow that the
government should own the packing industries of the
country. *Will any man say that the government should
go into the meat business? And yet if not, then why
should it go into the railway business?* The railway
business affects all the people, it is true; but so does the
meat business affect all the people — affects them vitally,
mortally. The railway business affects pocketbooks; the
meat business affects life.

So, if for the protection of the people the government
should own the railways, much more for the same reason should the government own the packing-houses.
And that is plainly impracticable, unwise. But government supervision is both practical and wise. It applies
to the sale of meats to the people as well as to transport-
ing the products of the people — applies to all industry
that touches all the people.

That is why government supervision is a principle and
not an expedient. But government ownership could not
apply to all industries so great as to affect all the people,

but only to some industries. That is why government ownership is an expedient and not a principle.

No business interest need fear the application to itself of this principle of government regulation unless that business interest itself compels it. The people require their government to prevent abuses only when abuses are persisted in.

When the manager of a business that affects all the people, recognizes the interests of all the people and manages it as a trust for the people's welfare, as well as a concern to make money for himself, the people will not only never ask government interference, but they will not tolerate government interference.

The fate of great businesses is in the hands of their managers. After all, the ancient legend of the man who, pursued all his life by a powerful but secret enemy whom he could never discover, when finally he had found him, stood before himself, is the story of us all.

Private management of all business so great that it affects all the people, the owner serving the people as trustee, taking just profits as a reward — this is the American ideal of business and this the ideal that must be enforced.

The question of Cain, " Am I my brother's keeper? " must never again fall from the lips of the humane and enlightened American business man. The American people want the American business man, like American business itself, to be the best and noblest in the world.

All hail to the American business man! It is the American business man who keeps the commercial blood of the American people moving. It is the American business man who is the captain of the Nation's prosperity. It is the mind of the American business man which discovers the possibilities of American resources and his is the heart that achieves them. It is the American business man who constructed our railways, organized our commerce, planned and built Chicago, split asunder our mountains and took from them their hidden wealth to serve the uses of the people.

It is the American business man that made American cities new wonders of the world, erected structures more marvelous than the gardens of Babylon — structures devoted to industry and trade and not to the pleasures of idle monarchs and corrupt courts. His is the imagination that has conceived the commercial conquest of the globe for the American people, and his the daring that has set these plans in operation.

The fruitful genius, the exhaustless initiative, the indomitable will of American business men constitute the mightiest force for material greatness in the Nation and the world — let it also constitute the mightiest force for righteousness in the Nation and the world. And the American business man is willing and anxious that this should be the supreme purpose of his life. He is willing and anxious for the world to realize that his intelligence is guided by his conscience. And all mankind will realize this when the American business man understands that he has become the first of modern *public* men — that when he becomes the trustee of a people's welfare he becomes the high priest of the religion of humanity, an agent of God Himself.

All this he will become when it is pointed out to him that he no longer lives for himself alone, but for all the people of this great Republic to whom the Most High has intrusted the leadership of human progress.   I be-lieve in the American business man.   Against appeals to his greed, I match the appeal to his conscience; for as the American business man possesses the most practical in-tellect on the globe, so I do not hesitate to say that he is the most upright man on the globe when a demand is made upon his righteousness.

This, the best of nations, has faith in its business men; and no power can shake that faith but those business men themselves.   Let the business man himself lead this his-toric movement for the moral regeneration of American commerce and finance.   So shall the watchman of the twentieth century, when questioned of the night, make answer in the words of Holy Writ, " Lo, the dawn ap-peareth."

But the business aspect of our national development is only a phase of that great uplifting movement that is animating the Nation.   I believe this people were estab-lished by the Almighty for the working out of His infinite purposes.

Who that reviews with historic eye the progress of this Republic, can doubt it?

Who that beholds the flag moving ever onward and bringing with it civilization, equal laws, unpurchased jus-tice wherever it floats, can doubt it?

Who that considers the world-wide movement toward law-regulated liberty which to-day manifests itself in every country of the globe — in Russia with its uprising of the masses; in Japan with its transformation to popu-lar government; in China with its awakening; even in Persia with its proclamation of a constitution — can doubt it?

Who can doubt it with the Philippines reclaimed; with Porto Rico free, prosperous and happy?

Who that considers the drift of affairs among the Cuban people can doubt it?

Six years ago, almost to a day, I stood on this platform to answer Mr. Bryan on imperialism, asserting in a word that American institutions were equal to the emergency of the Philippine problem; to-day I stand on the same platform answering Mr. Bryan, asserting that American institutions are equal to the railway problem.

But six years ago I went further and declared that the Teller amendment, adopted in the excitement of a declaration of war, pledging a destiny to Cuba separate to our own, was a false and foolish doctrine whose folly events would declare.

On this platform six years ago, almost to this day, I asserted that Cuban affairs could never be independent of American interests — that geography, civilization and the nature of our race made the future of the Cuban and American people one and the same. Six years ago almost to this day on this platform I declared that, in substance, what afterward was known as the Platt Amendment, would be adopted.*

All over the land political orators, even of our own party, acclaimed that utterance not only inopportune but impossible. And yet at the very next session of Congress that epochal statute, fathered by that then first of American public men, Senator Platt of Connecticut, was enacted by Congress and afterward made a part of the Cuban Constitution.

* Editor's note: See Senator Beveridge's speech in Chicago in reply to Mr. Bryan, entitled The Star of Empire.

To-day every Cuban patriot and every American citizen thanks God for the Platt Amendment. It gives us both in our own law and also in the fundamental ordinance of Cuba power to deal with those events which every student knew were absolutely certain to occur.

It gives us not only the power but lays upon us the duty to meet the present emergency. Not only were we given coaling stations — that was a measure of national safety; not only were we given practical supervision over Cuba's foreign relations — that was a measure of national prudence; not only were we given power over Cuban sanitation — that was a matter of national health; not only were we given power over Cuban foreign debts — that was a measure of national finance.

But we were also given power to send American soldiers to this geographical annex of Florida when a single house is burned, and a single man is killed, if, IN THE JUDGMENT OF THE AMERICAN GOVERNMENT, *the Cuban government was no longer effective and social order dissolved.*

When any man scoffs at the idea of a divine direction of American statesmen in the great crises of our history, let him read the Platt Amendment and tell us who inspired that immortal document. Let him read it by the flame of Cuban towns burned in the passion of contending factions. Let it be interpreted to him by the rattle of musketry within hearing of the President's palace at Havana. Let him read it in the prayers of Cubans who pray for that which is the common heritage of all Americans — life, liberty and the pursuit of happiness.

The Platt Amendment not only gives us the power

but lays upon us the duty of intervention if the Cuban people fail in their experiment of free government; *for free government is the important thing to the Cuban people; and if Cuban Administration fails to give free government American intervention means free government.*

It is practical liberty for which mankind craves — not theoretical liberty, as conceived of by cloistered dreamers; and practical liberty is what the American flag means wherever it floats.

Cuban trade is much to us — millions of dollars to-day and hundreds of millions in the future; and this is important. But Cuban trade is nothing to the American people compared with the realization of those American ideals of liberty to preserve and spread which the American people were established on this earth and American institutions were devised.

And practical liberty is what the American people mean that Cuba shall have. We prefer that they shall develop it by themselves — we have tasks in plenty to perform, duties in plenty to discharge. But if they can not realize it themselves we shall realize it for them. There is no burden too great for the American people to bear; for we as a Nation have learned what every individual has learned, that with increased responsibilities comes new strength, a higher inspiration, a broader vision.

Speaking for myself alone, I feel, as I have always felt, that the safety, the progress, even the civilization of the Cuban people can best be realized under the American flag. All students now admit that not only over Porto Rico, not only over Cuba, but over San Domingo and the Greater Antilles, the influence of the American Republic must continually increase.

Geographically — naturally — these islands are the territory of the United States. If the sovereignty of the world were to be redistributed on geographical lines the care of these islands would be assigned to our keeping by every statesman on earth. But whether or not any man subscribes to this statement, all men will agree that Cuba, which is but a prolongation of the Florida Peninsula, *is so near to us that we can not free ourselves of her destiny if we would.*

But we have pledged ourselves to her separate existence if she proves herself capable of a separate existence. That pledge we shall fulfil because American honor, plighted even in folly, must be redeemed. The fulfilment of America's word, given even in unwisdom, is, after all, the greatest wisdom.

But we have not only given her our pledge to support independence if she can maintain it; both she and we have given ourselves the power and laid upon ourselves the sacred duty of preserving the liberty of the Cuban *people,* whether she preserves the independence of Cuban *territory* or not.

And let us never forget that liberty of a people is more important than the independence of despotism, more important than the independence of anarchy. And between the independence of despotism and the independence of anarchy the first, although black as midnight, is preferable to the second, which is blacker than midnight.

The fate of the Cuban people is in the hands of the Cuban people. If they fail in this trial with which they have been tested by a wisdom beyond human wisdom; if for the preservation of practical liberty the American flag ought to float in Cuba, then let no man doubt that the American flag will float there.

And if it is unfurled from Santiago to Havana, that flag will mean for Cuba what it has meant wherever it has been raised — liberty regulated by law, peaceful industry protected by orderly government, human rights secured by independent courts upheld by all the force of the greatest government existing among men.

In the end, whether it be a decade or five decades or a century, Cuba must be American. History shows that the aspiration of the American people, even while yet we were colonies, was that she should be American — the colonists petitioned the English king to let them make Cuba American territory; and it was in most platforms until the Civil War distracted our attention from it.

And yet American government of Cuba can only come at the hands of the Cubans themselves. For the sake of the Cuban and the American people and the other people of the world, pray God it shall not long be delayed.

It can not be that American blood was shed in vain in Cuba. We did not go to war for liberty that liberty should be mocked. That conflict meant something more than a mere fight. It meant something more than driving Spaniards from the Western Hemisphere. It meant liberty; and if liberty be impossible under the Cuban flag it is certain under the American flag.

I ask all American producers this question: Is it best for you that Cuba continue the battle-ground of foolish factions, or that American law and order should regulate their industry?

I ask every American lover of liberty this question:

Do you feel that the cause of human freedom would best advance under the Cuban flag, or under that flag which, whenever it has been lifted, has meant practical progress and real freedom?

Liberty — that is the method of human progress. It is toward liberty that all mankind is struggling. And the Nation which, under God, is leading the world to liberty is this American Republic. It is for the realization of liberty and its fruits that all our laws are passed — for the preservation and spread of liberty that all our wars are fought. No American soldier ever died for his country but gave his life for liberty and civilization. It is as the agent and instrument of progressive liberty that the American people have written their record of usefulness and glory; and it is as workers for an ever purer, stronger liberty that the American people take their stand to-day.

THE ERA OF POLITICAL INDEPENDENCE

Extracts from speech opening the Massachusetts Republican campaign delivered at Boston, October 8, 1906.

THE only question before the American voters in this campaign is good government. There are no issues of policy dividing political parties — no conflict of principle to take the people's minds from the practical process of running the government. The individual and not the party at this moment dominates our political life, and the only question now before the individual American is which party can best administer the people's business.

Everybody is practically agreed on the money question. Everybody is practically agreed on recent legislation. No party struggle is thought of against a single statute enacted by Congress in the last five years. Everybody approved the Pure Food Law, and Democrats as well as Republicans voted for it. Everybody applauds the Meat Inspection Law, and Democrats were as earnest as Republicans in its support. Everybody now sees the statesmanship in the Irrigation Law, and it was passed by Democratic as well as by Republican votes. Everybody rejoiced at the enactment of the bill for free denaturized alcohol, and it became a law without party division. We are in an era of patriotic unity. Such, with all its trials, is the triumph of free government administered by honest men.

The whole people are satisfied with the legislation un-

der which the canal is being dug, and no party lines were
drawn in its enactment.   The enormous majority of the
American people demanded the passage of the Railway
Rate Bill, and Democrats and Republicans were practically unanimous when it was put upon its passage.
The most far-reaching law in its ultimate results since
the Civil War, the law creating the Department of Commerce and Labor, had practically the solid support of all
parties.   There was no party division on the anti-rebate
bill or on any law enacted for the correction of trust
abuses.

There is no practical proposition by either party to
which the other party is opposed with sufficient earnestness to make it an issue.   None but free-trade theorists
would destroy the protective system on the one hand,
and none but protection extremists would deny that tariff
schedules must from time to time be readjusted, on the
other hand; and *it is the safety of American institutions
that* EXTREMISTS ARE ALWAYS FEW AND THE MODERATE-
MINDED ARE ALWAYS MANY.   There can be no tariff issue because the party in charge of the government will
revise tariff schedules as soon as the party in opposition
could possibly change them.

The policy of administering just government under
equal laws in the Philippines, at least until the Filipinos
themselves are prepared for self-government, is admitted
as the proper policy by both parties; and what shall be
done when that time comes is a consideration so distant
that it is not yet an issue.   The question as to whether we
should have taken the islands in the first place is so many
years in the past that it is no longer an issue.

And so it is that the spirit of political independence is

awakened and the spirit of partizanship slumbers. This is always so in times of national contentment. The spirit of partizanship rules when vital policies are to be determined, and it should rule then; the spirit of independence reigns when the largest question is that of good government, and it ought to reign then. When the Republic is in danger, neither partizanship nor independence is dominant, for then Americans are unanimous.

[Senator Beveridge here detailed the work done by each department of the Government, showing that such work is well done.]

So much for the past achievements and present issues. The questions which we must now answer are great economic and social questions. There must be an ever-increasing morality in American business; an ever-increasing care for the life and health of fellow-men; an ever-increasing upbuilding of citizenship. The profits of greed must be replaced by the profits of honesty. Childhood must not be debased by labor — enormous fortunes must not be builded at the cost of the degeneration of children who to-morrow must constitute the Nation's citizenship. Classes whose very existence means death to free institutions must be prevented by giving ever larger care to the physical, mental and moral well-being of all the children of the Nation, the children of the poor as well as of the rich. A national child labor law is an immediate necessity.

In a word, the making of the Nation must go forward — the making of a nation of strong, sane, pure men and women; a nation of clean and wholesome homes; a nation of people and not of classes; a nation of millions of individuals and not a compact of petty sovereignties; a nation of brothers and not of groups; a single nation and not forty-seven nations; a single flag and not forty-seven flags; a nation which as the years pass and the centuries roll by increasingly becomes the mightiest uplifting power on all the earth; a nation which shall lead her sister nations along the paths of peace into the green fields and beside the still waters of universal human well-being; a nation which righteousness exalteth and whose God indeed is the Lord.

DUTIES OF THE PRESENT; NOT MEMORIES OF THE PAST

Speech closing the Indiana campaign, delivered in Tomlinson Hall, Indianapolis, November, 3, 1906.

THE American people are living in the present. The American people are thinking of the future.

Our past is glorious; but it is the past. We must consider to-day and to-morrow rather than yesterday and the day before, except as these by-gone days instruct us for the work and duty before us. Our fathers never camped for long on the battle-fields that they had won; they marched on to other victories. That is why Americans have accomplished more in a shorter time than any other people in history.

Important questions are now confronting us, confronting us *to-day*. And we must answer these questions or we are unworthy of our fathers' deeds. Our fathers' deeds — not our fathers' words alone. For what our fathers spoke and wrote they made good with laws on statute books or with bayonets on battle-fields.

To-day and not yesterday; the whole people and not special interests — this is the true formula of Americanism. Not the commercial viewpoint only but the moral viewpoint also; for we are building civilization as well as developing resources. We are making citizenship as well as money. After all, the highest human purpose is the development of the soul of man.

There are those who fear the open discussion of new questions. And yet nothing is so good for us as this very conflict of thought among the American people. The weave and play of opinion among our American millions is what keeps us intellectually alive, morally upright, politically sound, commercially pure. Running waters are aways healthful; death broods always over stagnant pools. It is the restlessness of its salty waves that makes the sea the physician of the globe.

Let us fear not the discussion of any question. Let us fear no opinion, however stoutly held, provided only it be honestly held. Let us fear only the counsel that declares inimical the discussion of any subject relating to the public interest. Let us fear only him who himself fears the ultimate wisdom and the final righteousness of the masses.

Honesty is the salvation of free institutions. Make your public men tell you what they stand for while questions are still unanswered — you do not care what they stand for after questions have been answered. Moral cowardice is as hateful to Americans as dishonesty. It is no discredit to be wrong — no human being ever lived who was always right. But it is not only discredit but disgrace to be a coward.

In this spirit let us go forward to the doing of our new duties as our fathers went forward to the doing of their duties. " Let well-enough alone " is not America's motto. That maxim would have kept every good law off the Republic's statute books. " Let well-enough alone " never sent a pioneer into the wilderness; never built a railroad; never set upon the ocean a single ship; never invented a machine. Columbus sailing into the

unknown seas flew no such ensign; no such spirit burned
in the hearts of the ragged Continentals who chose Valley Forge and its horrors rather than home and its joys.

No law securing the rights of man would have been
written; no step in human progress taken; no discovery
of science made; we should to-day have no telegraph, no
telephone, no steam or electric railways, not one of our
thousand modern comforts, had these words of reaction
been written on American hearts. Not "Let well-
enough alone," but "*Make well-enough still better*"—
this is the real motto of Americanism. Yes! "Make
well-enough still better"— let every school-boy and
school-girl write that in their copy-books as the real
motto of true Americanism.

The problems of to-day and to-morrow which now face
us affect both our national life here at home and our
national work out in the world. The first are those industrial and social questions which our development has
created; the second are those questions which our duty to
civilization has created.

In the last five years we have made certain laws that
mark the passing of an old and the coming of a new
epoch; just as was the case in Washington's, Jackson's
and Lincoln's day. These men did not make their times;
their times made them. They did not create the epochs
their life's work ushered in; human progress — the
thought of the people, the advance of civilization — created those epochs. These men only expressed the new
convictions of the millions. It is so to-day with the new
epoch ushered in by that first statesman of the contemporary world.

The new laws we have written are nothing but the

working out of a new principle which our complex social
and industrial order has developed; just as every new
principle has similarly been developed in the past.

That principle is the life of and reason for the Railway
Rate Law; the Pure Food Law; the Meat Inspection
Law; the Employers' Liability Law; and, greatest of all,
the law creating the Department of Commerce and
Labor.

That principle is this: When any business becomes so
great that it affects the welfare of all the people it must
be regulated by the Government of all the people. The
people can not permit individuals or associations of individuals to practise methods hurtful to all. And the people have no agency for their protection except their
government.

For example: The people eat prepared foods and use
prepared medicines. Under the old theory that all business is private and that the public has no right to interfere with it, manufacturers of foods and medicines were
adulterating both. They were making enormous fortunes at the expense of the health of the millions.

But this was intolerable. Our institutions are for the
benefit of the people — for their practical benefit and not
for their theoretical benefit. Our institutions contemplate that men shall make honest profits in business by
righteous methods that do not injure others; our institutions do not contemplate that men shall make dishonest
profits in business by methods that do injure others.

So the people had to be protected from poison in their
food and drugs. How? They could not protect themselves as individuals. The states could not adequately
protect them, because that business was nation-wide.

Therefore, the Government of all the people had to interfere with the food and drug business which affected all the people. So we passed the Pure Food Law and to-day the Nation's Government is supervising a business which is necessary to all the people, but which has been injuring all the people.

This same new principle that any business so great that it affects all the people must be regulated by the Government of all the people, also wrote the Railway Rate Law. The old principle was that railway managers could do as they pleased. "The public be damned," said Vanderbilt. The new principle is that the public's rights in railway management are as great as the rights of the railways themselves.

This new principle is the vital thing in the Rate Law. For the railways affect all of the people; and the government of all the people must see that they are just to all the people. The time has come in our Christian civilization when justice must reign in our business as well as in our courts. As a practical measure the present railway rate law will prove inefficient — a vexation and annoyance to the railways on the one hand and not a satisfactory remedy to railway abuses on the other hand. It is crude and not well worked out; but it recognizes the necessary principle of national regulation, which, in time, must take the place of state regulation. This is a great and historic advance in the solution of the country's transportation problem.

This new viewpoint that all great businesses are trusts to be administered for the people as well as organizations to be run for profit, is already being taken even by the captains of industry themselves. For example, we investigated the Pennsylvania Railroad the other day. That fact alone shows the revolution that is occurring; for if, five years ago, anybody had suggested the investigation of the Pennsylvania Railroad, he would have been considered mad.

But we investigated it and found some of the officers of this supposedly model corporation of the world holding stock given them in shipping companies to which therefore they furnished cars while refusing cars to other similar shipping companies in which they did not hold stock. One of the officers giving his testimony said, " This used to be considered all right, but we are looking at things differently to-day."

That statement shows the moral change which is now going on in American business. And this moral movement will not end until conscience dominates all our commerce. Righteousness must not be confined to the churches; it must illuminate the counting-house as well. Righteousness will prevail — is prevailing. No financier to-day voices Vanderbilt's profane contempt for the American people.

It is not necessary to take on the serious evils of Government railway ownership in order to be rid of the evils of private railway ownership. These latter evils are twofold: First, unjust rates and discriminations; and these, national regulation, finally, will cure; second, corrupt railway interference in politics, and this the penitentiary will cure.

The day of corrupt railroad and corporate power in American politics is drawing to its close. Any man who is nominated for any office, from President down, by railway or corporate influence ought to be overwhelmingly defeated, and hereafter such men will be defeated.

Laws are being placed on the statute books, making corrupt interference with free government a crime and these laws are being executed. More laws will be added until all corruptors of primaries, conventions, legislatures and Congresses will find themselves behind the bars of the people's prisons.

And there is where they ought to be. Every man who, on behalf of any corporation, or on his own behalf, spends a dollar to corrupt free institutions, ought to be sent to jail. For in a republic the worst of crimes is attack on the life of the republic. And that crime is all the worse if the hand that strikes the blow be a hidden hand and the dagger it holds be a dagger of gold.

This principle that all great business is not only a private organization for making money for its owners, which is right and important, but also a public trust to be administered for the people's welfare, which is even more right and important, placed on the Nation's statutes the Meat Inspection Law. That law was not passed in malice but in kindness. We did not want to hurt the Beef Trust's business; but we did not want the Beef Trust to hurt the people's health.

It is hard to understand why the Beef Trust fought that law. Of course, it prevents the sale of diseased meat and falsely labeled compounds; of course, it thereby forbids the use of hurtful materials; of course, it thereby reduces improper profits. But it puts the people's food under the eye of the people's Government. And the guaranty of the Government on the product of the Trust is worth to the Trust, as an advertisement, millions of dollars a year.

It was a bitter fight; I regretted at the time the folly of the Beef Trust, regretted that its savage, resourceful, cunning resistance forced the President to give the revolting facts to the country and the world. But now I am glad; for without that storm of national wrath raised by the Beef Trust's desperate struggle, we should never have got the Pure Food Law. It was the Meat Bill fight that forced the passage not only of the Meat Bill but of the Pure Food Bill as well.

What, after all, is the human meaning of this new principle that has written these laws? Merely this — that the people themselves are taking a greater part in their own government; that our industrial civilization, which frightens so many thinkers, is not making the people less important but actually is making the people more important; that the wisdom and righteousness of the masses is asserting itself in proportion as it is needed; that free institutions are being justified and proving themselves equal to all human problems; and that this Republic, established by the blood and lives of heroes, is being strengthened every day by the justice and intelligence of citizens.

To-day is better than yesterday; and to-morrow will be better than to-day. If not, our schools are failures, our churches mockeries, and our civilization hastens to inevitable tragedy.

What, now, are some of the new things we must do? Let us consider two or three, remembering that they are merely the advance of the people in the actual control of their own government. How fast we travel! Only yesterday in political campaigns we merely denounced the other party and praised our own. Only yesterday to

talk frankly of new questions on the stump was political
folly.   To-day in political campaigns party abuse is obsolete; and the open and honest discussion of problems
in the immediate future is political wisdom.

The first care of the people always is citizenship.   And
therefore governmental care first of all is for their children — the raw material for citizenship.   American pioneers reared school-houses as soon as they raised their
roof-trees.   American soldiers in Cuba and the Philippines turned teachers even as they stacked their arms.
Reverence for woman and the fostering of children are
the noblest of American characteristics.   We can say
with truth that we are not of that decadent breed which
regards not posterity.

Therefore we must have a child labor law in this Republic — not a clumsy, ineffectual tangle of state statutes,
but a national law covering the entire land.

To-day more than 1,000,000 American children, under
fourteen years of age, are doing men's work in factories,
mines and sweat-shops.   I do not object to children
working.   There is no training like labor.   But it must
be healthful and humane — not degenerating and brutal.
I myself worked from my twelfth year — worked as no
child should work.   But it was out of doors.   It was
in the fields glorious with the banners of the corn, frag-
rant with the smell of brown earth upturned by plow-
share, beautiful with the glory of the waving wheat.   It
was on the cuts and fills of building railways, with virile
surroundings — strong, rough but kind and simple men
all about me.   It was in the logging camps in touch with
the vitality, the silence and the wisdom of the forests.
It was hard work — bitter work; bending heavy and too

much for any child. And yet always above me was God's infinite dome of blue; always over me His golden sun shone by day, or His splendid clouds spoke of His protecting care; always above me at night His eternal stars kept their guardian watch; and always I breathed His life-giving and unpolluted atmosphere.

But such conditions are not true of the children I plead for. They draw into their lungs the poisons of the mine. They breathe the atmosphere of factory. They contract the contagion of the sweat-shop. They acquire the vile habits of the hopeless. They are spoiled for citizenship — ruined to be guardians of free institutions. And this must be stopped. We can not permit any man or corporation to stunt the bodies, minds and souls of American children. We can not thus wreck the future of the American Republic.

Shaftesbury said this a generation ago in England; but the English capitalists said that Shaftesbury was an "enemy of British prosperity"; and they rejected his counsel. To-day England can not raise an army of sound soldiers; and Curtis, the great correspondent, tells us that England is doomed by drink.

Such a fate must not — shall not — be America's fate. Protect free institutions, even if millionaires do not add other millions to what President Roosevelt calls their swollen fortunes. Save this Nation of men and women even if we halt the march of the Czars of wealth who are coining the blood of children into dollars. Manhood and womanhood with riches, if may be; manhood and womanhood without riches, if need be; but in any event, manhood and womanhood — this is our purpose and this is the reason for free institutions.

Why should these children be worked? The answer is cruel as it is true — to swell the profits of those who work them. But human souls are more important than profits. And there are some profits that have been and are too great.

I believe in full and overflowing reward for the mind and daring of those great masters of industry who develop mighty railway systems, create immense businesses, convert wildernesses into gardens and give employment to labor. Let all enterprise have its generous recompense. Let fortunes be builded, *no matter how great,* provided only they are honestly builded and are not the work of injustice and oppression. And let those fortunes be protected from demagogue or mob, from ignorance or passion.

But if vast masses of money are heaped up wrongfully; if tremendous riches in the hands of heirs who never earned a dollar go on increasing by their own power, as riches do; if the indifference and incompetence of these children of the rich do not work for the redistribution of their fortunes among the people from whom these came; and, finally, if these mighty accumulations become dangerous to the Republic, then first they must be regulated, and, second, limited.

One method is by an inheritance tax. It must and shall become a national law. Germany, France, even England are solving these intricate problems. Shall America, who first taught equal rights to all and special privileges to none, fall behind Europe, whose schoolteacher in human rights America was? The limitation and regulation of swollen fortunes; the more equal distribution of wealth and the destruction of unjust privileges that create it — these are matters requiring settlement.

This brings us to the tariff. I am a protectionist. The present law was fitted to conditions existing when it was passed. But it was passed ten years ago; and in that ten years more economic changes and greater industrial progress have been made than were made during the entire period from the Civil War to the election of McKinley.

Yet, so admirable is the Dingley Law, that with a few exceptions, it still answers the needs of the Nation. But in a few schedules it should be changed. And this, not alone because these few changes are needed; but also because, if they are not made, the whole law will be torn to pieces.

So, because we are protectionists and not fanatics, let us revise those schedules that everybody agrees need to be changed, first, in order to do our duty to the people; and, second, in order to prevent the whole system from being destroyed. Why do we have a periodical tariff revolution in America? Merely because needed changes are put off until so many accumulate that a purely economic mistake becomes a moral wrong; and when the moral sense of a people is aroused it often condemns the good with the bad.

If politicians and interests refuse to make individual changes when they ought to be made, and thus bring on the disaster of another tariff earthquake, *I want to put myself on record now as one of those who would have prevented that disaster. I want now to put myself on record as having told my " stand pat " friends that " a stitch in time saves nine."*

Some say: "You can not change one tariff schedule without changing all." Why not? There are hundreds of schedules in the law. When one needs change and others do not, why must we change those that need no change just because we change those that do need change? How absurd! And how untrue! Untrue, because we have practically proved the fallacy of the statement.

Did we not change the tariff on anthracite for a year without touching another schedule? Then why can we not change the tariff on steel without changing other schedules?

Why can not the people's government do in the people's business what every merchant does in his store, every manufacturer in his factory, every farmer on his farm — make changes when they are needed and as they are needed, and not years after they are needed?

The longer I am in public life the more I trust the wisdom of the masses. The people, I find, are thinking of their homes. The people, I find, are thinking how they can better their condition, put down injustice, build up civilization. The welfare of the people is our supreme concern.

That is why I was for railway rate legislation, pure food legislation, labor legislation. That is why I wrote the Meat Inspection Law. That is why I favor new child labor legislation, wealth legislation, tariff legislation. And that is why I favor legislation for primary reform in Indiana.

The candidates for office must, hereafter, be nominated by the people at the ballot-box instead of by politicians in conventions. If you people elect candidates, why should you not nominate candidates? The people have a right to elect whom they please to any office — for is not this the people's government?

But the people can not elect whom they please, because they must vote, not for candidates the people name, but for candidates conventions name. And sometimes these candidates thus named by conventions are selected by one or two men who manipulate conventions. Sometimes slates are arranged and put through without consulting the people or even the delegates.

Let the people really govern — not pretend to govern. Let the next Legislature pass a law putting all nominations for office in the hands of the people. And if your legislators, at their next session, do not pass such a law, ask them why? Put all party nominations, from Governor and Congressman down to precinct committeeman, in the people's hands. And make this not optional but compulsory. For under optional primary laws, nominations always are manipulated.

And let your choice for Senator be included. Your county officers are elected by the people. Are not your Senators as important as your county officers? Benjamin Franklin and most of the great men in our constitutional Convention thought so. It was chiefly the little men and the little colonies who thought otherwise — and the little men and the little colonies had the votes.

If your Congressmen, who pass only on laws, ought to be elected by the people, why ought not your Senators who pass not only on laws but also on treaties, be elected by the people? If we can not trust the people, whom can we trust? Is the average American legislature purer and more intelligent than the average American home?

There are those who shrink from these duties God demands us to do; those who close their eyes and ears to the mighty social and industrial questions; those who deny the validity of the question or the need of an answer. But what say human conditions to these self-made blind and deaf? What say the young men and women of America to these self-made blind and deaf? And human conditions and the young men and women of the Republic are the arbiters; for theirs is the future.

CHILD LABOR.*

Extracts from the debate in the Senate of the United States, Wednesday, January 23, Monday, January 28, and Tuesday, January 29, 1907.

The Senate having under consideration the bill (H. R. 17838) to regulate the employment of child labor in the District of Columbia, and the amendment proposed by Mr. Beveridge to prohibit the transportation by carriers of interstate commerce of the products of mines and factories employing child labor —

Mr. Beveridge said:

IT is to call the attention of this body and of the country to one of the gravest conditions confronting this Republic that I have risen to speak. I refer, Mr. President, to the employment of young children in factories, mines, and sweat-shops of this country.

The prevalence of this evil, I think, is hardly understood by the Senate. We have all of us been busy with other questions; and it is perhaps true that we know less than the people at large how far-reaching is this evil and how dreadful is its character.

* It is possible to give only extracts of this speech. A great volume of testimony was read by Senator Beveridge, two days being consumed in presenting affidavits which described the cruelty of child labor, its effect on health, on wages, on race deterioration, and showed the non-enforcement of state laws by states, etc. Also there was much debate throughout and the colloquies are necessarily omitted.

But I suppose that, little as we know about the matter, we are all familiar with the census figures. They are bad enough, but I shall demonstrate that they are far below the truth.

According to the census of 1900, there are not far from two million children in the United States under sixteen years of age working in " gainful occupations." Of these, according to the census of 1900, nearly *seven hundred thousand* are employed in industries other than agricultural.

This bill does not strike at the employment of children engaged in agriculture. Working children on the farm is good for them. Where children are employed within their strength and in the open air there can be no better training. All educators have now come to an agreement that the technical schools and the manual training schools in our cities are the best features of our educational system. I look forward to the time when, as part of the educational system of this country, children will be taught to work. There is no training like labor.

But, Mr. President, the evil at which this bill strikes is not such labor. It strikes at child toil, child *slavery* in mines, factories, sweat-shops.

The census figures, appalling as they are, are notoriously inadequate. Two million children under sixteen years of age is bad enough; seven hundred thousand in factories, mines and sweat-shops is bad enough; but there is not a man or a woman who has investigated this question who does not know that only a part of the children so employed were returned by the census enumerators.

Let me give the Senate some illustrations of the inadequacy of the census figures. For example, the cen-

sus of 1900 gives Maryland as having something over
5,000 children at work. The census bulletins of 1905
give 5,553 under sixteen at work in Maryland, of which
3,666 were in Baltimore.

Very well. In 1906 the Maryland law was amended,
requiring children under sixteen to secure permits testi-
fying to physical and educational requirements. The
law has been in force about five months and a half, and
already more than 11,000 permits have been granted and
between 1,200 and 1,500 refused; so we see that in Maryland alone the census of 1900 is more than one hundred
per cent. below the truth.

Again, the census bulletin in 1905, five years later
than 1900 gives the number of employees in cotton mills
in North Carolina as 31,231. The Labor Commission
of North Carolina gives 44,222 operatives, which would
make 52,025 for all the mills in the same ratio.

Again, it is estimated by the census of 1900 that the
total number of children employed in Southern cotton
mills, as for example, in North Carolina, Alabama, and
Georgia, is something under 30,000.

Yet the testimony of those who have investigated the
conditions upon the ground and who have not relied
exclusively upon the returns of manufacturers having
children in their employ is, that the lowest possible estimate, excluding children whose ages are questionable, is
at least 60,000.

So, Mr. President, we see that the census, terrible as
its figures are, is far below the truth. Anybody who has
studied this question knows why it is inaccurate. False
certificates, which are universal; the hiding of children
when the factory inspector comes; the exclusive reliance

of the census enumerator upon reports of interested parties; all these causes operate to give only a fraction of the awful truth.

Again, at the time mentioned the attention of the country had not been called to this evil. It is the conservative testimony of men and women who have given years of investigation to this subject that there are to-day, in this country, not less than 2,000,000 children at work, of whom *more than half are employed in factories, mines and sweat-shops.*

I suppose we may say, putting it upon a conservative basis, that as I speak to you there are now not less than 1,000,000 children under fourteen years of age (and I shall show by sworn testimony that some of them are seven, six and even *five* years of age) at work in the coal mines, in factories, and in sweat-shops of the Nation.

These are the figures, Mr. President; but figures give no idea of what this means. Figures can not, of course, describe it. Figures only give you an idea of its extent. I propose now to describe it. I propose to show to the Senate and the country precisely what it means; and I shall do this by the description of these children at work; of the manner in which their work is conducted; of its effect upon them; and in each instance I shall rely upon the testimony of eye-witnesses who have personally investigated this matter.

And, Mr. President, I shall not present a single statement that is not supported by an affidavit. I am perfectly well aware that no description of this evil will go unchallenged. Therefore, instead of stating facts by merely reading from an article and letting the statement go at that, as is our custom when debating, I have re-

solved to support each of the incidents which I shall give
by *the sworn testimony of the man or woman who gives
it.*

Then, if any of the great cotton factories, South and
North, if any of the mining interests in Pennsylvania
or elsewhere, if any of the railroad systems, if any
of the owners of glass factories think that they have
been injured by these statements, they will have an
opportunity to question men and women who will
stand the test of having made affidavit to the truth of
all they state.

The course of this argument will be this: First, to
state the facts; then to show the legality of the remedy
I propose. For if the facts convince the Senate that this
is a national evil of such a crying nature that it ought to
be cured; and if I can show that the method I propose
is within the power of Congress, of course the conclusion
is that the law must be enacted.

(At this point Senator Beveridge read a large number of descriptions of child labor collected from many sources. The facts in
each statement were sustained by the affidavit of the person who
investigated them.

The following, taken from *The Outlook,* and the accompanying
comment indicate the nature of the Senator's references.)

Mr. Durland says in *The Outlook:*

> Helen Sisscak, a wan mite of a girl, who spoke no English,
> told Judge Gray that she cleaned bobbins at *3 cents an hour.*
> *She went to work at half past six at night and worked until
> half past six in the morning.*

Here is a girl not nine years old, who for three cents
an hour begins work at half past six at night and works
until half past six in the morning. I tell the Senate that

if we do not give serious attention to conditions so in-human, we need not wonder at the creation of a class in this country which, when we contemplate its existence, makes every one of us tremble.

Mr. Durland continues:

> It took her nearly an hour to get from her home to the mill, and the road led across fields that were exposed to the storms that sweep down the valley.

Does the Senate find that amusing — a girl going a mile or more across a storm-swept valley to begin work *at half past six at night and work until six in the morning at three cents an hour?* If so, I shall present some examples from other states that perhaps will amuse the Senate still more.

Says Mr. Durland:

> I have gone over that very road in a winter afternoon when the bleak winds and snow were blowing from the hills, and it was a journey I should not care to make often. It was when this child had finished her story that Judge Gray exclaimed with much feeling: *"Here we actually find the flesh and blood of little children coined into money."*

Mr. Spargo gives the following description of child labor on the coal breakers:

> Work in the coal breakers is exceedingly hard and dangerous. Crouched over the chutes, the boys sit hour after hour, picking out the pieces of slate and other refuse from the coal as it rushes past to the washers. From the cramped position they have to assume most of them become *more or less deformed and bent-backed, like old men.*
>
> The coal is hard, and accidents to the hands, such as cut, broken, or crushed fingers, are common among the boys. Sometimes there is a worse accident. A terrified shriek is heard, and a boy is mangled and torn in the machinery, or disappears in the chute, to be picked out later smothered and dead.

Clouds of dust fill the breakers and are inhaled by the boys, laying the foundations for asthma and miners' consumption.

I once stood on a breaker for *half an hour* and tried to do the work a *12-year old boy* was doing day after day, *for ten hours at a stretch,* for 60 cents a day.

The gloom of the breaker appalled me. Outside the sun shone brightly; within the breaker there was blackness, clouds of deadly dust enfolded everything, the harsh, grinding roar of the machinery and the ceaseless rushing of coal through the chutes filled the ears.

I tried to pick out the pieces of slate from the hurrying stream of coal, often missing them; my hands were bruised and cut in a few minutes. I was covered from head to foot with coal dust, and for many hours afterwards I was expectorating some of the small particles of anthracite I had swallowed. *I could not do that work and live;* but there were boys of *10 and 12 years* of age doing it for *50 and 60 cents a day.* Some of them had never been inside of a school; few of them could read a child's primer.

Mr. Owen Lovejoy gives the following description of the same labor:

One group of little men, a picked squad from a company of twenty boys, only three *of whom claimed to be old enough to meet the legal requirements of employment,* were induced to tell the truth to one who was neither an "inspector" nor a "truant officer."

And their answers were as follows:

"Nine; goin' on 10."

"Nine years old."

"Ten; goin' to be 11."

"Nine last June."

"Ten; goin' for 'leven."

An examination of the school records confirmed the statement of the boys. Relations of almost intimate friendship sprung out of a brief visit to this breaker, due, perhaps, partly to the courage the boys may have ascribed to a stranger who would venture into the place of their daily labor.

The coal at this breaker is cleaned "dry," and the dust arises in a cloud that hovers above the building sometimes *for an hour after the day's work is done.* The boys wear mine lamps in their caps.

That is in the daytime, you understand.

Here twenty-two boys were interviewed at the noon interval, of whom all were under 14 years except one Scotch boy — 14 — whose age by the school record was found to be 10, and one Irish boy of 15, who has been out of school for over six years. Of the others, one was 9 — 8 by the school record — three were 10, two were 11, six were 12, and three were 13, although the school record showed one of the 13-year-old boys to be 11.

Now, Mr. President and Senators, mark the ages — 8, 9, 10, 11, 12 — although the law of that state requires that it shall be 14 at the minimum and 16 at the maximum for certain kinds of work in the mine.

Now, what kind of work is it that boys of that age are doing? Let us find out. Mr. Lovejoy tells us:

For nine hours a day these little fellows toil in the breaker, bending over the coal chute, with their feet in the coal, picking out the rock and slate. We are often asked whether this air is bad for the health! A five-minute visit to such a breaker will coat the lungs and throat with a black dust which twenty-four hours of pure air can not clear from the mucous linings.

This nine-hour day is broken by the dinner "hour," beginning in some breakers at 12.05 and ending at 12.25! — allowing the boys twenty minutes to swallow the contents of their dinner pails, with unwashed hands and dust-filled throat and lungs — and this is the visitor's opportunity.

Mr. Lovejoy, from having experience in the mines, from having gone into the breaker and trying to do a boy's work, describes just what that means. He says:

To sit bent over a stream of coal which pours out a cloud of dust so thick that the light can not penetrate; to be responsible for the exact separation from the coal of all slate and rock, depending often entirely upon the sense of touch, to endure the incessant rattle of deafening gigantic machinery; to suffer the

> stifling summer heat and the choice between the blasts that
> sweep these mountain tops and the cloud of smothering dust in
> the winter; to be conscious that the "boss" stands behind with
> a stick or small piece of coal to prompt to duty if the natural
> exuberance of childhood breaks out in playfulness or if back-
> ache induces a moment of forgetfulness; to have the hands cut
> and crippled and hardened by contact with the rough stones
> and bits of sharp-edged coal; to learn to control the nausea
> caused by swallowing quantities of coal dust, and by the feel-
> ing that one's throat and lungs are never clean —

That is the description of the work that these boys are
called to do in the breakers.

Mr. President, I wonder if when people find what they
call a "clinker" in their coal, they know just what that
means? This is what it means: It means that one boy's
eye has become dimmed after nine hours' work; that his
fingers are bleeding, and he has neglected to get out the
slate or the slag, which it is his business to pick from
among the coal, and that, going into the coal and finally
going into our furnaces, constitutes a "clinker."

So every time you find a "clinker" in your grate or
stove you may know that it represents the utter exhaus-
tion of a boy from 8 years old to, perhaps, 14 years old.

Then Mr. Lovejoy, who is a very conservative writer,
as you may judge from what he says, continues:

> If these were isolated instances of premature child labor, there
> would still remain cause for a protest against that which sacri-
> fices life for gold, for the progress of the race waits breathless
> upon the unfolding of every human life.
> But this appropriation of the days of childhood to the service
> of material gain *is a settled policy* of the coal region; against
> which the best public sentiment has hardly ventured to express
> disapproval.

Mr. Durland thus describes child labor in the silk mills:

The perpetual click of the rattling looms, the whir of belts, the crunch and rumble of wheels made a deafening din. The looms moved so regularly that I found my eyes easily tired watching them. It needed only a few moments of fixed gazing to appreciate the story told by one little girl who had had to quit the mill.

"When I first went to work at night the long standing hurt me very much. My feet burned so that I cried. My knees hurt me worse than my feet, and my back pained all the time.

"My eyes hurt me, too, from watching the threads at night. The doctor said they would be ruined if I did not stop the night work. After watching the threads for a long time *I could see threads everywhere* —

"When I looked at other things there were threads running across them. *Sometimes I felt as though the threads were cutting my eyes.*"

No wonder. She had been working twelve hours at night, looking at the ceaseless play of the threads; she was 9 years old; she had been standing on her feet; and this is going on in a country about which we make earnest and passionate Fourth-of-July orations.

Miss Irene Ashby gives this picture of work in the cotton mills:

During the latter half of December, 1900, and the first half of January, 1901, I visited *twenty-four* cotton mills in sixteen cities and villages of Alabama. I was prepared to find child labor, for wherever easily manipulated machinery takes the place of human muscles the child is inevitably drawn into the labor market, unless there are laws to protect it. But one could hardly be prepared to find in America to-day *white* children, *6 and 7* years of age, working for *twelve hours* a day — aroused before daybreak and toiling till long after sundown, in winter, with only *half an hour* for rest and refreshment.

I would not read the following if I did not have another witness to this fact —

One evening in December I stumbled through a totally un-lighted mill village, falling by the way into ditches and deep ruts, and knocked at the door of one of the wooden huts where I saw a light. I asked the woman who opened it if I might come in. Assenting, she ushered me in. She was surrounded by a brood of very small boys, and her consumptive husband sat beside the fire. The smallest child, a poor little fellow that looked to be about *6 years old,* nestled up to me as I talked to them. All worked in the mill except the mother, they told me.

" Not this one ! " I exclaimed, looking down at the wee, thin boy beside me.

" Why, yes." He had worked *for about a year;* the year be-fore he worked forty *nights.* He was *nearly* 8 years old. They left that mill because the night work was too hard on the chil-dren.

In answer to a query from me, the child said that he could scarcely sleep at all in the daytime.

At one place I heard of children working on the night shift, *turned out* for some fault *at 2 o'clock in the morning,* allowed by a compassionate clerk to go to sleep on a bench in the of-fice, as they were afraid to go home.

Ladies told me, too, of a common sight in the mill cottages — children lying *face downward on the bed sleeping with ex-haustion, just as they had come in from the night shift, too utterly weary even to remove their clothes.*

That is not on the coal breakers of Pennsylvania or in the cotton mills of the North. These are not foreigners' children. These are *American* children working in the South to-day. Continues Miss Ashby:

Often the whole family, except the baby actually in the cradle, is in the mill.

I have *seen* a boy *under 4* beginning his life of drudgery by pulling the yarn off bobbins to make bands.

Turning back once more to the purely human aspect of this uncivilized system I would say that no array of facts and fig-ures is needed by those who have *seen* it in operation. I am familiar with the slums of two continents, but I can say I have never seen a more pitiful sight than the mill children, nor known little ones for whom the outlook was more hopeless.

It is not only that they are pale, shrunken, and bowed — they look as if their brains were hypnotized and their souls paralyzed. A friend of mine in Atlanta, thinking to give some of these little victims a treat, asked a number out to her place in the country and turned them into the woods to play. What was her distress and amazement to find that *they did not know what the word or the thing meant.*

American children, not foreigners as in Pennsylvania and in New England, but American children in the Southern States that do not know what " to play " means. I shall quote some more from this book when I come to an examination of the impossibility of the States handling this evil.

Mrs. Van Vorst gives scores of typical examples of which two are quoted. She says:

A little girl had worked *twelve hours a day and was too tired to stand.*

She sank down beside me, leaning back against the post of the door-steps. Her face was hardly less white than the knitted woolen " cloud " which covered her head.

" I am tired enough to sit down," she sighed.

" Do you get tired in the mill? " I asked.

" I reckon I do. We live up on the hill yonder, and when I first started to work it didn't seem nights like I ever could get home. Now I don't mind it."

" How long have you been at work? "

" Over a year."

" And how old are you? "

" Eleven."

" What are the hours in the mill? "

" About twelve a day, I reckon."

" Twelve? "

" Well, there's the first bell at *half-past 4* — that's for ringin' us up; then there's the second bell for breakfast; and they don't give us more than a few minutes to eat before they begin callin' us at 20 minutes to 6."

" And you get out at —— "

" Twenty minutes a-past 6."

A girl awakened at half-past 4 A. M.; in the mill at 6; working all day until half-past 6 P. M.

Here is the case of a boy laborer. This is the best description of the best child that Mrs. Van Vorst specifically describes:

> His legs and arms protruded, bare and lank, from clothes long since outgrown, and his whole attitude expressed such physical exhaustion that instinctively I exclaimed to the woman who waited at the door-step:
>
> "Is that your boy?"
>
> Perhaps she detected something more than curiosity in my tone, for she answered:
>
> "Yes, mam. He's been sleepin'. He's on fer *night work* neow."
>
> He had never had a book in his hands or "scratched a line," as his mother put it; he had had no contact with that outside world of imagination and learning in which the rest of us dwell. He had been for years up before dawn and plied in the *service of a machine for twelve hours a day;* he had spent his childhood as a laborer, a bread winner, who earned food and shelter not only for himself, but for another; he had lived without pleasure, without amusements, without hope.

This boy was 15 years of age, and had begun to work at 7. He could not read or write and insisted that next year he was going to school. He was helping to support his mother. He was a fine type of boy.

Mr. Bacon: If the Senator will pardon an interruption at this point —.

Mr. Beveridge: I shall be glad to have the Senator's interruption.

Mr. Bacon: It is a very great injustice to present these isolated instances as representative of general conditions.

Mr. Beveridge: The Senator says that these are " isolated " cases. On the contrary, they are *typical* cases. The Senator will have an opportunity to disprove them if they are not true. Every one who has made these statements has made, or will make, an affidavit as to their truth.

When the Senator says that these are exceptional cases, what does he say about the estimate that there are to-day some 60,000 children 14 years of age or under that work in the cotton mills of the South? That is the fact, and the census figures themselves six years ago, when the industry was only in its infancy, showed there were some 30,000 children under 16 years of age working in the factories in the South. Does the Senator think that 30,000, does he think that 60,000 child slaves are " isolated " or " occasional "? It looks to me as though they are usual.

Before I get through I will take up other states. I will do so because the Senator seems to think we are not dealing with a great national evil, with a great sociological and humanitarian question.

Senators seem to think that they are the attorneys of the states here, and that when something is mentioned in which their states are named they must get up and denounce and deny it.

I am sorry I have to mention the fact that this occurs in Pennsylvania or New Jersey or Maine or Georgia or any other state. It is the evil I am after, and it is the evil that the American people are going to stop.

Mr. Elbert Hubbard gives the following personal experience in the cotton mills of South Carolina :

Boys and girls from the age of *6 years* and upwards are employed. They usually work from *6 o'clock* in the morning until 7 at night. For four months of the year they go to work before daylight and they work until after dark.

At noon *I saw* them squat on the floor and devour their food, which consisted mostly of corn bread and bacon. These weazened pigmies munched in silence *and then toppled over in sleep* on the floor in all the abandon of babyhood. Very few wore shoes and stockings; dozens of little girls of, say, 7 years of age wore only one garment, a linsey-woolsey dress. When it came time to go to work the foreman marched through the groups, shaking the sleepers, shouting in their ears, lifting them to their feet, and in a few instances *kicking* the delinquents into wakefulness.

The long afternoon had begun — from a quarter to 1 until 7 o'clock they worked without respite or rest.

That reminds me of what I read to the Senate concerning the silk girl of the Pennsylvania mill, who watched the thread until at night she could not sleep for seeing the threads that seemed to burn into her eyeballs. Mr. Hubbard continues:

They could not sit at their tasks. Back and forward they paced, watching with inanimate, dull look the flying spindles. The roar of the machinery drowned every other sound — back and forth paced the baby toilers in their bare feet and mended the broken threads. Two, three, or four threads would break before they could control the 20 feet — the threads were always breaking.

The noise and the constant looking at the flying wheels reduce nervous sensation in a few months to the minimum. The child does not think; he ceases to suffer.

* * * * * * * * * * * * *

He does his work like an automaton; he is a part of the roaring machinery; memory is seared; physical vitality is at such low ebb that he ceases to suffer. Nature puts a short limit on torture by sending insensibility.

* * * * * * * * * * * * *

At a certain night school where several good women were putting forth efforts to mitigate the condition of these baby

WORN-OUT BODIES

slaves, one of the teachers told me that they did not try to teach the children to read; they simply put forth an effort to arouse the spirit through pictures and telling stories. In this school *I saw* the sad spectacle of *half the class* — of a dozen or more — *sunk into sleep* that more resembled a stupor. The teacher was a fine, competent woman, but worn-out nature was too much for her. To teach you must make your appeal to life.

* * * * * * * * * * * *

Then he describes some of the other children he met, and here is an instance he gives. I want to say to the Senator from Georgia, about this evil being sporadic, that if I had given merely a large number of *figures* and nothing else it would have been said there is no inhumanity in that. "It is a good thing for children to work," we hear. "I worked," one Senator says, "and I have succeeded," etc.

So I have given specific instances, which are typical, because I wanted to place the finger on definite cases, at definite places, to show just what a child 6 years old working twelve hours a day does, and what such labor means. That is the reason I have read these descriptions that shock the Senator and will shock the country.

Mr. Hubbard grows specific and particular. He says — and *under oath,* don't forget that:

> I thought to lift one of the little toilers to ascertain his weight. Straightway through his 35 pounds of skin and bones there ran a tremor of fear, and he struggled forward to tie a broken thread. I attracted his attention by a touch and offered him a silver dime. He looked at me dumbly, from a face that might have belonged to a man of 60, so furrowed, tightly drawn, and full of pain it was.

That sounds precisely like the description that Durland gives, that Roberts gives, that Spargo gives, that Mrs.

Kelley gives, that Mrs. Van Vorst gives, that Miss Ashby gives. Can it be that all these men and women, as reputable and intelligent as any in this country, have told an untruth, *and then made affidavit to it?*

These witnesses say these examples are *typical* and not occasional. But of course all these people, who probably never saw one another, and who investigated independently, agreed in some mysterious way, some psychical way, to tell *the same lie,* and then, acting separately, have the audacity to swear to that lie. So Mr. Hubbard goes on:

> He did not reach for the money. He did not know what it was. I tried to stroke his head and caress his cheek. My smile of friendship meant nothing to him. He shrank from my touch as though he expected punishment. A caress was unknown to this child, sympathy had never been his portion, and the love of a mother, who only a short time before held him in her arms, had all been forgotten in the whir of wheels and the awful silence of a din that knows no respite.
>
> There were dozens of just such children in this particular mill.
>
> A physician who was with me said that they would all be dead probably in two years and their places filled with others. There were plenty more.

(A large number of other witnesses were quoted by Senator Beveridge, each one having made affidavit to the truth of his or her statements and giving similar examples to the above.)

It is said that certain interests even now are at work opposing this bill. Three-fourths of the cotton factories of the Southern States are determined that it shall be defeated — not all of them, Mr. President, for, I thank God, there are some mill-owners in the South who would rather have less money and more conscience, who employ children only because their competitors do, and who pray for the passage of this bill.

But it is safe to say that three-quarters of that tremendous industry, the extent of which you may see by looking at the map on my left, will resist this measure — are resisting right now.

It is said that the great Southern Railway system, a large part of whose business and a good fraction of whose profits come from these cotton mills, is also against this or any similar reform.

It is said that the enormous coal industries of Pennsylvania with their immense power, and the railroads that gridiron that portion of the state, and that carry the products of those mines — the Pennsylvania, the Lehigh Valley, the Delaware and Lackawanna, and the Delaware and Hudson — will also oppose and are now opposing it.

And these are not all. As this debate proceeds if it becomes necessary, indeed, if I have time and the geographer has time, maps will be presented showing the location of other industries and the extent of other interests which will fight this most humane of measures.

Mr. President, we are told this whole matter is a vast exaggeration; that the extent of child labor is not nearly so great as sympathetic persons are stating it to be; and that the allegations of cruelty are not borne out by the facts. But *the facts* which I give are susceptible of *proof in a court of justice.* With these facts before us the country can judge us if we do not act — *will* judge us if we do not act.

Mr. Spooner. Does the Senator think he is any more earnest in the discussion of Child Labor than the remainder of his colleagues?

Mr. Beveridge. Yes; I think a good deal more earnest than some.

Mr. Spooner. I doubt the Senator's accuracy.

Mr. Beveridge. I think I am more earnest — a good deal more. I have been earnest enough to spend nights and days and weeks and months in accumulating testimony. I have been earnest enough to appeal to the American people all over the country during the last campaign, from as far west as Nebraska to as far east as Maine. Has the Senator done as much?

* * * * * * * * * * * * *

Mr. Durland says this about the effect of child labor on health:

> Consumption, bronchial affections, anemia are all common ailments among the children of the mills. Their vitality is sapped. They enter the period of womanhood frail and worn out. Yet these are the women expected to bear sons who will carry on great industries that the state may prosper.

Mrs. Van Vorst, in the Philadelphia *Saturday Evening Post* of May 5, 1906, says:

> There is a wearing out among the mill hands, a gradual breaking down, an inward unhappiness, a sensibility different in kind from what ours would be under similar circumstances, because of the opposite esthetic chord to which their tastes have been attuned, but no less than ours in degree, and keen enough to make of their lives and of their children's lives one long, slow martyrdom.

Mr. Hubbard says — and don't forget that all this is under oath:

> Pneumonia carries off most of them. Their systems are ripe for disease, and when it comes there is no rebound, no response. Medicine simply does not act.

(A large number of similar examples were here quoted by Senator Beveridge — all under oath.)

Mr. President, we have seen that the evil exists. We have seen that it is not " isolated," as the Senator from Georgia says. We have examined instances which are typical, which are not two, five, six, ten, a dozen, a hundred, but thousands. We have all this given to us by men and women who have made oath that they themselves personally investigated the facts.

Now, what does it mean? In the first place, Mr. President, I have read one or two statements, under oath, that it means the literal death of these children. I have here, and shall put into the Record, abundant statements that it means the physical ruin, the mental and moral ruin, of the children who are not killed outright.

Mr. President, we might waive consideration of the ruin of the children themselves (millionaire manufacturers must get still more blood-made millions); but we are confronted with a far graver consequence — the deterioration of the race, the production of a degenerate class in this Republic.

According to the lowest — the very lowest — estimate, we are now pouring into American citizenship every year at least 200,000 London " Hooligans," boys and girls, who are broken in body and stunted in mind and soul, and who *know* it, and who are living engines of hatred toward society — and I do not blame them. And these become the parents of still other degenerates. We hear talk about the dangers of the " lower classes." Had we not better do something to stop the production of those " lower classes," those " dangerous classes? " Anyhow, I shall try to stop it.

Mr. President, the danger to national efficiency is be-

fore us. Great Britain is an example of a condition
precisely such as I have detailed — a condition that has
shocked mankind. The world did not know about it —
England herself did not know about it until the
United Kingdom had to meet 28,000 Boer farmers in
South Africa.

You will remember the newspaper accounts of the
unprecedented difficulty in getting soldiers for the English service, the descriptions of how small and feeble
were those obtained. Her army was the poorest ever
sent by England to a battle-field.

This began to come out. First there was a report
on the war — just a report on the war. And in this
report, commanding officers, in spite of their desire to
make their troops appear as well as possible, were truthful enough to say things like the following. I read
from the official report of the war made to the British
Government by Professor Ogston, in charge of the
service, who saw the men from the hospital point of
view:

> " Some of the regiments, especially some of the militia regi-
> ments, were physically very inferior. In one expedition, where
> a regiment was expected to take part in an advance, over 300
> of them — 380, I think — were sent for examination as to their
> physical fitness, and 212 of that part of the regiment so sent for
> examination were rejected as *unfit to sustain the toils of a
> march* and as being liable to disease."

*The Director-General says that from forty to sixty
per cent. of all the soldiers that England recruited for
South Africa in the Boer War were unfit for service.*
Over thirty per cent. of all attempted to be recruited
were rejected, *although the standard was purposely low-
ered by the British authorities.*

That was not the worst. Of those accepted two per cent. were almost immediately found unfit for military duty. And even that was not the worst; in the field, it was found that large numbers of them, when it came to going to the firing-line, *were incapable of the march.*

Still that was not the worst. Of those who actually got to the firing-line, fighting with that ancient British pluck never exceeded in history, thousands were swept off like flies with enteric fever.

The Sessional Papers of the British Government, showing these rejections, startled British statesmen as nothing has startled them in a hundred years. Think of these figures — I read from the Sessional Papers. Number medically inspected in 1897, 59,986; total rejections, 22,813; 1898, 66,501 medically inspected; number rejected, 23,287.

But even these figures do not represent the number of rejections. These were the rejections *only* of those who were taken by the recruiting officers and who were *medically inspected.* But the statement is made in these Sessional Papers that vast numbers of men were rejected offhand *by the recruiting officers and never were medically inspected at all.*

Of those who were "*passed*" by the recruiting officers and *afterwards* medically inspected, an average of *more than thirty-three per cent. were rejected.* The cause of these rejections were "undersize," "narrow chest," "bad teeth," "bad vision," "flat feet," and other causes that showed physical and racial deterioration.

When this was brought to the attention of the British nation it confounded British statesmen. They were suddenly face to face with the fact that, *upon land,*

England has not the men to meet any first-class nation.

They were suddenly confronted with the fact that while they had become the mistress of the seas in commerce, they had lost something of greater value. And so a commission was appointed to examine into and report upon the cause of this physical deterioration of the British people.

It was found that a general physical deterioration of the people, which had been revealed first by the lamentable lack of ability to meet the Boers in the field, did exist.

It began in England one hundred and fifty years ago with the invention of the spinning machines and bore its fruits in the Boer War.

Precisely the same process that is going on in Pennsylvania, in New York, in South Carolina, in Georgia, in North Carolina, in West Virginia, in New Jersey, and other states of the American Republic to-day was going on in England a hundred and fifty years ago.

As soon as the factories started up in England in the eighteenth century the mill-owners found themselves in exactly the condition in which the Southern mill-owners find themselves to-day. Word for word they used the same arguments to get the children into the mills. They soon found that the nimble fingers of the children could do the work of attending to the machines better than those of adults. Also they soon found that children were more " tractable," more easily " managed," and above all other things, *that they were cheaper.*

And so, first, the orphanages were emptied into the mills; and then the country was invaded by the mill-owners, just as to-day in the Southern states the hill people are being drawn from their farms to the factories. The strongest people from the country were induced to go to the factory towns. They left the inferior country people on the farms to run the farms and raise up the future yeomanry of the Empire.

These stronger young men and young women coming into the factories soon degenerated in health, and they produced children who were weaker still. And so the process went on from bad to worse.

Gradually there grew up in England a hundred years ago an agitation like that growing up in America now. It was resisted by British factory owners, as the agitation here is now being resisted by our factory owners. Sir Robert Peel began the reform in 1802. He did not succeed very well; but finally he got the Peel Bill passed, into the details of which, for lack of time, I can not enter.

This was succeeded by the agitation which resulted in the Sadler bill, limiting the hours of work to ten. In the treatment of this bill, we see again the experience of England parallel with our own. The manufacturers resisted the Sadler bill in every way they could. Finally they said: "This bill is being passed upon vague representations; upon the clamor of working-people; let us investigate it; let the whole subject be investigated."

Of course they knew it would take a year or two in which to "investigate," and in the meantime their enormous profits would go on. They carried their point. But so terrible were the conditions, and the report of the investigation committee so alarmed the nation, that the manufacturers aligned themselves for the purpose of delaying and, if possible, defeating action on that report. For the report showed conditions even worse than had been represented, just as the report of the " investigation " of this crime here in America, in the twentieth century, will show, if it is an honest report of a *thorough* investigation.

Finally, the cause of the labor-ridden children of England was taken up by a man whom every reader of English history loves and applauds — John Ashley, Earl of Shaftesbury. He gave his whole life to it. He gave up his official place; society turned against him; his noble associates reviled him. He was of the highest nobility of England. They all deserted him. " Shaftesbury," said England's better classes — England's " best people," to repeat the favorite phrase of the Senator from Georgia —" Shaftesbury," said they, " has joined the ' lower classes.' "

They did not succeed in stopping the outrage for seventy-five years — these English " reformers," these English sympathizers with the despised " common people," these English lovers of humanity; and it was not until perhaps twenty-five years ago that the evil was ended. The methods of resisting the reforms that are put forward here to-day were put forward there a hundred years ago, and down until a generation ago.

Does any man think that England pursued a wise policy? I hold in my hand the original notes of the statements by certain mill-owners in North Carolina, in resisting the improvements in North Carolina's wretched child-labor bill, all of which improvements the manufacturers of North Carolina defeated. One of them says: " We want more mills. It is all right to work the children. England is building more mills; and she has become the money center of the world and the commercial mistress of the seas."

Well, Mr. President, England has become " the money center of the world," and she has become " the commercial mistress of the seas." But does anybody think that she has not paid too high a price? Does anybody think that the proud eminence upon which she stands in trade has not been bought too dearly when it has been bought at the sacrifice of men and women?

The Boer War can teach us, as well as England, a lesson. England can not meet *on land* a single first-class power to-day. That is the price she paid for becoming " the commercial mistress of the seas."

I respect capital. I respect property. I like to see wealth grow, both in respect to the individual and to our Nation; but I tell you we are thinking too much about money *as money*. We are thinking too much about prosperity *as prosperity*. The chief use of prosperity is not to put food in your stomach or clothes on your back or a roof over your head. That is an important use; but the great use of prosperity is that it gives you time and strength to think on righteousness and to write conscience into laws.

So we see that the result of the labor of children to-day is not only the ruin of their lives, but the certain deterioration of the race and the establishment of an ever-increasing degenerate class in America.

Mr. President, it must stop. I have heard it whispered about the corridors, and so have other Senators, that " we must not go too fast;" that " we must have an investigation." Oh, no; let us not go " too fast." The evidence is before the Senate of the slow murder of these children, not by tens or hundreds, but by thousands. But let us not " hasten " to their relief " too fast." Let us " investigate," just as the manufacturers of England insisted upon doing when they were confronted with the same kind of reform. " Why not investigate? " said they.

No, Mr. President, this abuse must be stopped and *stopped now!* We all agree upon that — anyhow, everybody agrees in *saying* that it must be stopped; " only," say some, " let us be careful about the Constitution." The Constitution, it appears, is a very mysterious instrument. But child labor has got to be stopped some way. How? The states can not stop it. I hear that " states' rights " is to be used as the excuse for killing this bill. I say there are no " states' rights " involved in this bill.

But suppose " states' rights " were involved, even a little bit; well, last year we passed the quarantine law. For a century the regulation of quarantine has been recognized to be exclusively within the province of the states. The effect of the law last year was to make a national quarantine system. Still, there was no resistance to it. The people were not willing to quibble; not willing to make a strained construction of the Constitution when yellow fever was knocking at their gates.

There was no resistance in the Senate. There was some resistance in the House, made purely upon the " states' rights " proposition that quarantine regulation was the province of the state, and that the National Government was taking the right to quarantine from the states. I was very greatly struck by a one-minute speech made in the House by Representative Davey, of Louisiana, who said he could not see, as he had seen, the ravages of yellow fever down there and "quibble about the Constitution."

The practical effect of the quarantine law and the true intent of the bill was that we should have a national quarantine system, because everybody saw how foolish the other system was. If yellow fever got into the port of Mobile, though it was kept out of the ports of other states, it would cross state lines just the same. Yellow fever does not know anything about state lines.

If we would not quibble about the constitutionality of the quarantine law to protect the people from yellow fever, which does not kill a hundred people in twenty years, we ought not to quibble about the constitutionality of a law to stop a practice that kills thousands of people every year, *and these people children.*

Mr. President, why is it that the states can not stop this evil? Because if one state passes good laws and enforces them, and another state does not, then the business men in the former state are at a business disadvantage in comparison with the business men in the latter state. The business man in the state that has the good laws suffers from the very righteousness of that state's laws; and the business man in the state that has bad laws profits by the very wickedness of that state's laws. It is common sense as well as Americanism that all business men beneath the flag ought to have equal business opportunities so far as the law can give them.

Mr. President, the next reason why the states can not handle adequately this question is because neither in this nor in any other important question have the

states ever succeeded in having uniform laws; and it
is clear that this evil can not be remedied unless there
are uniform laws upon it.

Suppose, for example, that Ohio passes an excellent
child-labor law and my state repeals ours. Instantly
every manufacturing establishment in my state would
drain child labor from Ohio to us; and thus the manufacturers of Ohio would be at a disadvantage in comparison with the manufacturers of Indiana.

Not only that, but if every single state in the Union
but one were to enact a good law and execute it, nevertheless the one state that did not and that continued
to permit the child labor infamy that now exists in
many of the states, would be ruining citizens not of
that state only, but citizens of the Nation also.

A child that grows up in New York and becomes a
citizen is not a citizen of New York alone; he is a citizen
of the Republic as well. The citizen of North Carolina
does not vote exclusively for North Carolina candidates;
he votes for the President of the Republic; he votes for
members of the Legislature that elect a National Senator;
he votes for a congressman. He is as much a citizen of
the Nation as he is a citizen of the state; and when any
system of labor or a lack of education ruins him for citizenship in the state he is ruined for citizenship in the
Nation.

So not only, Mr. President, does inequality of law
produce inequality of business opportunities, but by that
first inequality the ruin of citizens in any one state,
the murder of innocents in any one commonwealth, affects the entire Republic as much as it affects that state.

Senators who are sincerely anxious about the question

of the rights, dignity and future of the states must not also forget the rights, dignity and future of the Nation. We have no right to permit any state to produce in this Republic a degenerate class unfit for citizenship, if any exercise of our power under the Constitution can prevent it.

Now, Mr. President, there can not be any uniformity in state laws. There is not. I have before me an abstract of the state laws upon the subject of child labor. There are not six of them alike. Some states have no child labor laws at all; others are in a worse condition, because their laws are but pretenses at labor legislation, which make the people think that something has been done, when, as a matter of fact, nothing has been done; and the ruin that went on before without the sanction of the law continues with the sanction of the law.

The truth about it is that the states are incompetent to deal with this question. *You have got to have a uniform law.*

You must make the manufacturer feel that at any time, upon the application to a court of justice of any citizen who sees a child put to work whom that citizen knows to be under age, that manufacturer may be haled by the United States district attorney before the United States district court, and compelled to face the prison bars. That will insure the manufacturer's watchfulness.

If you depend upon the parents to furnish certificates and thus allow the manufacturers to obtain the labor of these children, of course you can not get laws enforced; but when the manufacturer *himself* knows that he must err if he errs at all, upon the right side, and that if he errs upon the wrong side, he will find the penitentiary open to him as a consequence, he will take good care that he does know the age of the children whom he employs.

Mr. President, another reason why the states can not care for this matter is that in those states where this evil is worst — and I shall not now name them — the great interests, that are becoming rich from this practice, have all been powerful enough to prevent righteous legislation. Time after time they have defeated such legislation in Pennsylvania and in every one of the southern states. Even when the pressure of public opinion becomes such that a law is passed, as in the case with the North Carolina law now, it is constantly violated.

Mr. President, I shall ask the Senate to permit me to present affidavits from a large number of persons concerning law violations in a number of these states, particularly in the southern cotton mills and among the coal-breakers of Pennsylvania.

These affidavits demonstrate the violation of state laws. Here is a typical affidavit that I will stop long enough to read:

UNITED STATES OF AMERICA, *District of Columbia:*

Personally appeared before me, a notary public, F. C. Roberts, who on oath says that in March, 1906, he was in High Point, N. C., representing the American Federation of Labor; that he saw there the children employed in a knee-pants factory in operation in that town; that many of them were from *10 to 12 years* of age, to all appearances, and that one little girl, named Carrie Morgan, whose father was employed in one of the furniture factories of that place, was about 8 years of age, according to a statement made to him by her father; that her father furnished him with the weekly pay envelopes, showing the wages paid Carrie Morgan for the three months preceding, and that these envelopes showed that the child was paid from 19 to 49 cents per week.

F. C. ROBERTS.

Sworn to and subscribed before me this 26th day of January, 1907.

[SEAL.] WM. A. EASTERDAY,
Notary Public, District of Columbia.

And, Mr. President, here (exhibiting) are the original pay envelops for Carrie Morgan, *8 years of age, working ten and twelve hours a day.*

There is particularly one affidavit to which I want again to call the Senate's attention, of the observation personally on a train by Mr. McKelway of a load of children being taken from Tennessee, they having been got by an agent from some of the other cotton mills and " shipped " to other portions of the South. I should like very much to have the Senate hear it.

UNITED STATES OF AMERICA, *District of Columbia, ss:*

Personally appeared before me this day A. J. McKelway, who on oath says that in December, 1905, he was on board a train going from Knoxville, Tenn., to Spartanburg, S. C.; that he saw on board the train an immigrant agent of an immigration association of South Carolina, who was in charge of a company of about fifty people bound for the cotton mills of South Carolina, whom the agent had induced to leave their homes in western Tennessee; that the agent told him that he had made seven "*shipments*" of these people for the cotton mills from Newport, Tenn., averaging fifteen to the "shipment;" that seven more "shipments" had gone from Cleveland, Tenn.; that *there were several agents at work besides himself,* and that he had shipped personally about 500 people to the cotton mills; that he, A. J. McKelway, talked with some of the children in the company; that Harrison Swan said that he was "*going on*" *10 years of age* and was going to work in the Four Mills, at Greenville, S. C.; that Charley Matthews and a little fellow with him of the same size said that they were about 9 years of age and were going to work in the mills;

that the agent told him that there were a plenty of children *6 and 8 and 10 years* of age in the South Carolina mills, because their parents lied about their ages; that in the summer of 1905 the Rev. Mr. Abernethy, a Methodist minister living at Clyde, in western North Carolina, told him, A. J. McKelway, that 1,500 people had taken the train at Clyde for the South Carolina cotton mills during the preceding year.

A. J. McKELWAY.

Subscribed and sworn to before me this 22d day of January, 1907.

[SEAL.]   EDGAR L. CORNELIUS,
                   Notary Public, District of Columbia.

I have before me Mr. Lovejoy's report of one of his investigations. His affidavit to its truth is already in the record. Mr. Lovejoy gives examples, with names, dates and places. Many of the names are foreign names; but because these victims are the children of foreigners, is that any reason why they should be ruined for citizenship?

If it strikes any Senator here that because they are foreigners, therefore the matter is minimized, I shall make even worse citations from that portion of the country where is found, as the Senator from South Carolina (Mr. Tillman) the other day most truthfully said, the purest strain of Anglo-Saxon blood to be found on the continent. I shall show by sworn testimony that those children are being ruined for citizenship, pure American strain though they be, as surely as are the foreign children in the breakers of Pennsylvania.

(Senator Beveridge here presented a large volume of affidavits of eye witnesses, showing the extent of child labor in the south, all these children being American children.)

We have had much of this session taken up with a discussion of the race question. We have had the assertion of the superiority of the white race made time and time again; the assertion that the white race would never yield to the black race. Yet the children who are at work in the southern cotton mills are from the white working-class of the South; and this terrible situation stares the South in the face that, *whereas the children of the white working-people of the South are going to the mill and to decay, the negro children are going to school and are in the way of improvement.*

It is not in the power of any man to keep " superior " by asserting superiority. I am glad to see the negro children going to school, but it is enough to wring the heart to think that day by day you are permitting a system to go on which is steadily weakening the white race for the future and steadily strengthening the black race for the future.

There is another thing which we on this side — the Republican side — might as well take into account. I have here the present tariff law. I was reading before I came up to the Capitol the tariff on cotton, the tariff on glass, the tariff on coal. I ask Senators, who, like myself are protectionists, with what grace can we go to the country asking that the tariff be continued on these things, when the industries in these lines are supported by cheap child labor?

There is a tariff on glass, and I am glad of it. There is a tariff on soft coal, and I am glad of it. There is a tariff on cotton, and I am glad of it; and I also know some of the percentages of the dividends that are made out of these industries. I ask Senators and I ask them solemnly, how are the people to have any patience with us when we ask that those tariff rates be maintained if we refuse to deprive the very men who profit by these rates of the additional commercial advantage of child labor?

I have given my warning to the South. I have given my warning to my fellow protectionists. And now I give my warning to labor; and I shall ask permission to put into my remarks numerous statements made under oath to prove the need of such a warning. I want the laboring men and women of this country to understand what every labor leader knows — and if he does not know it he is not fit to be a labor leader or any other kind of leader — *that child labor tends to bring down manhood wages and womanhood wages to the level of child wages.* You are not only killing your children, laboring men, but you are reducing your own manhood wages.

(Mr. Beveridge here presented many affidavits proving the non-enforcement of state laws everywhere, and of the effect of child labor on wages.)

Mr. President, I come now to the constitutionality of this proposed law.

Why was the Constitution adopted? Under the Articles of Confederation there was an utter breakdown of government, because each of the states imposed its own commercial regulations and because the commercial regulations of the several states were various and contradictory. It became necessary, if we were to have any government at all, to give Congress all the power of the states over the subject of regulating commerce, so far as concerned commerce with foreign nations and among the several states. So the power given to Congress, so far as interstate traffic is concerned, is as complete as the power of the state over state commerce.

This absolute power was given to Congress in the following words of the Constitution:

> "The Congress shall have the power to regulate commerce with foreign nations and among the several states and with the Indian tribes."

" To *regulate commerce.*" That phrase had a definite meaning at that time. Also, it had a popular meaning at that time; and *they were the same.* The laws concerning the " regulation of commerce " with which the colonists were familiar, with which the statesmen and lawyers of that day were familiar, were the laws of England, from which country we had recently separated.

Nobody will deny that. Very well. There were in existence at the time the Constitution was adopted some twenty-seven acts of the English Parliament in which the phrase " to regulate commerce " occurs. In each one of them those words meant *" prohibition "* of commerce in some form or other or in some article of commerce.

It was not very long after the Constitution was adopted until there arose the very question which we have raised here; the question as to whether under the commerce clause Congress had the power, in regulating commerce, to *prohibit* commerce in any article; and that was decided in the affirmative in the case which every lawyer has had by heart since he went to law school — Gibbon vs. Ogden, 9 Wh. 1. In his great opinion in that case Chief Justice Marshall took up the question of embargo laws, going on to show, first, that the power over interstate commerce is precisely *the same* as over foreign commerce.

In the embargo act, one of the very first acts passed,

Congress had exercised its power to prohibit commerce and that was done exclusively under the clause giving Congress power over foreign commerce. Says the Supreme Court:

> "When Congress imposed that embargo, which for a time engaged the attention of every man in the United States, the avowed object of the law was the protection of commerce and the avoiding of war. By its friends and its enemies it was treated as a commercial, not as a war measure. They (its opponents) denied that the particular law in question was made in pursuance of the Constitution, not because the power could not act directly on vessels, but because a perpetual embargo was the *annihilation,* and not the *regulation* of commerce. No example could more strongly illustrate the universal understanding of the American people on this subject."

Then Chief Justice Marshall gets more directly to the question of "prohibition." Speaking of and defining the power to "*regulate commerce,*" he says:

> "The power over commerce with foreign nations *and among the several states,* is vested in Congress as *absolutely as it would be in a single Government,* having in its constitution the same restrictions on the exercise of the power as are found in the Constitution of the United States."

That "regulation" included "prohibition" the Supreme Court soon decided directly in the case of the United States vs. Marigold, 9 How. 560. Congress had passed a law exclusively under the interstate and foreign commerce clause, prohibiting the importation of counterfeit coin, and providing a penalty for doing it. It was conceded that the only authority for the law was to be found in the clause regulating commerce among the states and with foreign nations.

Marigold imported some of this coin; he was indicted under this law, and he resisted upon the ground, among

others, that there was no authority in Congress to pass
such a law — that the power involved in such a law was
a police power of the state.   Says the Supreme Court in
deciding this question:

> " Congress is, by the Constitution, vested with the power to
> regulate commerce with foreign nations, and however at periods
> of high excitement an application of the term ' to regulate com-
> merce,' such as would embrace *absolute prohibition,* may have
> been questioned, yet since the passage of the embargo and non-
> intercourse laws and the repeated judicial sanctions those stat-
> utes have received, it can scarcely at this day be open to doubt
> that *every subject* falling within the legitimate sphere of com-
> mercial regulation may be partially or *wholly excluded* when
> either measure shall be demanded by the safety or by the im-
> portant *interests* of the entire Nation.
>
> " Such exclusion can not be limited to particular classes or
> descriptions of commercial subjects; it may embrace manu-
> factures, bullion, coin, or *any other thing.* The power once
> conceded, it may operate on *any and every subject of commerce*
> to which the legislative discretion may apply it."

That was a definite declaration which the casuistry of
no lawyer can escape that the power of Congress to
regulate commerce with foreign nations and among the
several states is absolute and includes the power to
" prohibit " *any subject* of commerce from interstate or
foreign commerce.

In 1808 a case was decided which is so important and
so historic a case that it is included in Professor Lang-
ley's two volumes on *Leading Cases in Constitutional
Law.*   It is United States vs. Brigantine *William,* 2 Am.
Law Journal, 255, the only case, I believe, in either the
district or circuit courts of the United States or the Supreme Court where the constitutionality of the embargo
laws was ever questioned.   The court sustained their
constitutionality and I will call the attention of the Sena-

tor from Rhode Island to the fact that it was sustained not under the taxing power, not under the war power, *but exclusively under the commerce clause.* The court says:

"'Congress shall have power to regulate commerce with foreign nations, and among the several states and with the Indian tribes.'

"Such is the declaration of the Constitution. Stress has been laid in the argument on the word 'regulate,' as implying in itself a limitation. Power to *regulate,* it is said, can not be understood to give a power to *annihilate.* To this it may be replied that the acts under consideration, though of very ample extent, do not operate as a prohibition of all foreign commerce.

"It will be admitted that partial prohibitions are authorized by the expression; and how shall the degree or extent of the prohibition be adjusted *but by the discretion of the National Government,* to whom the subject appears to be committed?

"Besides, if we insist on the exact and critical meaning of the word 'regulate' we must, to be consistent, be equally critical with the substantial term 'commerce.' The term does not necessarily include shipping or navigation."

The court goes on:

"Much less does it include the fisheries. Yet it never has been contended that they are not the proper objects of national regulation, and several acts of Congress have been made respecting them.

"It may be replied that these are incidents to commerce and intimately connected with it, and that Congress, in legislating respecting them, acts under the authority given them by the Constitution to make all laws necessary and proper for carrying into execution the enumerated powers.

"Let this be admitted, and are they not at liberty also to consider the present *prohibitory* system as necessary and proper to an eventful beneficial regulation? I say nothing of the *policy* of the expedient. It is not within my province. But on the abstract question of constitutional *power* I see nothing to prohibit or restrain the measure."

So we see that what the word " regulate " means was settled just exactly ninety-nine years ago this year.   Then the court proceeds a little further:

> "It was perceived that under the power of regulating commerce Congress would be authorized to abridge it in favor —"

How abridge?   What for, abridge?   Why ——

> "— abridge it in favor of the great principles of humanity and justice?
> "Hence the introduction of a clause in the Constitution so framed as to interdict a prohibition of the slave-trade until 1808.
> "Massachusetts and New York proposed a stipulation that should prevent the erection of commercial companies with exclusive advantages.
> * * * * * * * * * * * * *
> "It has been said in the argument that the large commercial states, such as New York and Massachusetts, would never have consented to the grant of power relative to commerce, if supposed capable of the extent now claimed.   On this point, it is believed, there was no misunderstanding.   The necessity of a competent National Government was manifest.   Its essential characteristics were considered and well understood; and all intelligent men perceived that a power to advance and protect the national interests necessarily *involved a power that might be abused.*"

The question of the *abuse* of power, which is the *only* real argument made against this bill, I shall discuss pretty fully in a moment.

The next case in which this absolute power of Congress, under the interstate clause of the Constitution, is sustained in equally emphatic and unavoidable language, is the case of the United States vs. Forty-three Gallons of Whiskey, 93 U. S., 188.

This was the case of a libel by the Government of forty-three gallons of whiskey that had been brought into the county of Polk, Minnesota. That county was not within an Indian reservation. It had nothing to do with the Indians any more than a county in Ohio or Indiana. But forty-three gallons of whiskey had been taken into that county, and some of it was sold to an Indian who happened to be a member of a tribe living in some other portion of the state.

The owner of the whiskey resisted the libel upon the ground that his act was done exclusively within a state, not even within the limits of an Indian reservation; that it could not possibly be any trade with an Indian tribe; that in any event Congress had no power to " prohibit " whiskey from commerce with Indian tribes; that *" prohibiting "* was not *" regulating* commerce " with the Indian tribes.

And so the question that we have here was directly before the court in the case of Forty-three Gallons of Whiskey. The whole question of the power of Congress under this clause was examined, and the court says:

> " Congress now has the exclusive and absolute power to 'regulate commerce' with the Indian tribes — *a power as broad and as free from restrictions as that to regulate commerce with foreign nations.*
>
> " The Indian country, as defined by the act of 1834, was at that date so remote from settlements that there was no occasion to extend the *prohibition* beyond its limits. It has since then been so narrowed by successive treaties that the white population is now all around it and regarding it with a wistful eye.
>
> " In view of this changed condition it would be strange indeed if the commercial power, lodged *solely* with Congress and unrestrained as it is by state lines, did not extend to the *exclusion* of spirituous liquors intended to corrupt the Indians not only from existing Indian country, *but from that which has ceased to be so by reason of its cession to the United States.*"

Mark you, the *power* of Congress to "regulate commerce" with the Indian tribes is *precisely the same* as is the power to "regulate commerce" among the several states.

Perhaps as important a case in its indirect holding as any is the famous Rahrer case, 140 U. S., 545, which grew out of a provision of the Wilson Bill; and this provision of the Wilson Bill grew out of the decision of the Iowa liquor cases, did it not? The Senator from Rhode Island (Mr. Aldrich) will remember.

In its direct motive it is probably as important as the Marigold case, or as the case of Leisey vs. Hardin, 135 U. S., 100 — the Iowa liquor case. In that case — Leisey vs. Hardin — the court held that the state of Iowa had no power whatever over the importation of liquor into that state so long as it was kept in the original package.

To meet that a provision was put in the Wilson Bill, that articles of interstate commerce should be subject to the laws of the various states. The Rahrer case arose in the state of Kansas, which prohibited the sale of intoxicating liquors. The question was brought up on a test case, where the liquor was in an original package, and an attempt to dispose of it was made by the agent of a dealer who lived in Kansas City.

The Kansas law was strengthened by the section of the Wilson Bill which subjected all articles of interstate commerce to the laws of the various states. Rahrer, who was resisting the law, said that it was unconstitutional because it violated that clause of the Constitution which gives Congress power over commerce among the states.

But the Supreme Court held that that had been obviated by the Wilson Bill subjecting all interstate commerce to the laws of the various states, and in so holding here is what the court said:

"By the adoption of the Constitution the ability of the several states to act upon the matter solely in accordance with their own will was extinguished, and the legislative will of the General Government substituted. No affirmative guaranty was hereby given to any state of the right to demand as between it and the other what it could not have obtained before; while the object was undoubtedly sought to be attained of preventing commercial regulations partial in their character or contrary to the common interests. And the magnificent growth and prosperity of the country attest the success which has attended the accomplishment of that object. But this furnishes no support to the position that Congress could not, in the exercise of the discretion reposed in it, concluding that the common interests did not require *entire freedom in the traffic* in ardent spirits, enact the law in question."

This amounts, as was pointed out in every law journal and discussion in the United States when the Rahrer decision was handed down, to a *prohibition* of commerce in liquors or in anything else, that Congress by law might subject to the laws of the various states.

Every state might have a law prohibiting the sale of spirituous liquors or of anything else — of child-made goods, for example; and if an act of Congress putting all subjects of interstate commerce under the operation of the state laws is valid, then Congress has in itself prohibited from interstate commerce this article. That was the conclusion that so excited the bar and the country.

The next case to which I wish to call the attention of the Senate is the Addyston Pipe Company vs. United States (175 U. S.) and I read briefly from page 228. I am showing now that the tremendous scope of this power of Congress over commerce has been held by the Supreme Court to mean the *prohibition of anything*.

In this case it was held that the Sherman anti-trust law, which prohibited the making of a contract, was entirely constitutional. The court said:

> "The reasons which may have caused the framers of the Constitution to repose the power to regulate interstate commerce in Congress do not, however, affect or limit the extent of the power itself."

This was said because the question had been asked of the court, that is so often asked here in debates upon legal questions that are very close, "What was the intention of the framers? Did the framers intend this? Did the framers intend that?" As a matter of fact the framers never foresaw steam or electricity. The framers never anticipated the telegraph. The framers did not anticipate the Interstate Commerce Commission. The Supreme Court says that what may have been the framers' *purpose* has nothing to do with the limit of the *power*. The Court goes on:

> "In Gibbons vs. Ogden (supra) the power was declared to be complete in itself, and to acknowledge no limitations other than are prescribed by the Constitution.
> "Under this grant of power to Congress that body, in our judgment, may enact such legislation as shall declare void and *prohibit* the performance of any contract between individuals or corporations where the natural and direct effect of such a contract will be, when carried out directly, and not as a mere incident to other and innocent purposes, to regulate to any substantial extent interstate commerce."

Now I come to the most important case upon this subject that the Supreme Court has ever decided. Everybody knows that it is the famous Lottery Case.

About 1895 or 1896 Congress passed a law *prohibiting* the transportation of lottery tickets by carriers of interstate commerce. A law had already been passed excluding them from the mails under the post-office and post-roads clause; but that law was not effective because lottery companies used the express companies to scatter the lottery tickets throughout the country.

Many laws have been passed *prohibiting* various articles from interstate commerce. None of these has been questioned so far as its constitutionality is concerned; for in those cases no great business was profiting by the transportation of the thing prohibited.

But in the Lottery Case there was an immense institution, richly profiting by that business. So, of course, the law was fiercely resisted. Not only did the attorneys for the lottery companies see their clients' interests in preserving their unholy traffic, but they saw the tremendous scope of the decision. They understood thoroughly that the Supreme Court's decision would be as epochal as McCulloch vs. Maryland (4 Wheaton, 316) — that it would make history.

It was contended in the Lottery Case, 143 U. S., 110, that the law was void for two reasons. One was that lottery tickets were not subjects of commerce any more than insurance policies are, and that therefore the case of Paul vs. Virginia decided the lottery-ticket question at its inception. For, of course, if lottery tickets were not subjects of commerce, then Congress had no power to pass laws excluding them from interstate commerce. So the Court said upon that point:

"We are of opinion that lottery tickets *are* subjects of traffic and therefore are subjects of commerce, and the regulation of the carriage of such tickets from state to state, at least by independent carriers, is a regulation of commerce among the several states."

The other ground upon which the law was resisted was that Congress had no right to *prohibit* anything from interstate commerce. I call the attention of the Senator from Rhode Island to that. Their contention was exactly what was in the Senator's mind a moment ago, when he said that the only power confided in Congress was the power to "regulate," and that the power to "regulate" did not involve the power to prohibit; and that therefore the law of Congress excluding lottery tickets from interstate commerce was not within the constitutional power of Congress. But again the Supreme Court held that the power to "*regulate* commerce" *does* include the power to *prohibit* specified articles from commerce. The Court says:

"But it is said that the statute in question does not regulate the carrying of lottery tickets from state to state, but, by punishing those who cause them to be carried, Congress in effect *prohibits* such carrying; that in respect of the carrying from one state to another of articles or things that are, in fact according to usage in business, the subjects of commerce, the authority given Congress was not to prohibit, but only to regulate."

The Supreme Court continues:

"The Constitution leaves to Congress a large discretion in executing a given power.

* * * * * * * * * * * *

"We have said that the carrying from state to state of lottery tickets constitutes interstate commerce, and that the regulation of such commerce is within the power of Congress under the Constitution. Are we prepared to say that a provision

which is in effect a *prohibition* of the carriage of such articles
from state to state is not a fit or appropriate mode for the
regulation of that particular kind of commerce?

"If lottery traffic, carried on through interstate commerce, is
a matter of which Congress may take cognizance and over
which its power may be exerted, can it be possible that it must
tolerate the traffic and simply regulate the manner in which it
may be carried on? Or may not Congress, for the protection
of the people of all the states and under the power to regulate
interstate commerce, devise such means, within the scope of
the Constitution, and not prohibited by it, as will *drive the
traffic out of commerce among the states?*"

Could there be a more direct and emphatic answer to
the arguments made here against this bill?

But still more decisive of our power to prohibit any
article from interstate commerce, is the fact that the
power of Congress over interstate commerce is precisely
the same power as that over foreign commerce. Does
any Senator deny that? Does any Senator, any lawyer contend that the power of Congress over interstate
commerce and over foreign commerce is not *precisely the
same?*

If any Senator does so contend, I am compelled to
quote other decisions of the Supreme Court to the effect
that *they are the same.* It is conclusive of this case, if
possible more conclusive even than the Lottery Case,
though that alone is decisive.

        *   *   *   *   *   *   *   *   *   *   *   *

I read from the great case of Crutcher vs. Kentucky,
141 U. S., 47. Up to that time it was undoubtedly one
of the most important deliverances, outside of those
made by Story and Marshall, ever made by the Supreme
Court. It was made by Mr. Justice Bradley, whose mas-

terful ability and attainments are familiar to every school-boy in the law.

The state of Kentucky required a license from the agent of express companies before permitting them to do any business in that state. Part of the business of the companies in that state was *state* business and part came in from *other* states. Of course the law wàs resisted, and the Supreme Court held that such a law was void because it interfered with the power of Congress over interstate commerce, which was *exclusively* in Congress. In discussing this power the Supreme Court used the following language:

> "It has been frequently laid down by this court that the power of Congress over *interstate commerce is as absolute as it is over foreign commerce.*"

Is that clear language?

And the court goes on — this is the Supreme Court of the United States speaking, mind you:

> "Who would pretend that a state legislature could prohibit a foreign corporation — an English or a French transportation company, for example — from coming into its borders and landing goods and passengers at its wharves, and soliciting goods and passengers for a return voyage, without first obtaining a license from some state officer, and filing a sworn statement as to the amount of its capital stock paid in?
>
> "And why not? Evidently because the matter is not within the province of state legislation, but within that of national legislation. (Inman Steamship Company vs. Tinker, 94 W. S., 238.) The prerogative, the responsibility, and the duty of providing for the security of the citizens and the people of the United States in relation to *foreign corporate bodies,* or *foreign individuals* with whom they may have relations of *foreign commerce,* belong to the *Government of the United States,* and not to the *governments of the several states;* and con.idence in that regard may be reposed in the National Legislature without any

anxiety or apprehension arising from the fact that the subject-matter is not within the province or jurisdiction of the state legislatures.

"And the same thing is *exactly* true with regard to *interstate commerce* as it is with regard to *foreign* commerce. No DIFFERENCE IS PERCEIVABLE BETWEEN THE TWO."

It is not necessary to comment upon that. Language can not be clearer and more explicit.

In Brown vs. Houston, 114 U. S., 622, the Supreme Court says:

"The power to *regulate* commerce among the several states is granted to Congress in terms *as absolute as is the power to regulate commerce with foreign nations.*"

* * * * * * * * * * * * *

In the case of Stockton vs. Baltimore, etc., Railway Company (32 Fed. Rep., 9), while the language is not so clear and emphatic, there are some things which ought to be quoted:

Says the court — and this judge was later one of the justices of the Supreme Court of the United States, and one of its greatest justices; I was taught, as a law student, to admire and revere him — says this great lawyer:

"We think that the power of Congress *is supreme over the whole subject —*"

Over interstate commerce —

"*— unimpeded and unembarrassed by state lines or state laws;* that, in this matter *the country is one,* and the work to be accomplished is *national,* and that state interests, state jealousies, and state prejudices do not require to be consulted. IN MATTERS OF FOREIGN AND INTERSTATE COMMERCE THERE ARE NO STATES."

Can human tongue frame language more emphatic than these words?

Now, I have cited from Chief Justice Marshall, in Gibbons vs. Ogden, clear down to 141 United States, the definite, clear, direct, unconfused statement of the Supreme Court that the power over foreign and interstate commerce *is the same.*

But if this is true we have already done all that I ask the Senate to do. Because in the Dingley law there is the following section:

> SEC. 31. That all goods, wares, articles, and merchandise manufactured wholly or in part in any foreign country *by convict labor* shall not be entitled to entry at any of the ports of the United States, and the importation thereof is hereby *prohibited.*

I have here in my hand a list of the members of the Finance Committee of the Senate and of the Ways and Means Committee of the House, who inserted this provision, and it was inserted *without any party division.*

No lawyer found anything unconstitutional in this, although *this* clause of the tariff law does not fall at all within the *taxing power;* it is *exclusively* under the power *over foreign and interstate commerce.*

Mr. President, I have shown that under the interstate commerce clause of the Constitution the Supreme Court has time and again held that it meant the power to prohibit the transportation in interstate commerce of such articles as in the judgment of Congress were inimical to the interests of the Nation. Accordingly we have prohibited many things from foreign commerce.

For instance:

In foreign commerce we have had our embargo laws;

We have prohibited the importation of slaves;

We have prohibited the importation of counterfeit coins;

And we have prohibited the importation of convict-made goods.

We have passed a large number of laws, many of them quite exceptional, prohibiting *interstate commerce* in certain articles.

For example, the act of August 2, 1882, *prohibits* the transportation in interstate commerce of nitroglycerin in any vessel. The question of its being an explosive has something to do with the *policy* of prohibiting it, but not with the *power* of prohibiting it, for we in the same law permit its transportation within the limits of a state.

The act of March 31, 1900, *prohibits* the transportation of explosive materials in any vessel or vehicle in interstate commerce.

The act of July 1, 1902, *prohibits* the introduction or sale by another state of dairy or food products which have been falsely labeled or branded, although such products had *nothing the matter with them,* so far as hurting the health of the people was concerned.

The only objection to oleomargarine was that if they colored it, although the color was entirely healthful, still it deceived the people. So we can not say it was affecting the health or the morals of the people and that therefore the *power* arose from that fact.

The *power* was exercised because it was absolute; and in the *policy* of Congress, we thought it was a wise measure and beneficial to the " interests of the Nation " to exercise that power, and so we did it.

The act of February 3, 1903, *prohibits* transportation in interstate commerce of cattle without a certificate from the inspector of the Agricultural Department. And this, although a man has an absolute right to his property, and his property amounts to nothing unless he can transport it; yet Congress, acting under the power of *prohibition* in the interstate commerce clause, has *prohibited* the transportation of cattle without a certificate *whether those cattle are diseased or wholesome.*

Then, again, we have the act of February 21, 1905. On examining the debate I find that the senior Senator from New Jersey (Mr. Kean), who now occupies the chair, was the Senator who had charge of passing the bill through the Senate. It *prohibits* the transportation in interstate commerce of *gold and silver goods* with the words " United States Assay " or any similar words.

And this was *solely* under the *interstate-commerce clause* of the Constitution. When the bill came in it was referred to the Interstate Commerce Committee. It was reported favorably by that committee. We had absolutely no power whatever to pass that law *except under the interstate-commerce clause of the Constitution.*

There was nothing whatever in the gold and silver goods that could hurt the morals of the people, as was the case in regard to lottery tickets. The purpose of that law was to protect some jewelry manufacturers of New Jersey and New York who did not want the words " United States Assay " put upon anything, and because those words had been put upon some importations of very excellent gold and silverware that were then sent through interstate commerce.

But if we have the power to *prohibit* from interstate commerce the transportation of gold and silver goods with the words " United States Assay " upon them, *which do not hurt the physical condition or morals of the people any place,* have we not a right to *prohibit* the transportation of child-made goods from interstate commerce, so far as the *power* is concerned?

What have Senators who are troubled about the question of our *power* to say about that law? Nobody questions that law.

Again, the act of March 3, 1905, *prohibits* the transportation of loose hay and other highly combustible materials on passenger steamers. That is *exclusively* under the *interstate-commerce clause of the Constitution* and not under any other provision of the Constitution whatever.

If as a matter of *power* we can *prohibit* the transportation of loose hay, the only reason for it being a matter of *policy* — it might get afire — why as a matter of *power* can we not *prohibit* the transportation of child-made goods? Does it not subserve the " interests of the Nation," as Chief Justice Marshall says, and is not more involved in the ruin of our citizenship than in the possible burning of a steamer or the possible affecting of the business of some watch factories in New Jersey and New York?

The act of February 21, 1905, *prohibits* the transportation by carriers of interstate commerce of obscene books, and this although the Constitution *expressly guarantees " freedom of speech;"* and it has been held that printing is as much " speech " as words spoken by the tongue.

Yet, although the Constitution absolutely guarantees " freedom of speech," nevertheless, in spite of that guaranty, we have *prohibited* the transportation in interstate commerce of obscene literature, although that is held by the courts to be " speech " as much as anything else. We did that under the *interstate-commerce clause* as a matter of *power,* because, as a matter of *policy,* it subserved the " interests of the Nation," as Marshall says.

The Act of March 3, 1905, *prohibits* the transportation in interstate commerce of quarantined cattle, this quarantine being established by the Agricultural Department within the United States. And this, mind you, although the cattle *might* be sound and their transportation and sale *" a matter of right,"* to use the language of the Supreme Court in the Lottery Case.

The Act of March 3, 1905 — and I call the attention of the junior Senator (Mr. Latimer) to this act — *prohibits* the transportation by carriers of interstate commerce of *insects* of a certain kind.

(At this point Senator Beveridge quoted a number of prohibitory laws, illustrating the power resident in Congress.)

So far as the question of *power* is concerned, in none of these cases did the *power* come from the evil of the article prohibited. As a matter of *policy* we enacted those laws because they were good for " the interests of the Nation," to quote the language of the Supreme Court.

But if it is good for " the interests of the Nation " to prohibit the transportation of insects from state to state; if it is good for the " interests of the Nation " to prohibit the importation of convict-made goods; if the power over interstate commerce equals the power over foreign commerce, as the Supreme Court has said; if we have the power to prohibit convict-made goods in interstate commerce, as we have; if we have actually prohibited the transportation of gold and silver merely because the words U. S. Assay upon them inconvenienced the business of certain men in New York and New Jersey — all this upon the theory that it affected the " interests of the

Nation," again to use Chief Justice Marshall's famous phrase; if we have the power to do all these things — and we *have* actually done *all* these things — who can question our power to prohibit the transportation in interstate commerce of goods made by ruining children, whose present and future condition affects " the interests of the Nation "— aye, and the perpetuity of the Nation?

Why did we not hear of " the danger of the extension of Federal power " when Congress was enacting these statutes? Why is it that only when we attempt to stop the murder of children and the debasement of our race and the ruin of our citizens by prohibiting the transportation of child-made goods in interstate commerce, Senators are aroused about " the danger of Federal power? "

Now, Mr. President, every question that has been put to me this afternoon has one argument as its basis, the argument of the abuse of power. The Senator from Wisconsin (Mr. Spooner) says:

" Well, if you can do this, can you not also compel all the people of the United States to join the labor union? "

And the Senator from California (Mr. Perkins) says:

" Well, if you can do this, can not you also pass a law prohibiting the transportation in interstate commerce of the labor of men and women over fifty? "

In short, if you admit the existence of the power at all, where, says the Senator from Wisconsin, will its exercise end? Mr. President, that very question was taken up very early in our judicial history, and answered.

Undoubtedly the greatest man that we ever had on the Supreme Bench of the United States was Chief Justice Marshall. The very same arguments were made to him.

After holding that the *abuse* of the power was no argument against its *existence,* the Supreme Court, through Chief Justice Marshall, delivering the unanimous opinion of the Supreme Court of the United States, disposed of this "grave objection," which so "troubles" some Senators. Says Marshall (Gibbons vs. Ogden, 9 Wheaton, 1):

> "The wisdom and the discretion of Congress, their identity with the people, and the influence which their constituents possess at elections, are, in this, as in many other instances, as that, for example, of declaring war, the sole restraints on which they have relied, to secure them from its abuse. They are the restraints on which the people must often rely solely, in all representative governments."

There is the answer to the argument that the abuse of power is a denial of its existence. The remedy for all of our excesses of power is in the hands of our constituents at the ballot-box, says the Supreme Court of the United States.

Nor is that the only case. In Gilman vs. Philadelphia, 3 Wall., 713, the Supreme Court says:

> "The possible abuse of any power is no proof that it does not exist."

And again, says the Supreme Court in Brown vs. Maryland:

> "All power may be abused, and if the fear of its *abuse* is to constitute an argument against its *existence,* it might be urged against the existence of that which is universally acknowledged and which is indispensable to the general safety."

Says the Supreme Court in the famous Lottery Case:

> "But as often said the possible *abuse* of a power is not an argument against its *existence.* There is probably no governmental power that may not be exerted to the injury of the

public. If what is done by Congress is manifestly in *excess* of the powers granted to it, then upon the courts will rest the duty of adjudging that its action is neither legal nor binding upon the people."

But if what Congress does is within the limits of its power, and is simply an *abuse* of that power, the remedy is that suggested by Chief Justice Marshall — the ballot.

So, Mr. President, there is the complete answer, not in one quotation from the Supreme Court, but in many, to the only argument that we have heard here or will ever hear against the existence of this power, to wit: If we admit we have the power to do this then we have the power to do a great many foolish things. The answer to that is, in the language of the Supreme Court, the possible abuse of a power is no argument against its *existence;* and that if we abuse our power the remedy is at the ballot box and not in the courts.

Mr. President, if the possible abuse of a power is an argument against its existence where are we?

On that basis you might say that we have no power to require interstate carriers to use block signals, because, if we have the power to require them to use block signals we also have power to require them to station a man with a red lantern at every hundred feet. But that would be absurd. We have the power, but we would not pass a law requiring them to station men at every hundred feet with red lanterns because it would be absurd; and if we did such a thing as that the people would put us out of office.

Or if we have the power to require automatic couplings — and we have actually exercised that power — we also have the power to require all the railroads to use electric engines, which is absurd. Therefore, according to the

argument of the Senator from Wisconsin (Mr. Spooner),
we have no such power to require them to use automatic
couplings, because if we admit that power we must admit
that it might be exercised unwisely. " Where is the
limit? " asked the Senator from Wisconsin.

The limit is in our common sense and in our responsibility to our constituents.   If we do exercise our power
unwisely the remedy is in the hands of the American
people at the ballot-box.

Why are we afraid?   Of whom are we afraid?   Of
ourselves?   Are we then a conspiracy against the American people?   And if we are, have the American people
no control over their Government?

Consider laws which we passed only last year — first,
the meat law, which actually goes into the factories of a
state, requires national inspection and *prohibits* the
transportation of meats that are not inspected.   It does
not prohibit the transportation of diseased meats alone,
mind you — it prohibits the transportation of *all* meat,
wholesome or unwholesome, that is uninspected.

So the power does not spring out of the nature of the
commerce.   The meat law is far more questionable in its
constitutionality than the child-labor bill, but no one tries
to overthrow it.

Next, there is the railroad rate law.   It is packed with
illustrations of the absurdity of the argument of the abuse
of power.

So, Mr. President, it is not a question of *power*.   The
power we have.   It has been so held in decision after
decision of the Supreme Court.   The power has been
exercised by ourselves in over a dozen statutes, directly
prohibiting the transportation in interstate commerce of

any articles that Congress thought it was wise to prohibit.

So the *power* exists. It is exclusively a question of *policy*. But, Mr. President, all the time taken by me has been wasted if I have not demonstrated to the Senate that, having power, it is not only a matter of policy but a matter of duty for us to pass the bill which will end this infamy.

Some Senators seem to think that the words " delegated power " and " constitutional government " are mysterious terms by which the progress of the people and the safety of the people are imperiled. It is a curious thing to me that every " constitutional " fight that has been made in the Supreme Court against laws prohibiting something in interstate commerce has been made only when some business interest was affected by it.

Mr. President, all the subjects we have before us are important, but not one of them is a fraction as important as the suppression of this great evil, which involves the crime of murder, the degeneracy of American citizens, not only by the thousand but by the hundred thousand.

Why, Mr. President, when I think about these things I sometimes wonder what is the purpose of " free institutions " about which we talk so much. Why was it that this Republic was established? What was the purpose of the Constitution? What does the flag stand for? Mr. President, what do all these things *mean?*

They mean that the people shall be free to correct human abuses.

They mean that we shall have the power to make this America of ours each day a better place to live in.

They mean the realities of liberty and not the academics of theory.

They mean the actual progress of the race in the tangible items of real existence, and not the theoretics of disputation.

If they do not mean these things, then our institutions, this Republic, our flag have no meaning and no reason for existence.

Mr. President, to see this Republic of free and equal men and women grow increasingly, with each day and year, as the mightiest power for righteousness in the world, has been and is, and always will be, I pray God, the passion of my life — a nation of strong, pure human beings; a nation whose power is glorified by its justice, and whose justice is the conscience of scores of millions of free, strong, brave people.

It is to make this people such a nation that all our wars have been fought, all our heroes have died, all our permanent laws been written, all our statesmen have planned, and our people themselves have striven.

It was to make such a nation as this that the old Articles of Confederation were thrown away and the Constitution of the United States, about which we debate so much, was adopted.

And it is to make this nation still surer of this holy destiny that I have presented this bill to stop the murder of American children of to-day and the ruin of American citizens of to-morrow.

THE NATIONAL FOREST SERVICE

The Senate having under consideration the bill (H. R. 24815) making appropriations for the Department of Agriculture for the fiscal year ending June 30, 1908 —

Mr. Beveridge said:

MR. President: The question immediately before the Senate is whether or not the appropriation for the Forest Service which the other day, perhaps without full information, was reduced, is to be restored. After the very long attack upon the Government's policy, I may be permitted some time to explain and defend it. No debate which has occurred this session has been so useful as this in informing both the Senate and the country on a business of such high importance.

There are those of us who were deeply interested in this question and yet who were not informed about what this Service meant and about the priceless work for the whole country which it was doing. In the course of this debate statements have been made which require some attention; and it is to do this that I rise to address the Senate before we take any vote, if a vote, indeed, shall be necessary upon this amendment.

The Senator from Wyoming (Mr. Clark) the other day began his remarks by asking the question, "What does this great forest-reserve system," which he said included some 200,000 square miles, "mean?" It means, Mr. President, at the bottom the conservation and the distribution of the waters, upon which agriculture depends, and upon which the population of the Senator's state and of other states similarly situated depend for their growth more than upon any one other single element.

Mr. President, we are arranging to spend some $50,-000,000 for the irrigation of what once was thought to be the " arid West." I remember very well the great fight which was made for the irrigation law. It was finally put through the Senate and the House against the counsel of some of the most conservative members of each body; but I think its wisdom now is universally recognized by men of all parties and all sections.

But, Mr. President, you can not irrigate with words — you have to irrigate with water. You can not irrigate merely by digging a hole in the desert; not enough water is supplied. In the last analysis it must come from rainfall in the mountains. The Senator knows better, no doubt, than I do that unless the forests on those mountains are conserved irrigation is impossible. If the forests are felled the rain which falls sweeps down in torrential floods and either takes away the reservoirs or fills them up with silt. So the basis of the whole irrigation system, which means so much to the west, and therefore to the whole country, rests upon the foundation of the forest-reserve system.

Mr. F. H. Newell, Chief of the Reclamation Service, has repeatedly emphasized the very great importance of forest reserves in connection with the Government's irrigation work. In the second annual report of the Reclamation Service (1902–3) Mr. Newell stated: " One of the most important matters in connection with the permanent development of the water resources of the country is the protection of the catchment basins from destructive influences. It is essential to preserve in such locations a certain amount of forest cover, and to prevent the destruction of these by fire or by overgrazing. The headwaters of many of the important streams are already included within forest reserves, and some of the important reservoir sites are thus guarded from injury. In other localities the forest reserve boundaries should be extended to include the country from which comes the greatest part of the run-off. This land usually has no value for cultivation, is rugged, and suitable only for the production of trees. Grazing to a limited extent is practicable and will not interfere with the best use of the waters, but if unrestricted the number of cattle and sheep may be increased to such an extent that the grass is destroyed and the bare soil is washed by storms."

Forest reserves are created for these main objects: To conserve and regulate stream flow, and to maintain a permanent supply of timber. Some forest reserves are valuable for both these purposes; others are valuable mainly for their effect upon stream flow. In southern California, for example, forest reserves have been created in the San Gabriel Mountains, not with the chief purpose of the production of timber, because these mountains are largely covered with brush known as chaparral and have few trees growing upon them. But these southern California reserves serve a most valuable purpose in maintaining the flow of streams rising in them, which supply important cities, such as Los Angeles, and are essential for the development of water power, and, above all, in the conservation of streams used in the irrigation of arid lands. Again, large areas in these reserves are capable of growing trees, although no trees are growing upon them at present. As rapidly as its funds permit, and conditions warrant, the Forest Service is planting up these areas.

To make the boundaries of forest reserves conform exactly to the boundaries of existing forests would be to leave out of these reserves large areas which are of immense value as a protection to the water flow, and which have grown trees and will grow trees again under proper methods. Obviously the boundaries of forest reserves must be drawn not to conform to the boundaries of existing forests, but based on the actual character of the country in its relation to the objects for which reserves are created. Brush and grass covered areas of natural forest land in the mountains, even if they do not now produce trees, ought to be given exactly the same protection as existing forests receive, because they often exercise a not less important effect in conserving and regulating stream flow.

The Forest Service has never recommended the creation of a single National forest, in which the land does not serve its main purpose either by the regulation of stream flow or by the production of timber. No considerable bodies of open range are included in forest reserves. So far as open range is included, it has been included not as range land, but because it is necessary to the protection of stream flow or because it is suitable for forest planting.

Mr. President, the Senator from Wyoming (Mr. Clark) said further — and it was a most important charge, one that we should carefully consider, one that the country should know the truth about — that the reserves had been created without knowledge of actual conditions upon the ground. So far from that being accurate (and I am satisfied that neither the Senator nor any other Senator who spoke meant to make an inaccurate statement) the most careful, detailed and scientifically accurate examinations were made.

Mr. Clark of Wyoming: Will the Senator allow an interruption?

Mr. Beveridge: Certainly.

Mr. Clark of Wyoming: I ask the Senator if he refers to my statement — the only time I remember to have referred to it — when I spoke of the effort to create the forest reserves under the appropriation made by Congress of $25,000 when a special committee went out to make an examination?

Mr. Beveridge: I will state to the Senator that I do not know whether that was what he referred to at the time.

Mr. Clark of Wyoming: I made that statement, and my information was from the chairman of the special committee appointed, after he returned to Washington and the reservations were made.

Mr. Beveridge: I do not know whether the Senator was referring to that or not. That was some time ago — in 1896, to be exact. That was before the Government division of forestry had anything to do with examining land for forest reserves.

Mr. Clark of Wyoming: That is the only one I remember.

Mr. Beveridge: I hold in my hand, and I shall ask to

have entirely inserted in the Record in my remarks, the instructions to the field men who make the examinations.

Eight or ten pages are devoted to giving painstaking directions to the men, who are to make the physical examination of the ground in order to collect the information for the making of these reserves.

(Senator Beveridge here read the instructions of the Forestry Bureau to be followed by its field men in reporting on proposed reserves.)

Furthermore, I will exhibit that the Senate may see it, a map of the Shoshone or Coeur d'Alene Reserve in Idaho. The Senate will notice the various colors. This deep green here (indicating) in the southwest portion is the heavily forested portion of this reservation. These brown patches (indicating) throughout that reservation are the burnt-over districts, where millions of dollars, the property of the United States, have been destroyed by forest fires. The lighter portions here (indicating) are the young timber. There are other portions that represent sagebrush.

This green portion here (indicating), within these lines, heavily wooded, *is nearly all taken up by the state or by settlers.* That is the " ruthless " and " infamous " way in which the Government has destroyed the resources of the state, as Senators have charged.

Here (exhibiting) is another map of the same region which shows scientific care taken in ascertaining the facts by the men on the ground. This map shows the lands which are patented. They are these (indicating). They are the lands which are patented, where people have gone in. These (indicating) are the approved railroad lieu selections — and I am going to have something to say upon that subject, I will say to the Senator from Montana, pretty soon. The unapproved selections are these (indicating). The approved state selections are in blue, which Senators can see here (indicating). The school lands are here (indicating). So I might go on. I am exhibiting this map to the Senate in connection with the other one, to show Senators the extreme care with which not only the work is mapped out, but with which the work is executed.

Mr. President, having located a reserve, what occurs? In the first place, it is again carefully mapped, classified, and examined. The Department knows just exactly what kind of timber is in every part of the reserve. What is done with that timber? Two things are done with it. It is given away by the Government to the small users without charge — to the settler, to the homesteader, to those men that we have been led to believe were so badly treated by this "tyrannical" Government — and who with this timber build their homes. Lumber and timber are given free of charge. Not only is the place to build their homes given them, but all the timber they need.

In order to show how fairly and with what detail the law providing for the free use of timber and stone is applied, I will quote the regulation in this respect:

(Mr. Beveridge here read the regulation.)

To what extent this free-use privilege was actually availed of last year, the following statement very clearly shows:

Free-use Statement for 1906

February 6, 1907.

State	Total value	Number of permits issued
Alaska	....	....
Arizona	$3,807.79	401
California	5,880.53	1,106
Colorado	10,432.33	2,196
Idaho	10,804.90	2,448
Montana	12,089.77	1,414
Nevada	....	....
New Mexico	2,950.24	781
Oklahoma	147.67	7
Oregon	8,609.56	890
South Dakota	2,545.18	758
Utah	8,593.28	3,253
Washington	291.89	61
Wyoming	2,394.27	260
Total	68,547.41	13,575

Approximately 35,000,000 feet.

Next certain timber is sold, and to whom? To those who wish it, whether in small or in large quantities; not for their own use, but for commercial purposes. Ought the Government give it to *them?* Heretofore men have made millions sawing into lumber the timber that belonged to the people of this Nation. Shall we return to that policy?

Now, then, what timber is sold? I will come in a moment to the question of policy that was raised as to "the Government being a merchant."

Not only is what is known as "down" timber, to which the Senator from Wisconsin referred yesterday, sold, but what is called "ripe" timber is sold.

The truth about it is that these forest reserves are merely great natural wood factories; and unless reserves are so treated, and trees cut that *should* be cut and *when* they should be cut, the result is *bad* to the forest itself. It is blown down, it rots, and is itself a source of decay. What shall the Government do? Let it fall and rot? It is the Government's property, just as much as the chairs in this Chamber; just as much as the money we seem to be so afraid to appropriate is Government property.

The prime object of the forest reserves is use. While the forest and its dependent interests must be made permanent and safe in preventing overcutting or injuring the young growth, every reasonable effort is made to satisfy legitimate demands. Timber cut from forest reserves may be handled and shipped like any other timber, except that it is not sold for shipment in regions where local construction requires the entire supply, or is certain to do so in the future. Any one may purchase timber except trespassers. Forest rangers are authorized to sell timber in amounts not exceeding $20 in value; forest supervisors not more than $100 worth, and the Forester on larger scales.

We talk about " economy." Economy of what? Of the Government's *resources,* of course; and those resources consist in cash, in land, in trees, in ships, in anything else that the Government *owns.* So, if we are conserving these trees, and derive revenue from them, we are practising " economy " just as much as if we are careful of the actual dollars appropriated. " Economy " is a favorite cry with certain men — I had almost said certain demagogues. But there is true economy and false economy. To save the nation's resources is true economy; to refuse a reasonable appropriation to save those resources, thus playing into the hands of those who are exploiting and stealing them is false economy and worse.

In all, over 300,000,000 board feet of this timber was sold by the Government during the last fiscal year. Certain men would like to have got that for nothing; to have given it to them for nothing would have been " economy," I suppose. Of the benefits which flow to the community from the administration of the national forests the Secretary of Agriculture, in his last annual report, truly said :

> These National forests are being made useful now. The benefits which they are to secure are not deferred benefits. Through Government control the interests of the future are safeguarded, but not by sacrificing those of the present.
>
> There is now standing on the reserves not less than 300,000,000,000 board feet of merchantable timber. This is not locked up from present use as a hoarded supply against future needs; it is ready for the immediate demands of a developing country. It will not be rushed upon the wholesale market in competition with the cheap stumpage prices of private owners anxious for ready money, and it will not be disposed of under a shortsighted policy of utilization which would leave a gap between the end of the present supply and the oncoming of the second crop; but it is and will continue to be available, first for the small user — home-builder, rancher, or miner — and then for the needs of lumber concerns, large miners, and railroads for which a timber supply is indispensable, and which, in turn, are indispensable to the prosperity of the West.

So, Mr. President, that is what is done with that wood; and it is not only bringing a revenue into the Treasury, but it is creating a continuous revenue from the same source for the future. I ask any Senator who objects to the Government being a " merchant " as we have heard, whether or not any Administration could be justified in not saving to the people of the United States the revenue that comes from the sale of this timber. What else would you do with it?

Would you give to one man to receive freely and sell for his own profit the timber for which another man stands ready to pay two or three or five dollars a thousand feet — millions upon millions of feet of it? For there is no other choice than this — either some favored individual or the people of the United States must receive the benefit. Under sales already made the Government will receive hundreds of thousands of dollars. The timber sold can not be removed except in large quantities; expensive plants must be provided to make it possible to utilize the timber at all. Should the Government abstain from receiving this revenue that some private individual may gratuitously reap a fortune? If so, on what principle shall selection of the person to receive this princely favor be made?

But that is not all, Mr. President, nor is it perhaps the most important thing. We are developing this country, developing its resources. I very greatly doubt whether we have had any source of tangible wealth to the people so great as the aid that has been given the people in information, scientific direction, and help by the Department of Agriculture. An entire day might be most usefully spent, both so far as the people and the Senate are concerned, in reviewing the actual practical help to the people by the information that is gathered and given to the farmers of the country by the Department of Agriculture.

So the next thing the Forest Service does is constantly to test the trees and the various kinds of wood for new uses. It is found that some woods which formerly were supposed to be worthless are most valuable; so that, as one kind of timber is cut off, and the lumber disappears another kind of timber is found.

I cite as examples of that two trees with which some Senators here will be familiar. One is the western hemlock and the other is the southern gum. The southern gum was a tree which afforded excellent lumber, but which immediately warped, so that the stock expression of a lumberman was that if you were to go to sleep on one side of a southern gum board you would wake up next morning on the other side of it, because it would warp so. But the Department has found a method of cutting and treating it so that it has become one of the considerable resources of the states where it grows. It has taken the place of wood which heretofore was used almost exclusively, but which now has become practically exhausted, just because we did not have such forest preservation as is now proposed.

Another is the western hemlock. Up to a few years ago the western hemlock was supposed to be unfit for lumber. This Department has developed the fact that it makes an admirable lumber; and now it constitutes a source of real revenue to the states where it grows.

The Forest Service is active in finding new uses for sawmill waste; testing new woods to be used for paper in place of those which are becoming exhausted or too expensive; testing new woods for mine props, railroad ties, box boards, vehicle woods, wooden pavements, cooperage, and many other uses. It is studying methods of preserving woods against decay, and is thus increasing enormously the service that can be got out of wood in some of its commonest uses. In this one field its work is equivalent to increasing the timber resources of the country by creating out of nothing thousands and hundreds of thousands of acres of standing forest. Both by promoting economy in the use of wood and by preventing waste in harvesting the forest crop it has added millions of dollars' worth of material to the national wealth in private ownership.

Mr. President, that is not only creating wealth for the Government as such, but it is creating wealth for the people, because, of course, almost everybody knows that most of the forest land of the United States is held by private owners. I think perhaps less than one-fifth — the Senator from Wyoming may know about that, and I want to be corrected if the statement is wrong, and it is too high, if anything — is held in Government reserves.

Mr. Clark of Wyoming: It is very much too low.

Mr. Beveridge: You mean that much more than the amount I named is held by private owners?

Mr. Clark of Wyoming: Yes.

Mr. Beveridge: I think that very much more than I have stated is held by private individuals, but the private owners do not and can not, unless they operate upon a scale almost as great as the Government itself, make these scientific examinations which discover the unknown properties of their wood. So in this one way the Department is creating enormous wealth for the American people.

Mr. Clark of Wyoming: Is it not a fact that nearly all of the scientific experiments of the kind to which the Senator is referring are conducted by the private owners, and that nearly all these experiments are made upon private timber lands?

Mr. Beveridge: No; not all of them by any manner of means. I understand the fact to be about these experiments that they are conducted to ascertain the best uses of timber on the Government's forest lands, and also the best uses of timber on the lands of private owners. Where any private owner of forest land desires to test his wood, the Government coöperates very cheerfully, and even invites such coöperation. I am sure that every Senator here, no matter what may be his opinion upon any other subject, would approve that plan as a wise and common-sense thing.

In addition to coöperation work in timber tests, the Forest Service gives advice and assistance to private owners of timber lands all over the country. Unless these forests also are preserved, a timber famine not less dangerous than a coal famine is in sight. Applications for help of this kind come from both owners of small wood lots and holders of large timber tracts. What are called " working plans " are made; that is, certain rules are recommended for the proper protection, management, and utilization of the timber, to the end that the owner may be assured of a continuous supply of wood, at the same time cutting what is necessary for present needs.

The object of the wood-lot work is to give, free of cost to farmers and other small owners, advice and assistance in the improvement and use of their woodlands. The coöperation work on large timber tracts embraces the whole country, and in many cases the plans recommended by the Forest Service are now actually being carried out very successfully.

Coöperative work is also undertaken with the various states, and this branch of the work has been taken up with the greatest detail in California.

So, Mr. President, we see what the Department is doing. I am trying to forward the work as much as possible. Of course there is a far-reaching policy beneath it which I stated in the beginning, and that is the prevention of that portion of this country from continuing a desert or being made into one if it is not one already.. We are in a great work — and how characteristically American it is — the work of reclaiming, saving, developing. We have passed the period of destruction. We have abandoned that ruinous exploitation which was called " development," but was the reverse. We are replacing as fast as we can those gigantic resources which, in the strength and inconsequence of our national youth, we so ruthlessly and thoughtlessly destroyed. It is a great constructive policy designed to create conditions that will supply homes for hundreds of thousands in the near future and even a denser population in the more distant future.

I have described some of them. One part of it is the conservation of the water. That is a subject which ought to be spoken of perhaps for ten or fifteen minutes by itself, but I am not going to take two minutes with it. I think we all now pretty well understand the methods by which these waters are conserved. The rain falls on the mountains, and the leaves — not the trees — and the leaves and the leaf soil hold it like a sponge. The great reservoir of nature is the forested mountain, from which water is distributed over the surrounding country. This provision and plan of nature with reference to the conservation and the distribution of waters is as wise as it is beautiful.

It is to restore that condition that the Forest Service is laboring, not only with fidelity, but with intelligence that is not surpassed by any other Department of the Government, to put the statement very mildly indeed.

Now I come to a point that I see I have jotted down concerning the creation of game preserves. I have looked into that matter, and I find that no game preserves have been created except by Congress itself, and, of course, if we ever have acted unwisely in allowing the animals which nature placed there to be preserved there, the way is open to us, without any objection from the Department, or the right of any objection from the Department, to repeal our own acts. But this is what the Department has done. I find upon examination with reference to the laws of the states concerning game that where a forest reservation exists within the limits of a state the forest reservation is patrolled, guarded, and cared for by the foresters and forest rangers of the Nation. And the Nation's Forest Service, taking care of the Government forest reserves, *coöperates with the states* in the execution of the states' game laws even in those reserves. Mr. President, that ought to be satisfactory —

Mr. Clark of Wyoming: It is.

Mr. Beveridge: — to the most extreme states' rights man. I regretted when the question of states' rights was interjected here. It has nothing to do with this question. No friend of forest reserves would destroy the rights of a state, his own or any other, and I am sure, on the contrary, no national believer in that doctrine would deny that it was not only the right, but the duty of the Na-

tion to preserve its great forests for the large public purposes I have described, as much as it possibly could.

The Senator from Wyoming (Mr. Clark) said that
that was what he wanted them to do. He was glad of
that. My own sincere belief is that when we examine
one by one the points that have been made, and gather
information upon them from the original source, every
one of the Senators who have spoken against, not the
forest-reserve system itself, but its administration, will be
entirely satisfied — yes, and even pleased, as much
pleased as those of us who, on account of the exigencies
of the debate, were compelled to examine the facts.

I come now to a statement made yesterday afternoon
by the Senator from Colorado. The Senator from
Colorado yesterday described, with that vigorous eloquence which so characterizes him and charms us, the
establishment in Colorado of a great reserve, larger, he
said, than some states, without a single tree upon it or
any tree ever having grown upon it. I took pains to
look up the *facts* as to that statement; and what are the
facts?

It is true, in part, Mr. President, that such a reserve
has been taken up so far as the existing trees are concerned. But originally it was land every foot of which
was covered with magnificent forests, which have long
since been burned away until parts of the mountains
where that reserve is are as bare of trees as the surface
of this desk. But it is natural forest land. It is ideal
for reforesting; it is being reforested. But the reforesting is impossible if all the herds and all the flocks of
Colorado belonging to her great cattle and sheep kings
— and I have no objection to them, I should like

to be a king of that kind myself — are allowed to pasture their countless herds over that reserve at will and without control as well as without cost.

Mr. President, it was held out by intimation, if not by direct statement, that this land was fit for agricultural purposes and that the policy of the Department, therefore, had been despotically to take a principality in size, where no trees grew, and keep off the " sweeping tide of immigrants " from " founding homes." The fact is that it is above the agricultural line where homes are not " founded," and " immigrants " do not " pour in tides " or " pour " in any other way. Most of it is over 8,000 feet above the sea level, where farms are not practicable, except, I believe, a certain kind of farming, which is not worth taking into account. It is one of nature's forest reservoirs for the purpose of distributing water for the uses of the people where the land farther down is agricultural.

What exists with reference to that land now is this: It is grown over with grasses; those grasses are good for grazing, and over that great extent, which belongs to the Government of the United States, the cattlemen and the sheep men of Colorado have been fattening their herds *without paying the Government a dollar*.

Let us bear in mind the actual conditions. A forest reserve contains lands " chiefly valuable for timber." Yet if the farmer finds up and down some valley that creeps back into these mountains a site for settlement, it is open to him as much as any other part of the public domain, if he enters in good faith. The reserves have been pictured as vast stretches of unbroken wilderness, empty solitudes trod only by the Forester. In point of fact, they contain thousands of ranches; they contain hamlets, villages, and towns, to say nothing of lumber camps and railroad construction camps and mining camps. Wherever signs of mineral can be found the prospector stakes out his claim. In summer they are alive with those who resort thither for health and recreation — 50,000 of them in one season in southern California alone — and with the cowboys and sheep herders, who guard and care for the 7,000,000 head of animals that last year grazed in the forest reserves.

These forests of the West are unlike those of the East. They are often open and park like, with forage plants growing beneath the trees. These grasses, like the trees themselves, will be wasted if they are not used. For this reason the Forest Service permits grazing in the reserves, but in every case is careful to exclude grazing from areas in which it has been found harmful. For example, grazing is not permitted in forests "under reproduction," as the Forester speaks of it — that is, forests in which cuttings are in progress to invite young growth. Forest reserves have never been created out of lands which are merely grazing lands. Yet this resource is like the forest in that it may be greatly impaired and even destroyed by unwise use. Unrestricted admittance of all stock would bring, and in many cases has brought, a decline in the number which the range would support. By licensing only so many head as the range can well support the Forest Service has proved to the satisfaction of the stockmen themselves that the carrying power of the range season after season is actually increased.

It was said that this was the crowning " infamy " of

the Department, that the Department actually charged a " license fee " before any of these men were permitted to graze their cattle. I ask the Senate what else could the Government do? Ought the Government to give that privilege to the cattlemen and the sheep men, and if the Government ought not to give it to them can anybody imagine a safer or more practicable system of charging than the permit system? The legality of the regulations under which the permit is required, resting upon the act of June 4, 1897 (30 Stat. L., 34–36), has never been questioned by any court. It was established by the decision of the United States circuit court of appeals at San Francisco in 1903, in the case of Dastervignes vs. the United States (122 Fed. Rep., 30), in which that court affirmed a decree granting an injunction to prevent unpermitted grazing.

The district courts of Utah, southern California, and the Eastern District of Washington have, it is true, decided that unpermitted grazing is not punishable as a *crime* — that the act of June 4, 1897, in so far as it provides for criminal punishment is unconstitutional. But Judge De Haven, of the Northern District of California, in the cases of United States against Daguerre and the United States against Urarti, held that the criminal provisions of the statute *are* constitutional, though in so doing he overruled a decision to the contrary made by him before the Dastervignes case was decided by the circuit court of appeals. The supreme court of Arizona, a court coördinate with the district courts, also held, in the criminal case of Dent against United States (76 Pac. Rep., 455), relying on the authority of the Dastervignes case, and overruling its earlier decision, that the statute

is constitutional in making violation of the regulations
a criminal offense.

Now I come to the question of lieu land. I thought
when I heard the Senator from Oregon make his charge
the other day that he made a very serious charge, and
when it was renewed by the Senator from Montana it
appeared to me much graver. I knew that neither one
of those Senators would make such a charge as that
thoughtlessly. I have looked it up, and, in my opinion,
that charge is entirely true.

I think it is entirely well founded, and after my investigation I think the language of the Senator from
Montana, which I thought at the time was severe, is
wholly justified, when he said that the relations of the
Department at one time with the land-grant railroads
would bear looking into.

I find that it is true, as the Senator from Oregon described, that large tracts of land in Washington which
were worthless had been released and lieu lands taken
up in valuable portions of Oregon. But what has this
Bureau to do with that? What are the facts? Let us
be just to everybody. Nobody intends to accuse any
man falsely or condemn any man unjustly. The truth
is that it was done under a construction of the law by the
Land Office some years ago, *and one of the first objec-
tions to it that was made within the Government itself
was made by the Bureau of Forestry and personally by
Gifford Pinchot, the Chief Forester.*

The Senator from Minnesota, who was most active in
repealing that law to which a false meaning had been
given by this construction of the Land Office will bear
me out in that. Mr. Pinchot from first to last was ac-

tive not only in suggesting in his report, which I will ask to have inserted in my remarks, but in every other way, that that thing which he himself characterized as a wrong should be undone and that the impossibility of a repetition of that wrong should be absolutely assured.

Mr. President, I have examined briefly the policy upon which this forest-reserve system rests. Now, as to the question of administration, by which we mean the management of the reserves. After the reserves have been located in the painstaking way they are, as I have shown here by these maps and by the instructions to the locators of reserves, they are remapped. Then they are classified as to trees. There is now under the actual practical administration of this Bureau 128,000,000 acres, I believe. The Senator from Montana will correct me if I am wrong.

Mr. Carter: One hundred and twenty-seven million acres.

Mr. Beveridge: One hundred and twenty-seven million acres. Now, through that runs a great system of forest patrol. It is policed by a network of forest rangers. One Senator yesterday referred to the fact that the examination of the land could not have been thorough, because one man had gone over 4,000,000 acres in two weeks. What does that mean? Merely that instead of cutting down the appropriation for the proper care of the reserves it ought to be increased. As a matter of fact, the forest policing is very thorough. If any man thinks that a forest police is not valuable, I shall show in a moment that there is no individual service in this Government that is more valuable or difficult.

This policing is done by the rangers — 900 of them

employed last year to patrol 100,000,000 acres of land
— one ranger to 110,000 acres, or 172 square miles.
In the highly profitable forests of Prussia there is one
forest guard on the average to every 1.7 square miles.
Small wonder that the cost of administration in the
United States in spite of the higher scale of wages has
been kept below that of any other European country
except Russia. The cost of administration has been
officially reported for various countries as follows:

Year	State	Government forests	Actual expenditure on management of State forests		Percentage of gross income expended
			Total	Per acre	
		Acres			
1898......	Baden	231,082	685,972	$2.97	43
1895......	Bavaria	2,350,193	3,701,000	1.50	50
1899......	Switzerland	94,280	124,740	1.32	....
1895......	Prussia	6,846,733	8,408,000	1.23	50
1900......	France	2,691,581	2,801,949	1.04	......
1898......	Belgium	62,551	43,597	.68	22
1874–1893.	Austria	2,573,100	1,434,000	.56	72
1885–1894.	Hungary	3,512,700	1,690,385	.34	61
1899......	British India	51,192,000	3,450,000	.07	59
1898......	Sweden	18,640,300	358,600	.02	18
1900......	Russia	643,067,880	5,086,181	.008	18

The Forest Service is now expending annually, in administering the reserves, 1.6 cents per acre. Doubtless
it should spend more, and must spend more as use of
the reserves increases, for wise use means supervision
and supervision means expense. Every live tree that
is cut on the reserves is first marked by the forest ranger's ax; every log that is sold is scaled; and this is but
one of their many duties, which include guarding the
range against trespass and the forests against fire. And
all this with one ranger to 172 square miles! It needs

no further evidence to show that these are not invalids, or Eastern tenderfeet, or college-bred impractical theorists. They are men of the West, woodsmen, cowboys, lumberjacks — men who can ride the mountain trails and live a frontiersman's life. As to their efficiency, the record of forest fires throws some illumination on that point. I shall have something to say on that subject presently.

The next thing that the Forest Service does in the actual administration, after the test of the trees, after the marking of the " ripe " or mature timber, after arranging for the sale of that and the " down " timber, is to make trails and build roads, so that it is possible to communicate with one part of the reservation from another, and, further, so that if any agricultural lands are taken up by homesteaders there is a system of communication.

Then along this road there are built telephone lines, so that if in one portion of the forest a fire starts a ranger who finds himself unable to put it out may instantly telephone for help, so that men may be sent there and extinguish the fire while it is still young. Also, they build bridges, so that instead of a wild, ruinous, and rotting tangle of forest land you have a forest land which is woven together by trails, by a network of roads, by bridges, and by telephones. You have the " ripe " timber cut and taken off so as to increase the growth of that which is left. You have the " down " timber disposed of by selling it instead of permitting it to rot. You create a natural and healthy and perpetual forest, and therefore a profitable forest.

Mr. President, about the question of fires. In debate

yesterday I said that one of the most valuable services the Forest Service does is to preserve the forests from fires. I myself have had a little experience with forest fires and considerable observation of them, and there are Senators here from the West who have had a great deal more. It was suggested to me that the men who put out the fires are not the foresters, but the farmers. But that shows that there is still not so much knowledge in the Senate or the country as there ought to be as to what this Bureau is doing in the way of practical administration; because nearly all the fires that are now started in these mighty western forests are extinguished before they are old fires.

When a forest fire gets under way hardly all the farmers in a state could stop it; and I, in common with other Senators, have seen great areas of forest land, where millions — and I might also be accurate in saying tens of millions — of dollars' worth of Government property has been destroyed in less than two weeks' time. Then this is another part of its administration, and so excellent has it been that *the entire West has been practically clear of smoke during the summer time for the last two years.*

Mr. President, that last circumstance is something which, to those who live near great forest districts, is of incalculable consequence. I myself have seen in the forests of the Northwest mighty conflagrations raging which swept away villages and towns; and in one such fire, I remember, more than a hundred human beings lost their lives. I have seen, and the Senator from Montana has seen much more than I, the whole atmosphere clouded for weeks with smoke from these criminal acts

of negligence — because that is what they are.   When
the Forest Service of the United States stops *one* of
these fires it has saved more money to the Government than ten appropriations like this.   We speak of
economy, but we mean *economy of resources,* and trees
are resources as much as actual dollars.

The Forest Service keeps careful records of all fires on
the reserve.   These include even the smallest fires, which
are put out before they have covered more than a few
square rods — fires which, but for the vigilance of the
forest officers, might become great conflagrations, but
which are extinguished without cost beyond the salary
of the rangers who patrol these forests as a part of their
regular duties.   During the year 1906, out of a total of
97,000,000 acres under administration, one-eighth of 1
per cent. was burned over, and three one-hundredths of
1 per cent. of the estimated standing timber was destroyed.   Out of over 1,100 fires reported, 450 were extinguished without one cent of extra cost to the Government.   Nearly 700 large fires were fought, at a total
cost of less than $9,000 for extra labor and supplies.
That is pretty good evidence of the efficiency of the
protection which the Forest Service gives, at a lower cost
per acre, as I have already shown, than any European
country except Russia — and Russia's figure is so low
because the greater part of her forests are not under administration at all.

The next thing which shows how completely the Service is practical and results in a definite and tangible benefit to the people is the increase of the waterflow in the
streams.   If we can show that it has kept the West, that
mighty area of imperial forests, clear of smoke for two

summers, we have vindicated it. But now if we can show, as a matter of fact, it has kept the streams' banks full, we have done more than that.

As a matter of fact, actual stream measurements made in southern California show an increase of 25 per cent. in the flow of water since the reserves were created. No wonder the two Senators from California are hearty supporters of this policy.

So we see that in all the details of actual administration the Bureau is well-nigh perfect. I do not use that adjective lightly. I do not use it without having something of an official nature to support it. It is my purpose in the Senate to make no statement that I can not substantiate by something recognized as authoritative. I myself have never been greatly impressed by statements, however powerful they may seem, which could not be sustained by authorities.

(Senator Beveridge here read the testimony of Secretary Garfield before the House Committee as to the workings of the Bureau of Forestry.)

Now, I am permitted by the chairman of the House committee (Mr. Littlefield) to state with his express authority that after his committee had fairly heard all of the testimony which anybody chose to give on this subject, and the usual notices had been sent out and opportunity had been given to those who complained to appear before them; and after one of the Senators from this Chamber had appeared before them, that the report of his committee without a single dissent will substantiate in the fullest degree the testimony of Mr. Garfield, which is only a summary of all the evidence given before it.

Mr. President, in view of this showing, more formal and complete than any similar showing that I in my short public experience remember, I think the Senators who have suggested that the administration of the office might not be wholly admirable will do us all the credit to suggest that it was not with reference to the administration, but to the original policy, of these reserves in which the wrong was committed, and to correct which this Chief Forester was the speediest as well as the most vigilant man.

The next argument repeatedly made was, that the " Government ought not to become a merchant." Oh, that is merely a catch phrase.   Why should not the Government charge for the grasses growing on the great ranges which are in these reserves just as it ought to charge for the wood, the " ripe " and " down " timber on them?

Mr. Spooner: That argument —

The Vice-President: Does the Senator from Indiana yield to the Senator from Wisconsin?

Mr. Beveridge: Of course.

Mr. Spooner: That argument proves too much, because it would prevent the Government from selling its lands.

Mr. Beveridge: To be sure it would; one could say " The Government ought not become a real-estate dealer."   And here is another thought; if the Government ought to give the stockmen of the West land upon which to fatten their cattle, for instance, then why should not the Government furnish hay to the farmers in the East?   The analogy is complete.

I do not think that any tangible criticism can be made

upon the selling of timber instead of allowing what has occurred in the past to occur again — the thefts of the vast areas of timber lands belonging to the Government; the sawing of that timber up into lumber; the putting of the proceeds of that transaction into the pockets of men who became the great lumber barons of the West.

An extract from a published letter of the President written to Senator Heyburn under date of June 13, 1905, illustrates this matter:

(Here Senator Beveridge read President Roosevelt's letter.)

But Mr. President, I myself within the last five years have been over three mountains in Colorado and in California, which had been at no distant date heavily timbered to their tops. But when I rode over them they were as bare of a tree as the wall of this Senate Chamber, every stick of it having been cut off, every stick of it belonging to the Government, and every stick of it taken by some man or some company, upon the proceeds of which they became wealthy, and for which the Government of the United States never got a cent. I think it far better to preserve that forest, to sell off the down and the ripe timber, than to continue a policy that has devastated so much of the country as that policy devastated.

That was not all of that damage; for after those monarchs of the early western lumber camps had stripped the natural clothing from the mountains, and the rains descended, they swept off in torrential floods, filling the valleys and washing them out; whereas hereafter when retimbered the rain will go out gradually annually into the streams of the valleys.

Mr. Aldrich: I should like to ask the Senator a question.

Mr. Beveridge: Certainly.

Mr. Aldrich: Do I understand the Senator to say that timber from an entire section, including three mountains, had been taken by somebody without authority of law?

Mr. Beveridge: I say I myself have been over three mountains in Colorado and in California, altogether separate peaks. I have one of them in my mind quite as plainly as I see the Senator now, from which the timber had been stripped utterly, and I was informed —

Mr. Aldrich: Without authority of law?

Mr. Beveridge: The old stumpages looked as if it had been cut some years before. It was six years ago that I saw it. I was informed on authority sufficient for me to make the statement here that every stick of it had been taken without authority of law and that every stick of it actually belonged to the Government of the United States.

Mr. Aldrich: That is a very singular condition of affairs to exist in any community.

Mr. Beveridge: It is, and it did exist in that community. It was partially to correct such things as this that the forest-reserve system was established, and the result of the destruction of the forest-reserve system will be to restore such a condition.

Mr. Carter: Mr. President —

The Vice-President: Does the Senator from Indiana yield to the Senator from Montana?

Mr. Beveridge: Certainly.

Mr. Carter: I think I can throw some light on the legality of the proceedings referred to. More than

twenty years ago Congress passed a law, which remains
on the statute books to this day, authorizing the cutting
of timber upon mineral lands of the United States for
mining and milling purposes. No doubt the mountain
peaks referred to by the Senator from Indiana are classified as mineral lands, and, no doubt, further, the timber
was cut for mining and milling purposes. The peaks
have not been named nor have they been closely identi-
fied, but I venture the assertion that they are in a mineral belt and classified as mineral lands and lands of no
value for any other purpose.

Mr. Beveridge: I think quite likely they are in the
mineral belt, especially two of them. I have no doubt
that it may have been under cover of that that it was
done. I know that the act of June 3, 1878, to which
the Senator refers, has been used as a cloak for denuding
non-mineral lands of the United States, and I have in
mind a decision from the Senator's own state (Lynch vs.
United States, 138 Fed. Rep., 535) where damages were
recovered by the Government because of such a fraud.
The state referred to is no exception. The mineral
land laws are, themselves, made the means of defrauding
the United States of its timbered and non-mineral lands,
and I am informed that at this time an association of
sixteen persons, controlled by one of its members, is
asserting a claim under such laws for approximately
250,000 acres of heavily timbered land in the State of
California under the guise of compliance with the mineral laws and that no mines exist upon such lands.

Government geologists have examined a large part of
this land and the investigation is being continued at
great expense. California does not present an exception

to conditions existing in other states. Numerous frauds
of similar character explain the disappearance of timber
from the Government's lands. I do not know whether
those lands which I saw had been cut over as mineral
lands, but one thing I do know — there were not any
mines near them and not any mills near them, nor the
remains of any. As a matter of fact, we know that
before the establishment of this Service what very naturally occurs, because human beings are the same every
place and at all times, did occur, and shamefully occur,
and not only in the far West, but as the Senator from
Wisconsin said, in his own state. I refer to what I saw
myself in his own state, which he will confirm — a thing
that shocked me and every other man who learns about
it.

I spent many weeks in the very heart of what was
once a state reserve — there is not much of it left now
— and I was informed by those on the ground who knew,
that after the great lumber companies had stripped the
state as the Senator from Wisconsin described, and in
the manner he described, and had run out of forests upon
which to pursue their further slaughter, they went to the
legislature (this was many years ago) and by some
means or other the legislature was induced to repeal the
law creating that reserve, and the magnificent forest
reserve, which was conserving the water sources that
supply Wisconsin on both sides of the water divide will
within a year or two see the last of its existence.

Mr. President, it has been stated several times that
this policy was preventing the settlement of these lands
and the development of these states by homesteaders.
A rather pathetic and vivid picture was drawn by the

Senator from Idaho (Mr. Heyburn) of the prairie schooners, the white-covered wagons, sweeping through in great trains, and finding nowhere to deposit immigrants that they might build homes.

The truth is, Mr. President, that there is not a foot of these forest reserves that are fit for agriculture that are not open to entry under the act of June 11, 1906. There is not a bit of mineral land that is not subject to entry under the proper law. Where minerals exist and where the land is suitable for agriculture it is open to entry; but it can not be entered for the purpose of taking off wood and stone and mineral except by mining.

Now, to show the extent of this " flood of immigration," I have here an official list of all the applications for homesteads that have been made in these various states. It shows the great " tide," the mighty " inundation " of human beings that has been kept off the forest reserves in Idaho. Under the act of June 11, 1906, the *number of exactly 180 for all of Idaho,* and the applications for entries in the Shoshone Reserve reach the magnificent total of *4.* The total number of applications in those forest reserves of the entire State of Idaho is only 180. That is how many people have been made " homeless " by preserving the forests. In one reserve there were only four applications, and those, Mr. President, are being examined as to whether, first, they are really agricultural lands, and, second, whether or not the entries are genuine.

APPLICATIONS UNDER THE ACT OF JUNE 11, 1906

Arizona	221
California	100
Colorado	200
Idaho	180

Montana	299
Nevada	21
New Mexico	294
Oklahoma	70
Oregon	298
South Dakota	303
Utah	53
Washington	454
Wyoming	132
Florida	1
Total	2,626

Now, Mr. President, there is just one further point that I want to make as to this forest-reserve policy, and I make it in order that I may sum up in a compact fashion what would be the result if the Forest Service were destroyed, or even impaired. Senators were alarmed the other day when it was stated that this Forest Service controlled the distribution of water after it left the reserve.

Of course, we all know now that it does nothing of the kind. But here is what does occur, Mr. President, and this is what the Department was criticized for: The great water companies want to take water located within these forest reserves. They come into the Government forest land and get the exclusive use of the ground through which they run their pipes to the water, and they have that use. The Government charges them for that. Mr. President, what is the basis of that charge? Not only the exclusive use of the land for their pipes, but this:

The Government does not propose to charge for the water used. That is granted directly by the state. It charges only for the resources, opportunities, and services which it furnishes to the power company. These are of a twofold nature: First, the great storage reservoir formed by the maintenance of the forest cover which holds back the water so that it will flow during the dry season. Without this sponge reservoir the companies must spend millions in the construction of dams. Second, the Government furnishes in that part of the forest reserve traversed by the company's water conduits a fall, without which the water granted by the state and conserved by the forest reserve could not produce electrical energy. The Government proposes to charge for this conservation and this fall such reasonable amount only as can not make the prudent business man hesitate about carrying out his proposed water-power project.

These water companies now want these Government services for nothing. When that statement was made here the other day the Senator from California (Mr. Perkins), who is sitting on my left, said, " If that is done — these charges now made by the Department abolished — it will create one of the most enormous monopolies in all the West." No Senator more than another on this floor would want any great interest to be benefited that ought not to be.

The result of destroying the forest-reserve system or of impairing it would be to benefit *temporarily* just three classes of men.

The first are the water companies last named, who, instead of paying for the privilege of taking over the forest lands and the waters which the Forest Service conserves, want it exclusively and for nothing. Their benefit would last just so long as it would take for the effects of forest destruction to become operative upon the flow of their dwindling streams.

The second class of men who would be benefited would be the sheep men and the cattlemen, who heretofore have fattened their flocks and their herds upon Government land and given the Government no pay for it. Yet progressive deterioration of the range under unrestricted competition would soon work to their loss.

The third would be the great timber firms, which characterized a former but recent period of our history in the West and Northwest and in the northern portion of our country, who cut off the magnificent forests, the proceeds of which to-day constitute some of the greatest fortunes of the country, and who, if this Service, which prevents the ravaging of the Nation's forests, is destroyed or is impaired, would do exactly the same thing, to the ultimate ruin of their own industry.

Mr. President, there is the net result of either the destruction or the impairment of the Forest Service.

I do not know that I should have gone so much into the discussion if it had not been for the original question of the character of the services rendered by that remarkable public servant, the Chief Forester of the United States, whom I have known intimately since I was chairman of the Forestry Committee of the Senate years ago, and whose work I have observed with increasing admiration — a man who never spares himself mental or physical fatigue in his unselfish service to the Nation. Mr. President, when that man shall have completed his work on earth his monument will be no shaft of stone or image of brass. No! it will be our great and splendid forest reserves reclothed with nature's garment. It will be mighty mountain peaks now bare, then covered with the noble woods Nature once put there and which he has restored. It will be the streams now dry, running bank full for the welfare of the people. It will be all those material aids to human happiness.

STATE AND NATION

Speech delivered on the occasion of the anniversary of the birthday of Ulysses S. Grant, at Galena, Illinois, April 27, 1907.

AS Lincoln was the great leader of nationality in the council chamber, so Grant was the great captain of nationality on the battle-field. Both came from the common people, as all leaders must come; both developed in the heart of the Republic, as was fitting for men who were to be the statesmen and the soldiers of nationality. And above all things else, both were Americans. In the cabinet of Lincoln only the saving of the Nation was considered — states were trying to destroy it; in the field of Grant only the Nation's flag was carried — no state flag was permitted in battle.

The war which gave to Lincoln and to Grant their opportunity to serve the Nation, and in serving the Nation to serve progress and liberty, was the climax of the conflict between the national idea, as Washington understood it, and the states' rights idea, as Calhoun understood it. Slavery was the occasion of the contest, but the theory of national unity, on the one hand, and the theory of states' rights, on the other hand, was the profound and historic issue.

The supremacy of the Nation over the states, the sovereignty of the Republic over its sectional divisions; the common destiny of the whole American people, which

neither politicians nor " interests " can use for their purposes against the supremacy of small divisions of the
American people which supremacy politicians and " interests " can use for their purposes, was the argument,
conducted with bayonet and gun on fields of blood in the
terrible but splendid years from 1861 to 1865. Sumter
was states' rights defiant; Appomattox was nationality
triumphant.

You soldiers who followed Grant when the great national commander reviewed your final parade down
Pennsylvania Avenue in Washington and you disbanded
to your homes, thought that Calhoun's states' rights
were dead. But the old argument is on again; and this
fact compels a new discussion of this question. And it
is fitting that it be on this celebration of the birthday of
General Grant, the meaning of whose life-work was the
ever-increasing unity of the American people into an
ever-stronger growing Nation.

I do not mean that General Grant wished state lines
wiped out. Nobody wishes that. What his followers
to-day demand is that state and Nation shall occupy
natural instead of artificial relations to each other.

What is the natural and therefore the true and healthful province of state and Nation? It is this: the state
should be supreme in all matters affecting the American
people living within its limits and which do not affect
the great body of the American people living in other
states.

But the state should not be supreme in matters affecting not only that portion of the American people living
within its limits but also the great body of the American
people living in other states.

In a word, state government should mean local self-government, in which the Nation should not interfere; it should not mean participation in national government in which the state should not interfere.

On the other hand, the Nation should be supreme in all matters that affect the great body of the American people and which are not confined to that portion of the American people living in any particular state.

The Nation should not be supreme in matters which do not affect the great body of the American people, but only that portion of the American people living within any particular state.

In local matters, the Nation should not interfere; in national matters the state should not interfere.

If the provincial traditions planted in American soil by the English kings and which the American people's instinct of nationality has been steadily overcoming for two hundred years were not in the way; if the intelligence of our ninety millions were called upon to-day to establish upon clear ground a form of government, that intelligence would establish local government for local affairs, national government for national affairs.

The interference of those local agencies of government called states in matters which concern the welfare of the whole people would not be tolerated or even thought of. It is the artificial, unnatural Calhoun theory of rights-of-the-states, as against the natural and necessary functions of the Nation, which has caused most of our internal troubles, called forth Jackson's immortal assertion of nationality, brought on the Civil War and developed the comparatively feeble debate of the present day.

It is these artificial and unnatural Calhoun rights-of-the-states which, one by one, have been lopped off that the tree of nationality might grow in vigor and bear the fruit of the welfare of all the people that dwell beneath its life-giving branches. The sword of Grant was merely the pruning-hook with which these artificial and unnatural rights were cut away for the saving of the Republic.

How came to be the artificial and unnatural rights-of-the-states, of which Calhoun was and to-day remains the ablest defender.

The settlers who came to these shores were divided by the British Crown into colonies. The settlers themselves did not create colonial boundaries. The British kings did that. For example, how did the " sovereign state " of New York come to be? This is its origin: the dissolute Charles II., when the New Netherlands were taken from the Dutch, gave that province to his brother, the Duke of York. That was the beginning of the sovereign New York. How did the " sovereign state " of New Jersey come to be? The Duke of York gave a part of his royal gift to his friends Berkeley and Carteret. So began the " sovereign state " of New Jersey. North Carolina, by royal edict, was split off from Virginia. The Royal province of New Hampshire was severed by the English Crown from Massachusetts. These are examples of the origin of the states.

English governors were appointed over these colonies. Lord Baltimore reigned in Maryland, the Duke of York in New York, Governor Harvey in Virginia, Lord Calvert in Massachusetts. It was the policy of the British Crown to foster the spirit of colonial individuality — the spirit of unity among the American people was discouraged.

The colonists united into one people were a menace to British rule — their unity meant inevitable independence through a separate nationality. But if colonial pride, colonial individuality was sufficiently strong, British rule was easier, because the mutual jealousy of the colonists divided their strength, which if united was irresistible.

But in spite of the British royal policy, the spirit of unity developed in the breasts of the colonists — little by little they came to realize that they were one people and that their common destiny was a common nationality. Their common perils and their common interests caused this, just as their common perils and common interests, ever since, have strengthened the spirit of nationality and weakened the spirit of separate and divided " sovereignties."

This spirit of nationality grew until it brought on the Revolution. The Revolution nearly failed because the royal theory of colonial pride, suspicion and independence was so strong that the colonies which had transformed themselves into " states " would not obey the Continental Congress; and Congress had no power to enforce its laws.

Only the broad nationalism of the mighty Washington kept the American troops in the field and won America's final victory. The ragged soldiers of liberty, starving for their cause at Valley Forge, and Washington on his knees amid the snows of that awful winter, personify the American people's unconquerable instinct toward nationality and furnish a pathetic protest against the theory of states' rights which left those heroes and their glorious commander so uncared for and unsupported.

The desperate peril of the Revolution over, and the colonies transformed into states, the British theory of separation as evinced in the pride, suspicion and selfishness of the colonies asserted itself under the name of " the rights of the states." From this grew the first government of the Republic under the Articles of Confederation. This government was a government of the states, by the states and for the states, and therefore was no government at all.

Under it each state looked to its own interests, considering that the interests of every other state were antagonistic and that the hand of each state was against the hand of every other state. In a word, " states' rights " were supreme. There was no real government except local self-government. Commerce perished; misery reigned; the world despised us. What the soldiers of King George could not do on the battle-field, " states' rights " was surely doing on the farms and in the shops and homes of the people.

So all men, except little politicians, saw the absolute necessity of making a government that should be national. That is how the Constitution came to be. The Constitution is not a contract among the states. Its greatest interpreter calls it " our ordinance of national life." Its first words are " we, the people." Its supreme purpose is " to promote the general welfare." Whereas, the Articles of Confederation were adopted by the states, *as* states, the Constitution was ordained by the *people* and ratified by the people at the polls.

In this Constitution not one word about states' rights appeared. That was added by an amendment after our government had been in operation for a year under the Constitution. And that amendment was proposed by Congress and not by the people, as the Constitution itself was, and was ratified by the legislatures of the states and not by the people, as the Constitution itself was.

It was proposed and ratified to quiet Patrick Henry, in Virginia, and other like visionaries in other states, who opposed the adoption of the Constitution altogether. It was the reappearance in weaker form of the old royal British theory of colonial individuality, pride and suspicion. And that is how " states' rights " crept into our form of government at the back door.

Then to protect the institution of slavery, came the assertion of " states' rights " in greater vigor, with Calhoun as its apostle. The slave-holders saw that slavery could not prevail against the spirit of liberty in the breasts of the people as a single people, just as the British King saw that British supremacy could not survive against the spirit of liberty, in the breasts of the whole people as a single people.

It was against this doctrine that Jackson hurled his splendid defiance when he said, " I will hang as high as Haman any man who threatens secession." Jackson was great only because there was gathered into his heart the whole American people's instinct for national unity.

Finally came the epochal contest of the sixties, in which Grant became the great commander of embattled nationality. It was Calhoun " states' rights " that fired the first gun at Charleston. It was Lincoln nationality that received the surrender of " states' rights " at Appomattox; and, with nationality's great hearted tolerance, with nationality's divine kindliness, said through the mouth of nationality's greatest warrior, " Let us have peace."

To-day, we behold a recrudescence of Calhoun " states' rights." As has been the case from the beginning, it is caused by selfish interests which fatten on wrong to the whole American people, which resist the thought and conscience of the whole American people seeking to stop that wrong-doing. As always from the beginning, the theory of Calhoun " states' rights " defends itself upon the high ground of local self-government. Local self-government is sacred, and the use of that term to defend Calhoun " states' rights " is sacrilege.

It is said that the will and wisdom of the whole American people stopping national evils by congressional action would destroy local self-government; whereas, this process would preserve local self-government unadulterated by interference with the general government. It is said that the Congress of the whole Republic in obeying the commands of the whole people of the Republic would wipe out state lines; whereas such action preserves the lines of states as the boundaries of states, and not as the divisions between separate nations.

What nationality means is that the states shall perform the natural functions of local self-government, and that the Nation shall perform the natural functions of general self-government. What nationality means is that the states shall not be little nations paralyzing by jealousy and selfishness the welfare of the great Nation; but that the states shall be local self-governing bodies, supreme within the province of local self-government, but subordinate and even non-existent in matters affecting what the Constitution calls " the general welfare " of the whole Republic.

This is the issue to-day, as it was the issue in the time

of Grant. That great captain spoke two sentences that voiced the will of the American people then, as it voices the will of the American people now. Those two sentences are these: " We will fight it out on this line if it takes all summer." And this other one, equally applicable to the issue of the hour: " Immediate and unconditional surrender."

The national spirit of the American people in the beginning of the twentieth century, stronger even than in the middle of the nineteenth century when Lincoln was its oracle, or at the beginning of the eighteenth century when Washington, as warrior and statesman, was its representative, will not evade, will not truckle, will not compromise. It demands " immediate and unconditional surrender " and " it will fight it out on that line if it takes all summer " or a century.

Nationality has always achieved the victory. A hundred years ago the people needed good roads, navigable rivers, safe harbors. " States' rights " said that the nation could not build roads, dredge rivers, equip harbors; that this work was the province of the state. Madison vetoed a bill to do these things, upon the ground that it violated the rights of the states. But the people needed these things; the states did not and could not do them; so the Nation did them, and nobody complains to-day that internal improvements by the National Government violate " states' rights," although Madison vetoed the first internal improvement bill because he said it did violate " states' rights."

The people demanded that the morals of the young should not be debased by obscene literature. To stop the scattering of this pestilence through the Republic it was necessary to exclude obscene literature from inter-state commerce. " States' rights " said that the Nation could not do this because the guardianship of the morals of the people of each state was a matter to be decided by that state; but the Nation did it; and nobody to-day. complains that the rights of states are violated because express companies and railroads are not permitted to carry obscene literature.

With the growth of national unity, which always marks and measures the growth of civilization, the American people demanded the suppression of lotteries. This could be done only by forbidding railroads and express com-panies scattering lottery tickets over the country. States' rights said that the Nation could not do this — that the suppression of lotteries was exclusively a state affair. But the states did not and could not suppress them. So the American people, through their Congress, kept them out of interstate commerce, and that suppressed them. And nobody to-day contends that this law and the his-toric decision of the Supreme Court upholding it violate the rights of the states.

With the necessary concentration of the meat-industry into great meat-preparing centers and with the increase of railways which brought every spot in the Republic in touch with every other spot, it became necessary to super-vise the preparation of meats, so that diseased meat products could not be sold to the people. But this meat industry was located within the limits of certain states.

" States' rights " said that the supervision of industries within a state was the exclusive province of the state. But the states could not correct their evil practices; so it became necessary for the Nation to correct them. Thus in the Meat Inspection Law the Nation did this work, necessary to the welfare of the whole people; and although this law was passed only a year ago, nobody now contends that it was a violation of the rights of the states.

The same thing is true of the Pure Food Law. The states did not and could not stop the sale of adulterated food and medicine to the American People. Nothing could stop it but to exclude such poison from interstate commerce. For five years " states' rights " fought this measure upon the old familiar grounds. But at last upon the demand of the American people that their health and lives should not be sacrificed to an artificial theory of government, the people's Congress passed this law; and although it is scarcely a year old, nobody now contends that the Pure Food Law is in any sense a violation of " states' rights."

The railroads are the means of the people's communication with one another — the agencies by which they travel and exchange their products. Their uses extend to the whole people; their profits are drawn from the whole people; they are the servants of the whole people. They were indulging in rebates, discriminations and other unfair methods. They were in league with the great shippers who were exploiting the people.

It became necessary that the Government of the whole people should regulate these servants of the whole people. The states could not and did not do this. So the Nation did it. And although the Rate Law is scarcely a year old, nobody now contends that it violates " states' rights."

That law is not perfect. It is as yet crude and incomplete. But for the first time in our history, it places in concrete form on the statute books an assertion of the principle that the Nation should control the highways of the Nation.

The next great struggle in the railway problem will be between separate regulation of interstate railways according to the law of each particular state through which they pass, on the one hand, and, on the other hand, exclusive national control of interstate railways through all the states through which such railways pass. This contest will not end in a day or a year. But its conclusion is inevitable.

The railways, properly managed, are by far the greatest agencies in our well-being. They are the largest practical force that holds the American people together. Our prosperity depends absolutely on our commerce; and our commerce depends absolutely on our railways. Our culture depends absolutely on the quick and easy communication of every part of the Republic with every other part of the Republic.

In a word, the railways are of universal importance. Their evils are general evils; their benefits are general benefits. They are the most distinctly national of the elements of American life. Therefore, their control must be national as are their benefits or their evils. But if the National Government regulates them, as it should and must, and if at the same time forty-seven other governments also interfere with them, we shall have the Nation's highways, which are purely national in their activities, harassed by forty-eight governments. No system of communication can be perfect under such a tangle of conflicting laws.

The time must come when states must cease to interfere with national highways passing through them.

That time will be delayed because of selfish interests; because of the recrudescence of "states' rights" with which we are now troubled; but chiefly because of demagogues who seek position and power by attacking these most conspicuous of public corporations. The American people are as much in danger from the demagogues who selfishly and ignorantly seek to inflame their passions as they are from selfish interests which seek to exploit their resources. When a great railway passing through many states is controlled by the Nation's Government and also by the government of each state, through different and hostile laws, a situation is presented which taxes the human mind to manage.

Still another advance in nationality is necessary. Another step in safeguarding the welfare and promoting the prosperity of the American people through the government of the American people is inevitable — a step which the states do not take and can not take. Most large business is now carried on by corporations. Our business is so big that no single man or partnership is big enough to do it. Therefore corporations which combine the capital of hundreds and thousands and even hundreds of thousands of stock-holders are indispensable. But these vast corporations which are great only because the business of the American people is so great, while greatly serving the American people also in some cases greatly wrong them. One form of this wrong is in over-capitalization.

Men create these corporations; charge the people too much for their service; sell the people stock based on this overcharge; and therefore continue and increase this overcharge upon the plea and excuse that the people who have bought this over-capitalized stock must be paid dividends upon it. All these largest corporations do business throughout the entire Nation. Therefore their problem of over-capitalization, upon which they tax the people of the entire Nation, must be solved by the Government of the entire Nation.

We must have a national law compelling all large corporations that do a nation-wide business to publish to the whole country the exact truth concerning every possible element of their assets, liabilities and business that would influence any purchaser of stock. This will end over-capitalization; for, if any man who would like to buy stock, knows that it is "watered," he will not buy it. And, of course, if corporations can not sell this "watered" stock they will not issue it; and that means the end of over-capitalization and of the robber charges based upon it.

In time, too, there must be national incorporation of all incorporated enterprises which do a nation-wide business. This last will come slowly, because these interests themselves which are powerful will fight it; because "states' rights," prejudice inherited from the policy of the British Kings, though fast dying, still feebly survives; and because of the purely selfish and temporary interests of certain states that use the theory of "states' rights" to fill their own coffers at the expense of the whole American people.

This latter is the chief obstacle. To-day these nation-wide corporations are chartered to do business everywhere as they please, by states in which they do little or no business at all. Indeed, such states are in competition with one another for the business of issuing to such cor-

porations letters of marque and reprisal, called state charters, upon the American people.

Look at New Jersey; look at Delaware; look at Nevada
— the feeblest members of the American Union — authorizing corporations to do as they will, to issue stock as
they like, to over-capitalize and prey as they choose.
While it is true that other states may keep such corporations out of their borders, the fact is that they do not.
In all human problems we must deal with facts which
support theories, not with theories unsupported by facts.

And yet another reform which the Nation must work:
Thousands of little children this very hour are being
maimed and murdered in coal mines, cotton mills, glass
factories and sweat-shops. Hundreds of thousands of
the little ones who survive are being made into degenerates, poured into the great body of American citizenship to poison and pollute it.

No word is vitriolic enough to condemn the savage infamy of child labor in this free country. It has got to
be stopped. States have not stopped it — can not stop it.
The Nation can stop it, must stop it, will stop it. The
combined factories, mills and sweat-shops that practise
this brutality; the immense mining interests that increase
their already swollen profits with the blood of little children; the vast railway systems that haul products of child
labor, all have united to resist the passage of a national
law to end this national evil.

And as was the case with the dealers in lottery tickets
and obscene literature, the argument these interests use
is the moth-eaten doctrine of Calhoun " states' rights."

We are told that such a law is " unconstitutional " —
that it violates the rights of the states. But it is as con-

stitutional as the lottery law, which was also denounced as a violation of the rights of the states; as constitutional as the obscene literature law, which was also said to violate the rights of the states; as constitutional as the law prohibiting the importation of convict-made goods which nobody says is a violation of the rights of the states. Such absurd contentions weaken the people's respect for the Constitution.

The Constitution was made for the people; not the people for the Constitution. It is interpreted not only by courts but by events — all its great expositions by the Supreme Court have been called out by emergencies which " states' rights " declared the Constitution did not permit the Nation to meet and overcome. It was Grant who said in his second inaugural, " The theory of government changes with general progress."

As the years pass new problems rise because continually the people advance. For the evils of the hour the Constitution permits us to apply the remedies of the hour. On the question of ending the barbarism of child slavery in the Republic, Nationality says to " states' rights " what Grant, the captain of Nationality, said to the captains of " states' rights " more than forty years ago — " Immediate and unconditional surrender," and " We will fight it out on this line if it takes all summer."

Thus we see that the solution of present and future problems is merely a continuation of the mighty work of Lincoln in the statesman's cabinet and of Grant on the stricken field; just as their work was a continuation of the labors of Washington and of the great men who achieved our independence, wrote our Constitution and breathed into the Nation the breath of life.

THE MEANING OF THE TIMES

*Address before the Students of Yale University,
January 17, 1908*

THE meaning of the times is the organization of honesty. We are in a moral movement, not a political phase. Ours is a period of history, not a moment of passion. The Nation is writing into law for all men to obey those rules of fair dealing which, without any law, most men already obey.

It is said that we need no such statutes. But you Yale men, who so often win in athletics, know that you can not leave the game to the mind, will or moral sense of any man or set of men. So you make rules of the game, which every man must obey. The purpose of these rules is order and fair play. A game won by fraud is not a victory, but a disgrace. These rules apply equally to all. Nobody can be above the rules of the game, no matter how strong or wise he is. If any man among you took the stand that he would play the game by his own notions, instead of by the rules which govern all the rest of you, you would apply those rules to him harder than to anybody else; or else you would not let him play at all.

This simple example shows how wrong it is to let exceptional men do big business in their own way regardless of law, instead of having common rules for making them do business in everybody's way in obedience to law. It shows how necessary it is to make the extraordinary man do business by the same rules by which the ordinary man must do business. That, and only that, is what we started to do in the laws we have passed; what we will keep on doing until the work is finished.

This is the meaning of the times — a meaning that is simple and plain, just as the meaning of every historic movement has been simple and plain. All great things, all things that last, are simple and plain. The Bismarck period in Germany meant the unity of the German people; all other matters connected with it were mere incidents of the march and not the march itself. The Washington movement in America was mainly nationhood; everything had to give way to that, whether British or Hessian bayonets without, or local and selfish ideas within. The meaning of the Lincoln movement was mainly supremacy of the general will of all the people over the local will of some of the people — the never-dying and ever-growing idea that we are one people with one flag, instead of many peoples with many flags; and as time goes on, all the problems of our Civil War, important as they appeared, are seen to be little when we look at them side by side with this overwhelming issue.

So all great movements have had a plain and simple meaning — a clear principle running straight through and explaining their every phase. And every one of these movements went on until its meaning was thoroughly worked out. All of them were resisted by the wrongs which those movements had come to make right. Able and wicked men who fattened on those evils resisted them with money, pen and sword; and even good men who saw with the eye of the hour instead of the eye of the future, grew weak and faint-hearted, and sometimes thought it better to endure the things which hurt the people than to suffer the pains that come with their cure.

For nothing wrong is ever made right without pain. There is no such thing as a comfortable reform. Suffering is the price of putting righteousness in the place of wrong. But it is worth the price. Valley Forge was terrible, but the birth of the Republic was worth a thousand Valley Forges. Vicksburg and the Wilderness were fearful, but the unity of the American people was cheap at the cost of those red years, those storms of death, those fields of blood.

Throughout all these great movements for the betterment of man there were seasons of despair, and the despair of the good was strengthened by the courage of the bad. So in our Revolution we see Washington and his patriots surrounded within his own camp by scheme and plot to end the struggle; but Washington and his patriots kept straight on, and in the end they won. In Lincoln's day even pure and able men said of the seceding states, " Let the erring sisters go "; and a political party nominated for President a Union general upon a platform that " the war is a failure." Lincoln and those who thought that nothing could fail which was right, and nothing could win which was wrong, went straight on, and in the end they won.

So we see that our own movement to-day is just like every other similar movement throughout all history. It, too, is fought by the same kind of forces that fought the same kind of movements in the past. It, too, has its dark hour when those who have battled for it lose their nerve, and when those who oppose it come to the fight with fresh bravery and skill. It, too, has its plain and simple meaning — the organization of honesty; or as I named it two years ago, the moral regeneration of American business. This is the clear light by which all the laws we have passed and intend to pass may be read easily, and by which future generations will behold and understand our times.

Each of these movements grew out of conditions, and so does ours. We have been busy with material things, making money, building railroads, sinking mines, occupying land; busy with trade and the development of resources. All this was good. But finally we became so busy with material things that we forgot ideal things; so busy with results that we forgot methods. Development of resources too often became exploitations of resources; trade too often became trickery; government too often became graft; building industry too often became juggling with industry; the praiseworthy spirit of gain by fair methods too often gave way to the evil spirit of gain by any methods.

Men felled and sawed into lumber forests belonging to the Nation, and called it enterprise; men sold poisoned food and diseased meat to the people and called it business; men watered stocks, overcharged the people to make the stocks pay dividends, and called it finance; men forced secret rebates from railroads, built prosperous plants upon the fraud, and called it industry; men bought the mastery of cities and states, got corrupt privileges and contracts, and called it government; men purchased high office, and called it career.

When we stopped the robbery of the Nation's forests the robbers called it paternalism; when we stopped the sale of poisoned food and diseased meats the sellers called it socialism; when we are trying to stop stock-juggling, criminal rebates and the like the jugglers call it a raid on prosperity; when we try to stop government by graft and politics by purchase, those who grow rich by graft or go to high places by purchase call our work interference with private affairs in the one case, and assault upon respectability in the other case.

Yet such of these things as we have already done are now agreed to and it is found that nobody is hurt but that everybody is helped by them. Even those businesses which for the moment sold less of their goods, soon sold more of their goods than ever; and instead of selling hurtful things, they are now selling wholesome things. Examples of this are the meat and food businesses. Months ago when certain men were saying that we had gone too far, I pointed out that these very men did not even suggest a repeal of any of those statutes. If we have gone too far, is it not strange that nobody proposes that we go back?

Those who cried out that we were wrong when we began to make laws for the moral regeneration of American business; that we had gone too far when we wrote the laws which we have now passed, are the same persons who now declare that we must not pass any more such laws. But, if you were building a railroad between two points, what would you think of a man who, when two-thirds of the railroad was builded, objected to going ahead until he saw how the part already done would work? Yet this is just like those who say that the present movement must stop — just the men who throughout all history have always objected to every great moral movement being finished. Indeed, such men, now and throughout history, have not only resisted the finishing of these movements, but have been against the beginning of these movements. No, the road will be builded to its terminus; the movement will go on to its natural, wholesome, helpful end. And when it is all over, as it will soon be, it will be found that another historic step forward has been taken for the good of the Nation and the world, which will never be retraced.

Not many more things need to be done — the road is nearly finished. Only a few more rails must be laid. Let me briefly describe them. First, we must revise our tariff, and that is a big thing; but we must do more — we must make sensible, up-to-date plans for revision, and that is a bigger thing. There are several hundred items named in our tariff laws and every year new articles are put on the market which are not named but which are covered by general terms of the law. It is plain that just and intelligent duties can not be fixed without a knowledge of the facts upon which every one of these duties is supposed to rest. We have made our tariffs heretofore through committees of Congress working a part of the time, for a few months, not only to find out these facts but also to fix duties to these facts, study how those duties will work out with foreign tariffs, how our trade will thereby be helped or hurt, and all other things that must be thought of in making a tariff. Yet it is plain that even experts could not learn all the facts in so short a time, to say nothing of the other work our congressional committees are now forced to do in making a tariff law.   Other nations have seen this plain truth and therefore made the common-sense plan of finding out the facts upon which their legislatures can act with knowledge and wisdom.   So Germany and Japan, whose tariffs are the most careful of all tariffs, had a body of tariff experts find out the facts and then make their tariffs fit those facts.

These German and Japanese experts know more about the tariffs of their own and other countries, more about every industry of their own and other countries, than any other men in the Japanese and German nations. They were the fittest men to do the work that Germany and Japan could find.   Then, armed with the special knowledge they looked into everything that had anything to do with German and Japanese industries and with the trade those industries carried on.   All this took not only hard work but much time.   A body of thirty-two German experts worked for six years consulting two thousand trade experts and investigating every industry in the Empire, not only by itself, but in relation to other German industries and those of other nations.   Then the work of these experts was laid before the Reichstag and with all these facts the Reichstag made the present German tariff.

The same is true of Japan, except that the work of the Japanese experts is never finished.   Some of the Japanese experts are all the time going quietly to other countries and finding out about the trade and industry of those countries.   On one of my trips to the far East, I found three such men going back to Japan from two years of such work in one European country and our own country. France does the same thing, but not so well as Germany and Japan.

Of course, this is merely good sense. What man can be against this way of handling our tariff except the man who does not want the facts to be known? And it is by not knowing the facts that all dishonesty, if there is any dishonesty, gets into our tariff. If anybody says that we have no right to know the facts about anybody's business, the answer is that if that business asks the people to put a tariff on what it makes and sells it should tell the people the facts so that the people can put the right kind of tariff upon these things; otherwise, those who run that business would be putting their own tariff upon what they make and sell. They would be making a tariff law instead of letting the people make a tariff law for them. Further answer is that at the bottom all honest gain in business comes from the fact that its goods are better than other goods and the men who run the business abler and more forceful than other men. So the next thing we must do in finishing up this movement of putting honesty into law is to make a body of tariff experts who shall do for the American Congress what has been done for the German Reichstag, the Japanese Parliament, and the French House of Deputies.

Nothing that we are doing puts any limit on honest business. On the contrary, we would lift from honest business the burdens it now carries. For example, the first law against trusts, called the Sherman Law, was passed eighteen years ago. The business of this country has traveled a century forward since then, both in methods and results. That law does not fit the conditions

that have thus grown up. It forbids all trade combinations, no matter how much they are needed or how helpful they may be. Therefore, we must make that law
over again so as to permit reasonable and honest business
organization. We must put into the Sherman Law the
word " reasonable." All students now know that the big
businesses called trusts are necessary, and that trade can
hardly be carried on without certain railroad and business
combinations. The law must be changed to permit these
when they are reasonable and honest. Nobody but
demagogues and ignorant men object to the mighty organizations called trusts; but every informed and honest
man does object to the robberies of some of these trusts,
just as we object to the same thing by individuals. What
we are after is justice and fair dealing both by the trusts
and railroads toward the people and by the people toward
the trusts and railroads.

We must have a law that will stop the watering of
stocks. Ultimately, all interstate railroads — that is, all
national highways — must come under exclusive national
control; but the necessity for this is only ripening. Our
labor legislation must be brought up to date. We are
one quarter of a century behind Europe in the matter of
laws for the safety and general benefit of working-men.
That great scheme for conserving our national resources,
fathered by one of the most useful men Yale ever gave
to the Nation — Gifford Pinchot — must be well worked
out. Our forests have been slaughtered — they must be
replaced; our streams have been neglected — they must
be improved; our wealth of timber, minerals and water
power has been wasted and stolen — we must save and
nourish it.

All of this is the statesmanship of construction, not of destruction. We are building up, not tearing down; we are working for the whole Nation, instead of for a few individuals, and for the future as well as for to-day. We are not tearing down the house; we are taking out the rotten bricks that threaten the whole structure and putting sound ones in their place. Those who say we have hurt business know better than anybody else that if what has been done had been neglected, this country would have had, three years ago, the worst panic in our history. These may know better than anybody else that businesses based on sand and builded with cardboard would have fallen; that financial adventures blown up to the bursting point would have exploded and that the utter ruin of the wicked and heedless would have also crushed the careful and the good. The wild horses of financial recklessness were dashing straight over the cliffs; we have merely tightened the reins, checked their flight and turned into the safe, straight and solid road of fair and honest dealing.

When these laws that I have outlined have been passed, the work of the moral regeneration of American business will be practically finished — the road will have been builded to its terminus. Nothing more will be needed except making those laws better as time shows us how and where we can make them better. The whole movement is the evolution of the people's conscience, not the revolution of the people's industry. Indeed, it does not go so far as the English laws of business have already done. The English people did this same work and more over a decade ago, and that work did not hurt, but helped, English business. It is truthfully said that the business laws of England are the safest, as English business itself is the soundest, in the world.

Yet our work in America to-day, which is raising such an outcry by those who have been doing wrong, is the same, though not so great, as that accomplished by the English people. Those who are doing this work in America to-day are called very bad names, and if anybody introduced in Congress to-morrow the English Companies Act he would be painted as an enemy of business, a foe to prosperity, by the very men in America who praise these same laws in England.

So we see that this movement is nothing but the people in action; the moral making of the Nation is catching up with the physical making of the Nation. The people's government is getting more into the people's hands. This is right if government by the people is to live. The fight between the people on the one hand and special interests on the other hand is as old as the world. Until these later days the fight was between aristocracies and the people. The people won that fight here and are winning it all over the world. There is now manhood suffrage in England; in France the people are in the saddle; in Italy the government is almost as democratic as our own; the German Emperor is called the " Arbeiter Kaiser," the working-men's emperor; in Russia thirty million white slaves were freed with the pen before our comparatively few black slaves were freed with the sword, and now these men who yesterday were serfs are making themselves felt in the rule of Russia. The rights of man are invading the Orient; we see it in China; last year the Persian people formed a Constitution; all

over the world the people of every race are winning their
fight with aristocracies and kings.

With us in America, the fight is between interests
which do not want fair play on the one hand, and the people who mean that everybody shall play fair on the other
hand. Here and now, as everywhere and at all times,
the people are winning and will completely win. But
it is a hard fight. Every man is needed. Especially
young men like yourselves are needed. If the Nation
were at war — and it may be at war before many years
— every one of us would gladly give his blood and life
for it on the field of battle. But this is not enough;
every one of us must give his time and strength to the
Nation in the field of politics. The man who will not do
this does not deserve those rights which his indifference
compels others to win for him. The young man who
will not take part in the Nation's civil struggles for honesty and righteousness is unworthy of his fathers, who
gave not only their time and strength in the same struggle, but gave their blood and lives on war's red fields for
the same great purpose.

DATE

GAYLORD